THE BODY IN INTERPERSONAL RELATIONS

Merleau-Ponty

Mary Rose Barral, Ph.D.

UNIVERSITY
PRESS OF
AMERICA

LANHAM • NEW YORK • LONDON

Copyright © 1984 by

University Press of America,™ Inc.

4720 Boston Way
Lanham, MD 20706

3 Henrietta Street
London WC2E 8LU England

All rights reserved

Printed in the United States of America

Copyright © 1965 by
Duquesne University

Originally published as
*MERLEAU-PONTY: THE ROLE OF THE
BODY-SUBJECT IN INTERPERSONAL RELATIONS*

ISBN (Perfect): 0-8191-3755-3

TO MY BROTHER

PREFACE

Merleau-Ponty's philosophy has been attracting more and more the attention of scholars outside the pale of the French philosophers and psychologists, but it has been little known in English-speaking countries, lacking as they did translations of his works as well as of the works of the critics. Recently, however, some of his writings were translated (*Phénoménologie de la perception, Eloge de la philosophie, La structure du comportement*), others are being translated. Some commentaries and criticisms are also now available in English, and a number of articles have also appeared to add to the abundant French literature on the topic.

Our purpose in the present work is to present the philosophy of Merleau-Ponty as an introduction to his works and to point out the importance the author attaches to the body as the bearer of a dialectic; this presentation does not include a study of his political writings. To offset the danger of misrepresentation, we have retained as far as possible Merleau-Ponty's own manner of expression: it is very difficult (and those who know the thought of Merleau-Ponty will bear us out; Kwant says, "almost impossible") to summarize Merleau-Ponty's thought without in some way distorting or mutilating it.

We have remained rather close to the various texts used, in the hope that this work may prove useful as a guide in approaching the writings of the author, which, even in translation, present some difficulty.

Although it is quite difficult to understand Merleau-Ponty's thought apart from that of other philosophers, we have avoided involving other thinkers as far as possible. Likewise, in spite of the fact that his thought can be so easily related to that of others—it almost compels one to make all sorts of connections and to see innumerable similarities with other thinkers—it has been our study to omit all but the necessary references to such relations.

ACKNOWLEDGMENTS

Sincere thanks to Professor Joseph A. Kockelmans for graciously reading the manuscript and for his constructive criticism; to Seton Hall University and particularly to Fr. A. Hakim for his assistance in the preparation of the manuscript for the press; to Fordham University Library Staff—particularly to Miss A. M. Murphy, Mr. A. E. Merkl, and Miss M. Tighe—for their help in securing needed material.

TABLE OF CONTENTS

PAGE

CHAPTER ONE—INTRODUCTION
1. Contemporary Philosophy and the Personal Dimension 1
2. Phenomenology as a Movement 2
3. Range and Scope of Phenomenology 8
4. Existentialism 17
5. Phenomenological Existentialism 21

CHAPTER TWO—THE PHILOSOPHY OF MERLEAU-PONTY: PHENOMENOLOGICAL AND EXISTENTIAL
1. Specific Object of Investigation 28
2. Scope of His Phenomenology 42
3. Existential Phenomenology 44
4. Existential Dialectic 55
5. Critique of Existentialism 60
6. Marxist Leanings 66

CHAPTER THREE—THE REALITY OF MAN AS A BODY: THE NOTION OF STRUCTURE OR FORM
1. Investigation of Behavior: Reflexes or Structures? 79
2. Levels of Structuration 87
3. Body-Soul Dialectic 90
4. My Body Perceived and Experienced 101
5. Directness and Unity of Perception 107
6. Genesis of Consciousness 110
7. Limitations of Phenomenology 116

CHAPTER FOUR—CENTRAL ROLE OF THE BODY IN ITS RELATION TO SELF, OTHERS, AND THE WORLD
1. Prerequisites for an Investigation of the Body 128
2. The Body as Object 130
3. Spatiality of the Body 136

	PAGE

CHAPTER FIVE—MAN: A SEXED BEING
1. Intersubjectivity 143
2. Sexuality, an Original Form of Intentionality 146
3. Affectivity and the Incarnate Spirit 151
4. Existential Signification of Sexuality 158
5. Some Implications of the Doctrine 166

CHAPTER SIX—THE ROLE OF THE BODY IN MAN'S POWER OF COMMUNICATION
1. The Word: Authentic or Empirical 175
2. Relation of Word to Concept 181
3. Language, an Encounter 185
4. Communication with Words: Through the Body 186
5. Gesture: Natural or Conventional? 189
6. The Phenomenology of Language 196
7. Philosophical Implications of the Phenomenology of Language 200
8. Aesthetic Expression 204
9. Silent Expression 208

CHAPTER SEVEN—INTERSUBJECTIVITY AND PERSONAL RELATIONS
1. Being-in-the-World 217
2. Intersubjective Relations 226
3. The Other and Solipsism 229
4. Existence and the Social World 233
5. The Phenomenon of Love 237
6. The Cogito: Merleau-Ponty's Interpretation .. 242
7. Presence and the Subject 247
8. Human Liberty 249

PAGE

CHAPTER EIGHT—CONCLUSION
    1. Prevailing Ambiguity 259
    2. Experience and the Absolute 263
    3. The Personal 267
    4. Groundwork for Development 270

APPENDIX ONE—PHENOMENOLOGY 273
APPENDIX TWO—EXISTENCE AND THE EXISTENTIAL 275
APPENDIX THREE—BIOGRAPHICAL NOTES 277
BIBLIOGRAPHY 279
INDEX OF NAMES 291
INDEX OF SUBJECT MATTER 292

ERRATA

p. 135 — note 38, line 3: know, should be knows
p. 169 — par. 2, line 7: phenomena, should be phenomenon
p. 193 — last line: paint on, should be paint about
p. 202 — line 1: omit period (.) after "perception"
p. 209 — par. 2, line 5: meaning, should be meanings
p. 283 — Kaelin's title, line 1: Aesthetic, should be Aesthetics
p. 292 — line 12: aesthetic, should be aesthetics

CHAPTER ONE

INTRODUCTION

1. *Contemporary Philosophy and the Personal Dimension*

Contemporary cultural life presents a fascinating and at the same time a disquieting aspect. Modern man has been moving away more and more from conventional modes of expression towards ever bolder and more novel manifestations of his restless spirit. All forms of art have undergone a rather astonishing change. Classical order, logic, rational communication have given way to the freest forms of personal expression—so personal at times that they have ceased to be communication at all. In painting particularly, the classical order has been discarded to such an extent that now some critics claim that there is not any order at all, nor beauty of form, nor indeed any form of communication, because the artists' message is understood by no one except himself. This trend of contemporary culture is disquieting; yet there are aspects of it which are fascinating; such rebellion discloses novelty and reveals potentialities and thoughts which would have remained hidden if freedom of expression had not prevailed.

Philosophic thought is no exception to the general trend. Just as all arts are said to be wanting form or a definite order, philosophy is said to lack rationality, and to be no longer a system of thought, but the dubious expression of individual thinkers, who, perhaps after the example of Kierkegaard, generalize and universalize their own private, individual experience. Hence, philosophy is no longer considered a rational interpretation of reality (whatever that may be taken to mean) but a subjective, individual interpretation of experiences, most often expressed in descriptive, poetic language, through drama, and without any real regard for logic or for conceptual clarity and consistency. The age of the system seems to be gone and forgotten; now the emphasis is on process, dialectic, tension, development, and openness to the ever changing phenomena of lived experience. But, is all this philosophy? Or is it merely a preparation for philosophy, though a very important and necessary one?

The new living force of contemporary philosophy has met with considerable criticism—as is always the case with new movements—and as a result, its proponents have gone to great lengths to emphasize the values of this new thought, which claims to be genuinely philosophical even if not garbed in pure, clear, and well defined concepts. It is precisely this lack of conceptual expression, of system and, in general, of a definite direction which has caused this movement to be looked upon as a regression into irrationalism, almost to the point of absurdity.

However, this is really not the case. In fact, a patient and unprejudiced study of the new patterns in philosophy will disclose genuine values and an unsuspected rational ground upon which the investigation is founded.

2. *Phenomenology as a Movement*

Several important movements have developed in contemporary philosophy: linguistic analysis, Marxism, phenomenology and existentialism. Of these, the last two are particularly relevant to the present study. Phenomenology, as a movement, can be traced back to Hegel; was taken up by Husserl and has become common property—though with profound differences—of both existential and phenomenological philosophers. These generalizations need to be specified.

Hegel's *Phenomenology of Spirit*[1] opened the way to the phenomenological movement. Needless to say, the phenome-

---

[1] Translation with Introduction by J. B. Baillie (2nd ed.; London: George Allen & Unwin Ltd. [1955]). Hegel's *Phenomenology* . . . "is a comprehensive and connected survey of the ways in which experience appears." Introduction, p. 41. Cited hereafter as *Phenomenology* . . . .

Introduction

nology of Husserl is not a sequel to that of Hegel, but it bears nevertheless resemblances to the latter: Husserl was influenced by Hegel's phenomenology. Likewise, Husserl's own disciples, while following, consciously or not, the inspiration of the master, pursued a phenomenelogical investigation of their own.

Since phenomenology is the science of experience and it does not concern itself with either the object alone or the subject alone, but with the point of contact at which subject and object meet in the intentionality of consciousness, it follows that the phenomenological method will lead different philosophers along various paths. Thus we see that phenomenology has branched off in many directions, to such an extent that it is now no longer possible to speak of phenomenology without at once qualifying it as Hegelian, Husserlian, Sartrean, etc.; for every philosopher who adopts the phenomenological method is likely to reach conclusions different from those of others.

Is there, then, no possibility of a generic definition of phenomenology, that is, one which might meaningfully express just what is meant by the word itself? All phenomenologists have in common one thing: they turn their attention to the "phenomenon"—to that which appears in consciousness. At the risk of seeming to use a circular definition, we must say that a phenomenon is that which appears or presents itself, reveals itself or manifests itself to consciousness. It therefore presupposes a being which manifests itself or appears and another being—gifted with consciousness—to which the first manifests itself. Hence, generally speaking, a phenomenon is itself the manifestation of a being[2] to another being capable of experience.

---

[2] The use of this term—being—is rather ambiguous at this point: the phenomenon is *that* which appear (actually one is not justified in calling it "being," for this is already an assumption; phenomenology does not disclose this at once.)

The term itself—phenomenon—has assumed, at different times, various meanings: a real (true) appearing as in idealistic or realistic philosophy; the object of an empirical investigation; deceptive appearance or illusion; the appearance or that which appears; object of an eidetic intuition.

For Kant the whole world is phenomenon—and a well founded phenomenon, in the subject, "dependent upon the way the thing-in-itself affects us in sensation, or the way the mind looks at it."[3] But the phenomenon postulates being, that is, a reality in itself (noumenon) which transcends it, for the phenomenon implies that there must be something corresponding to it which is not phenomenon. Hence Kant, to avoid a vicious circle, must posit something in-itself, independent of our sensible constitution.

Hegel's way of understanding the phenomenon runs counter to the Kantian: he opposes the distinction between phenomenon and noumenon. His conception of the phenomenon is realistic, with this qualification: for him the real is *spirit*. For Hegel, the phenomenon is not merely an appearance to the mind, but the appearance of that which manifests itself. He criticises the Kantian notion of phenomenon versus noumenon because, according to such view, the noumenon, far from being "the reality" is seen to be, is merely illusion. The Hegelian phenomenon is not a mere appearance indicating some unknown reality; rather, it is the reality itself as it appears to consciousness. For Hegel, furthermore, phenomenon is considered both at the phenomenological and at the metaphysical level. Thus he asserts:

> . . . Appearance is just not the world of sense-knowledge and perception as positively *being*, but this world as superseded and established in truth as an inner world. It is often said that the supersensible is *not* ap-

---

[3]*Dictionary of Philosophy and Psychology*, ed. by J. M. Baldwin, Vol. II (New York: The Macmillan Co., 1928), p. 289.

Introduction

pearance; but by appearance is thereby meant not *appearance;* but rather the sensible world taken as itself real actuality.[4]

And, he maintains that the essence is not behind or beyond the phenomenon; and precisely because essence is that which exists, existence is phenomenon. "Essence must appear. It appears as existence. Essence does not exist outside, or apart from, or behind, or beyond its existential appearance."[5] Therefore we can say that

> The phenomenon is a "moment"—the second—in the category of essence: of these, the first moment is the *reason of being* (Grund), the third, the *reality* (Wirlichkeit). The character of the essence is its reflecting itself. Reflection in itself is the organizing principle of the essence, the foundation; reflection in another is the phenomenon, that is, the manifesting of the essence.[6]

Jean Hyppolite points out that the best characterization of Hegel's philosophy is precisely his phenomenology, wherein he states that the proper object of philosophy is "effective reality (Wirlichkeit), that category of the Logic which designates the concrete unity of essence and appearance, that manifestation which manifests only itself, and demonstrates its necessity not by a separate intelligibility, but by its own movement and development."[7]

---

[4] *Phenomenology* . . ., p. 193.
[5] Hegel, *Encyclopedia of Philosophy*, tr. G. E. Mueller (New York: Philosophical Library [1959]), par. 82.
[6] *Enciclopedia filosofica*, Vol. II (Firenze: G. C. Sansoni, 1957), col. 331. Cited hereafter as *Enciclopedia filosofica*.
[7] Jean Hyppolite, *Logique et existence: Essai sur la logique de Hegel*, Épiméthée, Essais philosophiques (Paris: Presses Universitaires de France, 1953), p. 4. Elsewhere he adds: "Le savoir empirique—celui qui est étudié, décrit comme tel dans la Phénoménologie—l'expérience en général avec son développement, est le Phénomène du Savoir absolu, le savoir absolu en tant *qu'il apparaît*, et il n'est phénomène qu'en tant qu'il ne sait pas encore que c'est lui-même qui *s'apparaît* à lui même. . . .," p. 77.

Husserl's notion of the phenomenon differs from both the Kantian and the Hegelian. He upholds the objectivity of the phenomenon, but with a new meaning, which he expresses thus:

> ... The phenomena of transcendental phenomenology will be characterized as non-real (irreal). . . . Reductions, the specifically transcendental, "purify" the psychological phenomena from that which lends them reality, and therewith a setting in the "real" world. Our phenomenology should be a theory of essential Being, dealing not with real, but with transcendentally reduced phenomena.[8]

Thus Husserl has introduced a new understanding of reality; to make the world appear as a phenomenon is really to consider the world no longer as reality or existence, but rather as "meaning." And this phenomenon—the world—is constituted by consciousness, that is, consciousness constitutes the meaning of the world.

Merleau-Ponty, although admitting his indebtedness to Husserl, understands the phenomenon in a still different way. At this moment we will only note that he strives for an existential rather than an essential philosophy, and therefore it will soon be apparent that for him Husserl's reduction, if accepted at all, will have a different meaning. In fact, we might say at the outset that with him the possibility of the reductions is at least questioned. It seems very clear that for Merleau-Ponty, the phenomenon, far from requiring a stripping of its existential character, must in fact be considered within its existential condition, which alone can permit its full revelation. This is not to say that Merleau-Ponty is merely indulging in a sort of phenomenalism yielding no

---

[8]Edmund Husserl, *Ideas: General Introduction to Pure Phenomenology*, tr. W. R. Boyce Gibson (New York: Macmillan Co., 1931), p. 44.

Introduction

philosophical insight; on the contrary, his intention is to penetrate fully the significance of the phenomenon so that it may stand revealed in its essence. It is his conviction that the philosopher—the phenomenologist—cannot hope to arrive at an understanding of man and of the world except through a phenomenological reflection based on the very facticity of the world and of man in the world. All this does not in the least prevent Merleau-Ponty from maintaining that phenomenology is a transcendental science; on the contrary, the very acceptance of the phenomenon as it appears clothed in existential conditions assures the achievement of the philosophical aim he sets himself.[9] To consciousness, which is itself steeped in existence (this will later on be seen as the condition for ambiguity), the phenomenon appears as ideal content and yet enriched with its existential significance. In other words, for Merleau-Ponty there is no such a thing as (the possibility of experiencing) a phenomenon disengaged from its relatedness to the phenomenal field of space and time wherein both the experience and the experienced are inextricably related to the experiencing consciousness.

> The paradoxical and profound result is that what consciousness intends and recovers without ceasing is the world of which it is a part and out of which all its undertakings (and all reflexion) come forth. This is not what traditional philosophy calls the external world, the object of cosmology, but the existential relationship of man to the world.[10]

---

[9] Maurice Merleau-Ponty, *Phénoménologie de la perception* (Bibliothèque des Idées. Paris: Librairie Gallimard, 1945), p. I. Cited hereafter as *P.P.*

[10] Pierre Thévenaz, *What is Phenomenology: and other essays*, tr. by J. M. Edie et al. (Chicago: Quadrangle Books [1962]), p. 86. Cited hereafter as *Phenomenology*.

Merleau-Ponty

The first revelation of the phenomenon will undoubtedly be a perceptive experience. At this level, the phenomenon will not yet be an object of consciousness involving an intellectual judgment, but it will be a knowing of the body, without judgment—an immanent and sensible confrontation. In fact, Merleau-Ponty renounces the analysis which brings us to distinguish consciousness *which situates* and *situated* consciousness. If consciousness is passing judgment on the world, then it must itself be outside the world, aware of phenomena, but itself outside the phenomenal. But for Merleau-Ponty, as will appear, consciousness is part of the world. Hence, he

> rejects at once the two correlative ideas of absolute objectivity [the phenomena over against consciousness] and of the absolute subjectivity [transparent consciousness] of the World in Itself and of the Spirit; instead of making them alternate as both true, he considers them as both false. That from which he wants to begin is human thought in its factual condition [as a phenomenon] and we find here the integrated humanism which forms the foundation of existentialism.[11]

Actually, when Merleau-Ponty will speak of reduction, he will, in fact, mean not a bracketing of characteristic of the object of consciousness, but, rather, a radical consideration of the phenomenon in its primordial revelation of itself to a subjectivity itself steeped into the same originary pre-objective existence.

3. Range and Scope of Phenomenology

Just what is the range of the phenomena which are the concern of phenomenological reflection and analysis? Ob-

---

[11] Ferdinand Alquié, "Une philosophie de l'ambiguïté, l'existentialisme de Maurice Merleau-Ponty," *Fontaines,* Vol. II (Avril 1947), p. 54. Cited hereafter as "Une philosophie . . ."

Introduction

viously, even here there cannot be a univocal answer, applicable to any and every phenomenological inquiry. Since a phenomenon is that which manifests itself, broadly speaking, anything which manifests itself—which is capable of appearing in consciousness—can be the object of phenomenological reflection.

Sensible appearances alone are not the whole field of phenomenology; as a matter of fact, the sensible as sensible is not the most important field for phenomenological reflection; it is by no means the most "real" phenomenon. Whatever manifests itself is phenomenon: thus a philosophy, a political view, a feeling, a desire, a doctrine, an expression of personal likes or dislikes, can be just as real phenomena as the configuration of a solid or the color of a flower; for all these appear and manifest themselves in consciousness. Inner feelings manifest themselves to me just as clearly and are just as real as any exterior events. As a matter of fact, if properly considered, these immanent acts are even more clearly manifest to me that those coming from others or from the exterior, for, in the last analysis, I really only know that which comes from without on condition that it appears to me from within. In a very true sense, therefore, whatever is more properly "subjective" is, for all purposes, more properly "appearance to me" and therefore fit subject for phenomenological investigation.[12]

Phenomenologists have chosen to investigate this or that group of phenomena, according to their own personal preference—a philosopher's thought is very much determined by the kind of person he is—but all have been concerned with the same thing: to discover the reality of the phenomenon as it appears in consciousness.

If we want to go as far back as Kant's philosophical inquiry, we can say that for him the whole world was a

---

[12]But this also represents a difficulty: at which point do I draw the line between that which is merely subjective and that which is the "real appearing" or the phenomenon?

phenomenon and consequently everything could be object of phenomenological reflection. But the problem, with Kant, was really not that of a phenomenological analysis. His main concern was to show that only the appearance of being is susceptible of scientific classification, whereas being itself (the thing-in-itself) forever eludes us. Hence, we may, if we want, consider Kant as the remote influence of modern phenomenology; but we may not, properly speaking, call him a phenomenologist.

It is precisely with Hegel that we come to the consideration of a vast array of phenomena. He begins with an analysis of perception, then goes on to the understanding, and examines all phases of human consciousness in relation to the various experiences, at all levels. It can be said with truth that Hegel's phenomenological inquiry embraced the whole range of human experience, natural, social, and cultural, so that for him no phenomenon which appeared in consciousness was neglected. And this for a good reason: for Hegel, to be "fully conscious" of self is to be fully conscious of all reality. For him, up to the attainment of this goal (the ultimate self is all reality) there is no departure from the original phenomenon: his dialectic insures the continuity of the chain which has its first link in experience.[13]

---

[13] This seems very significant to us: in Hegel we already have some aspects of contemporary philosophy: phenomenology and existentialism. This is not to rashly label Hegel either one or the other, or even both. By his own admission, Hegel was an absolute idealist, hence, it would seem, he belonged to neither of the movements mentioned above. And yet, because his approach was definitively phenomenological (although neither in the Husserlian nor in the existential sense), and because his point of departure—experience—became the first link of an unbroken dialectical chain of being, is it not correct to say that his philosophy has a definite grounding in experience? Further, if, as Hegel maintained, the concrete *only* is the true embodiment of the universal, there seems to be quite a good reason for stating that Hegel's idealism is such that it does not deny the individual existent, on the contrary it presupposes it. Now, as will be seen later, if the "existence" with which the existentialists are concerned is the direct return to the only existence we know—that of the existent—then the phenomenological approach of Hegel to reality, his whole philosophy is not an

Introduction

But it was Husserl who came to be looked upon as the founder of phenomenology even though he was influenced by Hegel and admitted his indebtedness to Franz Brentano: he borrowed Brentano's meaning of the term "phenomenon," which he used differently. In fact, after accepting from Brentano the insight he had reached, namely, that the psychic phenomenon always has as referent an object (i.e., no seeing without something seen, no believing without something believed) he detached himself from the master to such an extent that the trend of his thought became strictly his own. The chief difference lay in this: Brentano was a psychologist and his concern was with the psychological aspect of the phenomena which he discovered to be "acts" (another valuable insight); Husserl's concern was for the phenomenon as the appearing of the intentional object of consciousness, an object immanent to consciousness; although he started with events of psychology as phenomena, he did not consider these ideal or real entities from a purely psychological viewpoint.

Husserl sought a radical point of departure. He deliberately placed himself in the Cartesian tradition claiming as he did that transcendental phenomenology is the completion of the radicalism of Descartes. In order to found a science on a secure basis, one must first of all consider the knowledge one already has. Thus Husserl began by re-examining the knowledge already available in terms of psychology, positive science, facts, and all the "real" objects with which we are already familiar.

His first task was to get rid of a first level of naive evidence which is too obvious; the aim was to acquire a more profound insight and reach a deeper level of evidence. Husserl did not institute any sort of artificial doubt, but rather attempted to realize a position of detached spectator

---

abstract system entirely detached from experience, but a return to the concrete by a true dialectic leading up to the Absolute spirit which is all reality.

of the world in order to better grasp its meaning insofar as it presents itself to consciousness. Thévenaz says that for Husserl transcendental intention is attention to the world, and that which is revealed therein is the relation of the world to its transcendental source.[14]

Thus Husserl's point of departure was the intentional recapturing of the world—the coincidence of consciousness with the world. Whereas the Cartesian Cogito, from which Husserl claims to take his cue, is an intensified attention to consciousness of self in the act of thinking (it does not matter what); for Husserl consciousness is entirely intentional—consciousness of self is a continued effort at recapturing the world by ever new intentionality. Consciousness is openness to the world.

Again according to Thévenaz, it is not possible to speak of coincidence of consciousness with itself, unless one means by that the coincidence of transcendental consciousness with "the totality of its intentions," which is coincidence with the world. The point of departure Husserl sought therefore was not being, but transcendental constitution. In all this Husserl still maintained the possibility of a consciousness as detached spectator to the world.[15]

However the Husserl of the pure phenomenology is not the only Husserl we can speak of. Although his thought did not undergo any radical change after the publication of the second edition of *Logische Untersuchungen* (Halle, 1913), the philosophy of his later years has often been considered different from his earlier one.[16] We think it is only a question

---

[14] Thévenaz, "La question du point de départ radical chez Descartes et Husserl," *Problèmes actuels de la phénoménologie*, ed. H. L. Van Breda (Actes du Colloque International de Phénoménologie, Bruxelles, Avril 1951; Paris: Desclée de Brouwer, 1952), p. 21. Cited hereafter as *Problèmes* . . .

[15] Thévenaz, *Problèmes* . . ., pp. 24-25.

[16] We do not enter into the discussion of the various opinions held by contemporary thinkers on the matter. The reference to a change of position should be to Husserl's first edition of the *Logische Untersuchungen*—but this is hardly possible since the subsequent editions are the ones currently used.

Introduction

of elaboration and clarification, so that he developed a phenomenology wherein the world of consciousness appeared more clearly as an intersubjective world, a community of persons in an intentional transcendental relation in and with the world as phenomenon. The ambition of his philosophy was now to explore this world of common experience (Lebenswelt) and to describe the pre-predicative experience of man in the world.[17]

This Lebenswelt which Husserl undertakes to describe, presents itself in experience, whether actually or virtually, that is to say, in perception, imagination, memory, etc.; this world of common experience, whose presence is at least silently recognized by our conscious selves, is the presupposition and the ground of all our activities. But this common world is not a purely natural world; it is, rather, a socio-historical world, relative to a certain milieu wherein conscious subjects live. Now, for Husserl, phenomenology has the tremendous task of accounting for the world at large as well as for "mundane existents in particular and ... for all objective entities whatsoever, in terms of experiences, acts, operations, and productions . . . of consciousness."[18] How does Husserl effect this accounting? By a systematic and comprehensive study of the relation which attains between all being (to which we are accustomed to direct our attention in a naive approach) and our consciousness of the same—that is, by studying the relation between such being and the acts of consciousness through which being appears and in which such being of consciousness originates.

But the world for Husserl is also made up of other subjects and therefore it can be called an intersubjective world.

---

[17]It will be seen how much Merleau-Ponty owes to the insights of the late Husserl. In this we can find justification for Merleau-Ponty's assertion that his phenomenology is modeled after Husserl's.

[18]Aron Gurwitsch, "The Last Works of Edmund Husserl," *Philosophy and Phenomenological Research*, XVIII (Sept. 1956-June 1957), p. 379. Cited hereafter as "Last Works . . ."

Merleau-Ponty

It is clear that each subject will have a different view of the mundane objects which appear in his consciousness as phenomena; but all these varying presentations are phenomena of the same world and only prove the truth of one's own experience; that is, individual experiences complement and correct one another:

> Besides being *objects in the Lebenswelt,* we are at the same time *subjects with respect to the Lebenswelt,* insofar as it derives its meaning and the sense of its existence from our collective mental life, from our acts (concatenated and interlocked with those of our fellow men) of perceiving, experiencing, reasoning, purposeful acting, etc. Collective accomplishments become part and parcel of the *Lebenswelt* which not only is as it is conceived of by the respective community, but also comprises all its creations, both material and mental.[19]

Just how Husserl will account for the intersubjective relations and for intersubjective constitutions in the light of his famous "reductions" and his "intentionality"[20] is a question which Merleau-Ponty will discuss and criticize; it is interesting to note, however, that the former tries to overcome the difficulty by having recourse to the notion of the Ego-pole in transcendental function. In this transcendental intersubjectivity the Ego-pole enjoys a privileged position— a claim which Merleau-Ponty will contest—by which the other Ego-poles will always appear to me, the privileged Ego-pole, as "other Ego-poles." The world itself is experienced as common precisely because it is seen to be the correlate of transcendental intersubjectivity.[21]

---

[19] Gurwitsch, "Last Works . . .," p. 372.
[20] We will have occasion to return to this topic. Cf. Bibliography for works on Husserl's phenomenology.
[21] Gurwitsch, "Last Works . . .," p. 386.

Introduction

The problem of solipsism which may seem to be the necessary consequence of Husserl's "constitution" is really overcome by the intersubjective communication: the perceiving subject cannot be a solipsist, because the very world he perceives includes and implies other subjects, if not actually present at least virtually so; the world of common experience is precisely not "the world" unless subjects make it so by communication resulting from intersubjective perceptions. Gurwitsch expresses this very clearly:

> It must be pointed out that the thing as it objectively is, is given to nobody, since it is, for the consciousness of everybody, nothing other than the systematic unity of an indefinitely open multiplicity of perceptual experience, his own as well as those of his fellow men.[22]

It must not be forgotten, however, that in spite of all efforts towards a phenomenology grounded on the *Lebenswelt*, Husserl's philosophy remains an idealism and a systematic analysis of the phenomena. Fink, Husserl's disciple, comments on the grandeur of the Husserlian works by emphasizing the incomparable subtility of the analysis, the extremely critical approach. He affirms that Husserl has developed in his phenomenology a tremendous capability for questioning intentionality. Intentional analysis, as envisaged by Husserl, is capable of making explicit the hidden meanings of which life is a bearer. But this explicitation requires an infinite patience and a high degree of attention, together with a calm observation of the enfolding meanings of life appearing in consciousness, through the intentional threads which make up the tissue of the Lebenswelt. The importance and the value of this intentional analysis cannot be overstressed, and Husserl's works have precisely demon-

---

[22]Gurwitsch, "Last Works . . .," pp. 382-83.

strated that this is so, by opening the way to its accomplishment.[23]

And Van Breda, concluding a study on Husserl's reductions affirms that

> the philosopher—being by definition the man who attempts to discover the origin of all data [of the given] and who makes an effort to live an authentic life—must practice phenomenological reduction if he does not want to betray his vocation. The transcendental epoche imposes itself categorically and imperatively to his liberty.[24]

Summing up, phenomenology as intended by Husserl, and this includes his first developments as well as his later works, is meant to be a philosophical endeavor based on a presuppositionless approach to the immediately given, the world of common experience, the *Lebenswelt*. That is not to say that reason should be discarded. As a matter of fact, Husserl claims that phenomenology opens new dimensions in rational thinking by establishing a rationalism which is utterly radical—radical in the sense of going to the roots of things.

> *Reason is not an accidental de facto ability*, not a title for possible accidental matters of fact, but rather a title for *an all-embracing essentially necessary structural form belonging to all transcendental subjectivity.*
>
> Reason refers to possibilities of verification; and verification refers ultimately to making evident and having as evident . . .

---

[23] Eugen Fink, "L'analyse intentionelle et le problème de la pensée spéculative," *Problèmes* . . ., p. 81.
[24] Van Breda, "Note sur: Réduction et authenticité d'après Husserl," *Revue de Métaphysique et de Morale* (Jan.-Mar., 1951), p. 5. This brief work is well worth studying for its faithful rendering of Husserl's thought.

Introduction

> . . . in the broadest sense, evidence denotes a universal primal phenomenon of intentional life . . .[25]

Therefore Husserl's phenomenology far from being irrational, brings rationalism to a new level.

The basic notions of phenomenology, as discussed above, are valid whether we consider it (with Husserl) a "strict science," a "manner or style of thought" (as Merleau-Ponty puts it in his Preface to *Phénoménologie de la perception*), or just a method of approach to an existential philosophy (as has been used by existentialists).[26] Whether phenomenology actually is a philosophy in its own right some have doubted. That one ought to approach philosophy without presupposition is a good philosophical tenet; that one ought to accept every intuition as final and complete revelation of reality is not a valid position.[27] However, there is hardly a phenomenologist who would claim this; and it is not very likely that anyone be inclined to mistake Husserl's phenomenology for mere phenomenalism, or to ignore the profound influence of Husserl's phenomenology on modern philosophy.

4. *Existentialism*

As was previously hinted, phenomenology as a method has been used by philosophers with widely differing viewpoints, leading to different interpretations and conclusions of which an outstanding one is existentialism. Although Husserl himself had undoubtedly prepared the way for this by his theories of subjectivity and intersubjectivity, he was prob-

---

[25] Edmund Husserl, *Cartesian Meditations, An Introduction to Phenomenology*, tr. Dorion Cairns (The Hague: Martinus Nijhoff, 1960), p. 57.
[26] E.g., Sartre, Heidegger, Marcel.
[27] E. P. Welch, *The Philosophy of Edmund Husserl: The Origin and Development of Phenomenology* (New York: Columbia University Press, 1941), p. 168.

ably very far, even in his later years, from anticipating the existentialist movement. He was concerned with a science of essences, and his "Ego-poles" were no less "reduced phenomena" than anything else; the existentialists instead center their attention on existence rather than essence; for them the Ego-subject is to be experienced in the richness of his being-in-the-world rather than investigated as pure phenomenon.

The reason why phenomenology lent itself so readily to the existential interpretation is quite obvious: since the existentialist is concerned not with the *notion* of existence, but rather with the existent, there is an appeal common to both phenomenology and existentialism in the phenomena to be described as well as in the revelation of the consciousness experiencing the world of phenomena. However, the conscious subject experiencing the world could never be a "disinterested spectator"; on the contrary, the existentialist is precisely the philosopher of the subjective, of the personal, of the engaged individual. Existential philosophy is interested in the human subject, who is always free to choose his own actions and thus give direction to his own life, making himself "unique." The mainspring of existentialism is then the personal commitment—within the world of one's experience. The subject is then vitally concerned with facts and circumstances involving his personal being, and he cannot divorce himself from that which refers to him most intimately. Thus we may say that the subjectivity of the existentialist is the realm of those realities which are more profoundly human and personal. From an existential point of view, philosophy will be concerned not so much with problems to be solved as with mysteries to be penetrated. Discussion, analysis, philosophical reflection will not have as point of departure some principle or abstract generalization, but the human question here and now confronting this concrete human being, whose concern will also be the focal

Introduction

point of the investigation. In other words, where traditional philosophy attempted to solve abstract and hypothetical problems relating to man in general, existentialism is concerned with the concrete human existent in the world, and attempts to illuminate and direct precisely this individual existent. It is for this reason that, ultimately, man becomes his own measure, his own "creator" of values.[28]

From the beginning of the movement, Existentialism has stressed the human affective element and has placed it in the realm of philosophy, along with conceptual expressions and reason. Thus, the existential philosophers developed certain themes which form the tissue of man's concrete and existential facticity.

Historically, the movement goes back to Kierkegaard, whose opposition to the systematization of Hegel and the conceptualization of rationalism brought him to emphasize the existential experience of the individual and the significance of the personal commitment. Existence is, for him, steeped in the cares and anxieties of this world: yet, "It is Kierkegaard who gave the term existence the meaning it has kept in the subsequently so-called philosophies of existence, and who closely linked the feeling of existence with the feeling of transcendence [towards God]."[29]

Heidegger, unlike Kierkegaard, accepts a transcendence without God, looks forward to the future as oriented towards death—death is the end of existence.[30] The feeling of

---

[28]Obviously, a commitment to the human condition, or a realization of one's involvement in the world, need not lead one to the ultimate "self-creation" or to the denial of the Absolute. Cf. Frederick Coplestone, *Contemporary Philosophy: Studies in Logical Positivism and Existentialism* (London: Burns & Oates, 1956).

[29]Jean Wahl, *The Philosopher's Way* (New York: Oxford University Press, 1948), p. 41.

[30]See Appendix II, p. 275. Most commentators maintain that Heidegger is an atheist—that is, he does not know whether there is a God, though he thinks it would be a good thing if there were. However, others maintain that Heidegger's meaning in allowing a transcendence without God is this: we cannot know God in a positive way—therefore

contingency is closely linked with the experience of existence. Each existentialist will call this contingency by a different name, will stress human helplessness before life, will seek a way out of life's absurdity and meaninglessness. Thus Kierkegaard's "dread" will call for the "leap of faith" in God; Sartre will counteract his experience of nausea[31] by his limitless free choice, his own "project" and his own values; (Jasper also had recognized, with Kierkegaard and Nietzsche, that existence is "choice"). Camus will strive to overcome absurdity by rebellion, and will be saved by human love, if not by the divine. Marcel will bring to the existential scene a genuine light: hope;[32] but Marcel, more serenely than Kierkegaard, has directed his movement of transcendence toward the Absolute, and therefore has given a meaning to life.

The main contentions of the existentialists is that man is condemned to exist, to make his own projects; to be responsible for others (Sartre); there is no essense;[33] that is, existence is without content. True, existence cannot be deduced from essence; but pure existence is no existence at all. The isolation in which the individual finds himself in existentialism is precisely the result of this "contentless" existence. Beginning with Kierkegaard's "secret" the existentialist finds himself alone, unique. To be an authentic

---

we cannot speak of Him as if we did (this is an implicit criticism of classical philosophy's claims that a knowledge of God as He is can be had by man). Kockelmans—Personal correspondence.

[31] Jean P. Sartre, *Nausea*, tr. by Lloyd Alexander (London: New Directions, 1949).

[32] Gabriel Marcel, *Homo Viator*, tr. E. Crawfort (Chicago: Regnery, 1951).

[33] "There is no essence" has come to be almost synonymous with existentialism; however, this does not apply to phenomenology; an existentialist like Merleau-Ponty most emphatically maintains quite the opposite; (cf. *P. P.*, Avant Propos, especially pp. I and IX ff.) Moreover, even for the existentialists the expression means not literally what it says, but that man does not have a static essence—a definitive nature; that he can, and does make himself what he wants to be. It is a way of emphasizing the role of man's project and the extent of his liberty.

Introduction

individual one must be away from the crowd, and, by definition, "the exception." To be an existent is to be "this" individual existent, not a nature, not a "copy" of which there are many, but a being who wills himself what he is not and "becomes" by his own absolute choice.

Marcel differs by declaring that one is authentic only in communion with the other—although for him also the necessity of avoiding the "crowd" is emphasized; not however, for the sake of a solipsistic position, but to avoid anonymity. Marcel's existentialism is, in a way, very closely related to Personalism.[34]

5. *Phenomenological Existentialism*

Although Existentialism has incorporated much of the phenomenological method, not all existentialists are phenomenologists, and phenomenologists are not necessarily existentialists.[35] In general, whether existentialists or phenomenologists, contemporary thinkers have delimited their investigation to some few aspects of reality: phenomenologists usually select a specific field wherein to conduct their investigation. Professor Lauer gives a listing of such philosophic trends, and adds that in each case the authors are concerned with "essences" while at the same time they contribute "sociological, linguistic, epistemological, and logical developments."[36] This fact is an affirmation of the value of phe-

---

[34] Mounier and Nédoncelle, among others, have developed their thought along these lines. Cf. Emmanuel Mounier, *Personalism* (London: Routledge & Kegan Paul Ltd. [1952]); Maurice Nédoncelle, *Vers une philosophie de l'amour et de la personne* (Paris: Aubier, Montiogne, 1957). Also cf. R. O. Johann, *The Meaning of Love* (Westminster, Md.: The Newman Press, 1959).
[35] William A. L. Luijpen, in his book *Existential Phenomenology* (Duquesne Studies, Philosophical Series 12, Pittsburg: Duquesne University Press, 3rd impr., 1963) makes a profound study of the development of phenomenology as existential philosophy—a re-thinking of eternal problems in a new light. Cited hereafter as *Phenomenology*.
[36] His classification is as follows: Heidegger, Jaspers, Marcel and Conrad-Martius, ontological implications; Pfänder, Geiger, Merleau-Ponty, Ricoeur, and Binswanger, psychology; Von Hilde-

nomenology and also of the interdependence of philosophic disciplines.

One of the philosophers who made the most of phenomenological possibilities in relation to the existential approach is Maurice Merleau-Ponty. He detached himself from both movements in that he did not opt for either in an exclusive manner. Yet, he belonged to both in a sense. Jean Hyppolite observes that Merleau-Ponty has been able to confront and penetrate that primordial "massive" existence which can never become completely transparent to itself and that nevertheless is at the same time apart from and within things though it cannot transcend itself in its temporality.[37]

Merleau-Ponty could not conceive the philosopher as a mere disinterested spectator. Yet, he maintained it was possible to reflect on the "irreflexive" in such a way as to make the world *be* for consciousness. However, as will be seen, his answers to the questions which arise are always, at best, ambiguous, precisely because the subject doing the investigation is himself—existentially—within that reality which he investigates phenomenologically.

A study of the works of Merleau-Ponty will help to answer some of the questions raised by modern philosophy, with a special emphasis on the role of the body in interpersonal relations.

In the study which will follow, we will attempt to bring to light Merleau-Ponty's valuable contributions to phenomenology as well as to existentialism and try to show how his

---

brand, Hartman, and Scheler, ethics and general theory of values; Otto, Hering, and Van der Leeuw, religion; Simmel, Ingarden, Malraux, Duffrenne, and Lipps, asthetics. J. Quentin Lauer, *The Triumph of Subjectivity: An Introduction to Transcendental Phenomenology* (New York: Fordham University Press [1958]), pp. 1-5. Cited hereafter as *Triumph* . . .

[37] Jean Hyppolite, "Existence et dialectique dans la philosophie de Merleau-Ponty," "*Les temps modernes,* 17e année, Nos. 184-85, Numero special: Maurice Merleau-Ponty [July-Aug. 1960], pp. 228-44; p. 230.

Introduction

insights may be useful in constructing at least a theory of intersubjective relations, for the question of truly personal relations does not come up clearly in his thought.[38]

---

[38]After learning the meaning given by Merleau-Ponty to "intersubjective" we will find it necessary to distinguish between intersubjective and personal relations. The two terms are not interchangeable.

CHAPTER TWO

THE PHILOSOPHY OF MERLEAU-PONTY
PHENOMENOLOGICAL AND EXISTENTIAL

In order to understand the philosophical thought of Merleau-Ponty it is necessary to see it in relation to both his phenomenological approach to reality and his existentialism, keeping in mind that he does not intend to elaborate a metaphysics, and is therefore concerned with that which "appears" and not directly with the ontological implications thereof. Further, the terms he uses have a meaning neither like to nor comparable with the traditional one.

It seems therefore imperative to approach Merleau Ponty's philosophy directly, without trying to explain it in terms of any philosophical system. Merleau-Ponty, in the Preface to *Phénoménologie de la perception,* tells us just how far he considers phenomenology a method of philosophical investigation and in what sense he maintains that phenomenology is already a philosophy. His position makes him at once a disciple of Husserl and an independent phenomenologist. Like Husserl, he defines phenomenology as "the study of essences," but immediately detaches himself from the master by adding that, in addition to attempting to define essences, phenomenology is also a philosophy which "replaces essence in existence"; with Husserl, he affirms that it is a transcendental philosophy; yet his phenomenology is existential, because "it is also a philosophy for which the world is already there [déjà là] before reflection as an inalienable presence. . . ."[1] In subsequent discussions Merleau-Ponty will come to disclaim any idealistic tenden-

---

[1] *P. P.,* p. I. Cf. A. De Waelhens, *Une philosophie de l' ambiguité; L'existentialisme de Maurice Merleau-Ponty.* Bibliothèque philosophique de Louvain (Louvain: Publications Universitaires de Louvain, 1951) Chapter XVIII. Cited hereafter as *Une philosophie.*

cies as incompatible with phenomenology, although this is precisely the position of Husserl.[2]

The phenomenological method of Merleau-Ponty excludes both reflexive analysis and scientific reflection; it is a movement distinct from idealistic self-reflection, and aims at the pure description of the pre-objective world, that is to say, the world prior to all constructions either of science or of conventional everyday concepts, of the world prior to knowledge and of which knowledge speaks.[3]

For Merleau-Ponty the world of my experience is the natural field of all my thoughts and perceptions. The return to the things themselves advocated by Husserl really means almost a protest against science in favor of a return to the world of experience, in which at each moment my perceptive field is filled with lights, noises, tactile impressions so fleeting that I can hardly connect them in my perception of the whole, but of which I am certain: I recognize them as belonging to the world and I never confuse them with my dreams.[4] Why is this so certain to him? Because, he answers,

> the real is a solid tissue; it does not wait for our judgment to take up the most surprising phenomena, nor to reject our most plausible imaginations.[5]

It is for this reason that our perceptions are living, warm, in a sense intimate to the self experiencing them; and that is why the experiences are unhesitatingly held to be

---

[2] On Husserl, cf. Marvin Farber, *The Foundations of phenomenology: Husserl and the quest for a rigorous science of philosophy* (Cambridge: Harvard University Press, 1943); J.Q. Lauer, *Edmund Husserl: La philosophie comme science rigoureuse* (Epiméthée, essais philosophiques; Paris: Presses Universitaires de France, 1955); cited hereafter as *Philosophie*. Lauer, *Phénoménologie de Husserl: essais sur la génèse de l'intentionnalité* (Paris: Presses Universitaires de France, 1955).
[3] *P. P.*, p. IV.
[4] *P. P.*, p. IV-V.
[5] *P. P.*, p. V.

real, not a conjecture, not a probability. Hence, Merleau-Ponty can say with conviction that man is not "interiority," but that his truth is the truth of "being-in-the-world." Man does not find the truth except in his commitment to the world.[6]

This commitment makes it impossible for man to be a detached spectator of the world.[7] Man can at best suspend his engagement and his movement within the world, or render it inoperative in order to have full awareness of it—it is necessary to step out of a situation in order to view it. Commenting on Husserl's "reductions" Merleau-Ponty finds Eugen Fink's formula best suited to express the real meaning of this abstension from the world: "astonishment" before the world.[8]

> Reflection does not retire from the world towards the unity of consciousness as foundation of the world. It only withdraws in order to see the transcendences stand forth clearly. Reflection distends the intentional threads which link us to the world in order to make them stand out. It alone is consciousness of the world precisely because it reveals it as strange and paradoxical.[9]

Can we not see in this strange and paradoxical world the world of the existentialist? The obviously essentialist interpretation of Husserl would not be (or have been) misunderstood by the existentialist "dissidents" if the true import of the reduction had been grasped: complete reduction

---

[6] *P. P.,* p. V.
[7] Herein Merleau-Ponty differs sharply from Husserl. Cf. Lauer, *Triumph* . . . p. 80, Note 31. Cf. also: Kullman and Taylor, "The Pre-objective World," *The Review of Metaphysics,* Vol. XII, No. 1, Issue No. 45, Sept. 1958, pp. 108-32; cited hereafter as "The Pre-objective." Cf. also Nicola Abbagnano, *Storia della filosofia,* Vol. II, Part II (Torino: Tipographia Sociale Torinese, 1954), pp. 641-42. Cited hereafter as *Storia* . . .
[8] *P. P.,* p. VIII. Eugen Fink was Husserl's assistant.
[9] *P. P.,* p. VIII.

is impossible. Hence Husserl constantly questioned himself about the possibility of reduction. This rupture with the world, this retirement from the world in order to see it, does not really reveal to us anything more than this: the world springs forth, unmotivated, and we have the task of giving it meaning—this is the existentialist's creed. But for Merleau-Ponty, complete reduction being impossible, it is never possible to see the world at a distance and with a detachment sufficient to allow us to see it clearly.

> If we were absolute spirit the reduction would present no problem. But since on the contrary, we are in the world, since, likewise, our reflections take place within the temporal flux which they attempt to capture . . . there is no thought which embraces all our thoughts.[10]

It is precisely because the world is never seen in the proper perspective—that is, without our being enmeshed in its threads—that our thought about it can never be absolutely clear or total. Because of this incompleteness of our thought, if we want to be faithful to the phenomenological method, we must always begin anew:

> philosophy . . . is a renewed experience of its own beginning, and it consists entirely of a description of this beginning . . . this radical reflection consists in consciousness of its own dependence with respect to a nonreflective life which is its initial, constant, and final situation.[11]

---

[10] *P. P.*, p. VIII-IX.
[11] *P. P.*, p. IX, Professor Lauer puts the matter thus: the phenomenologist insists that "although phenomenology is a science of reflexion, it is greatly concerned with 'prereflexive' consciousness. In a certain sense, this aspect of phenomenology has been accentuated more by the followers of Husserl than by Husserl himself [Merleau-Ponty in particular] but the latter did not fail to signalize its importance. If consciousness is by definition consciousness-of something, and if reflexion is consciousness of consciousness, then, prior to any reflexion there must be a consciousness of something. Thus even though phenom-

Merleau-Ponty

Merleau-Ponty concludes—evidently referring to Husserl—affirming that the phenomenological reduction is not the formula for an idealistic philosophy, but for an existential one. It is necessary to point out here that the author, at the very beginning of his philosophizing, makes very clear man's position in the world: he is a presence, not an event in the world; his existence does not come from certain "causes," in certain "circumstances," physical or social; he is not the result of certain "conditioning forces"—on the contrary, he is the conditioner, the very being which gives meaning to and sustains the "world." In this sense, Merleau-Ponty speaks of man as the "absolute source," he is the one who "makes" the world in which he is—for the world would not "be" if he were not there to become its center.[12] To speak of man as "the absolute source," in terms of this philosophy is not to make it an idealistic one: the subject is the "absolute source of sense", not of being. Herein is the truly significant distinction between idealism and existentialism. That it is so is clear from the many references of Merleau-Ponty to the world as "already there" before I consider it reflectively or scientifically. But it is also clear that I cannot approach the world reflectively unless, as a conscious being, I become aware of it in a primordial, prereflective encounter. This leaves no room for doubt about Merleau-Ponty's existential stand.

1. *Specific Object of Investigation*

Merleau-Ponty's primary interest in phenomenological research is in the field of knowledge, of which he feels the

---

enology properly so called begins with reflexion, the objectivity with which it is concerned is present in consciousness prior to reflexion, and if objectivity is to be understood, pre-reflexive consciousness must be understood as that wherein objectivity first resides." *Triumph* . . . , p. 88.

[12]*P. P.*, p. III, "Je suis non pas un 'être vivant' ou même un 'homme' ou même 'une conscience', avec tous les caractères que la zoologie, l' anatomie sociale ou la psychologie inductive reconnaissent à ces produits de la nature ou de l'histoire,—je suis la source absolue. . . ."

fundamental fact is perception; by it, man finds himself in immediate and originary contact with the world—that world to which man is indissolubly bound. For Merleau-Ponty, man is in the world, and the world is in man, as man is in other men. The world can be defined as the intersection of the experiences of men.

> The phenomenological world is not pure being. The meaning which appears at the intersection of my experiences with those of others, by the enmeshing of the ones with the others, is therefore inseparable from the subjectivity and the intersubjectivity which form their unity by taking up my past experiences in my present experiences and those of others in my own.[13]

Because of our engagement in the world, which does not permit us to stand off as disinterested spectators, we cannot, strictly speaking, submit our perceptual experiences to a philosophical reflective search without being at the same time involved in the very world we are trying to define. Therefore our concern is precisely with that very effective engagement in the world which we must try to understand and conceptualize. For our author the knowledge of essences is not the end, but the means to an understanding of our own existence as contingent and then to the nature of this existence. Essences, ideas, are not the object of philosophy but rather the means by which our existence—too caught up in the world to know itself precisely as existence—can know itself through reflexive thought.

However, even this knowledge of ourselves as existents will be, at best, ambiguous for a very significant reason: essences, for Merleau-Ponty, are never separated from existence; then, one might ask, how can they be the means by which we know ourselves as existents? Obviously, there is need of interpretation of the term "essence" as used by

---

[13] *P. P.*, p. XV.

Merleau-Ponty. It is not used in the traditional sense: for him, to speak of an essence is not to speak of an abstraction, or of the mere meaning of the verbal expression "essence"— already a step removed from the primary datum. When he tells us what the essence of consciousness would be, he gives us a very good example: to seek the essence of consciousness is not to seek the idea of it once it has been expressed intellectually. It means, instead, to seek that which is prior to any formulation—in this case to recover the presence of self to self, "the fact of my consciousness, which is in the last analysis that which one wants to express by the word and the concept."[14] It is because we have this direct experience of our own consciousness that language has a meaning. He reads the same interpretation of the notion of essence into Husserl's philosophy. He even claims that Jean Wahl is incorrect in maintaining that Husserl separates essences from existence: the separation is merely in terms of language. But even this separation of essences is only apparent, because they are still founded on the pre-predicative conscious life.[15]

Yet, according to commentators of Husserl, there is in his transcendental phenomenology a clearly expressed essentialism. Professor Lauer maintains that it is the very summit of essentialism to hold, as Husserl does, that the being of anything is its being constituted as what it is. Moreover, he adds, for Husserl the reference to existence is not significant; the spectator's attitude is therefore possible for the philosopher.[16]

Abbagnano comments that it is somewhat of a paradox that Husserl, so firm in rejecting every form of naturalism, has not been able to disengage himself from naturalism in

---
[14] *P. P.*, p. X.
[15] *P. P.*, p. X.
[16] Lauer, *Triumph* . . . , pp. 80, 90-95. Cf. also: Lauer, *Philosophie* . . ., p. 167, Note 246; Pos, Problèmes . . ." for discussion on Husserl's essentialism.

his notion of philosophy. In advocating for the philosopher a complete detachment from the world in order to contemplate it as a pure spectator, Husserl overlooked the fact that a contemplative attitude is a particular manner of looking at the world, and therefore involves a choice, an effort, a constant application. He did not see that a purely contemplative philosophy is an illusion: "the attitude of the disinterested spectator *qualifies* the world, that is, it modifies it, as any other attitude would; so that the implicit pretension of seeing the world 'such as it is' is illusory."[17]

T. W. Adorno is of the opinion that Husserl's position is nothing but idealism. To maintain that every primary intuition is to be accepted as it is given, or as it presents itself to consciousness, reverts back to the idealist principle of consciousness as the ultimate source of all our knowledge, so that an analysis of consciousness is sufficient for the attainment of a sound philosophical position. Thus the doctrine of essences, which should have been Husserl's strongest anti-idealist move, turned out to be "the summit of idealism: the pure essence, the objectivity of which seems to spurn any subjective constitution, is nothing but subjectivity in its abstractness . . ."[18]

It is with these considerations in mind that Merleau-Ponty's criticism of both sensism and transcendental idealism must be viewed. He maintains that both positions "reduce" the world, the first by making it nothing but "states of consciousness" that is, "states of ourselves"; the second, by making it immanent to consciousness thus destroying the aseity of things. But the eidetic reduction respects the world as it appears prior to all reflective consciousness: "It is the ambition to equate reflection to the unreflective life of consciousness."[19]

---

[17] Abbagnano, *Storia* . . . , p. 642.
[18] T. W. Adorno, "Husserl and the problem of Idealism," *Journal of Philosophy*, Vol. 37, (1940), pp. 5-18; p. 18.
[19] *P. P.*, pp. X-XI.

Merleau-Ponty

How Merleau-Ponty tries to attain his aim is seen in his two major works, *La structure du comportement*[20] and *Phénoménologie de la perception*. Both works are phenomenological in intent, although only the latter is an express declaration of it; *La structure du comportement* has for its aim "to understand the relations between consciousness and nature"; the vast meaning Merleau-Ponty assigns to "nature"—organic, psychological or even social—gives us an inkling of the range of phenomena his investigation will embrace. The whole of the first work could properly be viewed as a great reduction—a preparation for *Phénoménologie de la perception*. He attempts to do so by dropping the scientific garb with which things are presented to us, as well as the psychological interpretation which accompany them, in order to arrive at "the thing itself" as it is in pre-reflexive consciousness. But to do this, he undertakes to examine the phenomena which psychology—especially Gestalt—reveals, with a view to discover their meaning without allowing any "pre-judgment" to influence his description.[21]

In *Phénoménologie de la perception*, he then goes further, and carries on the investigation by a further reduction: he tries to purify the "things" and the "world" even of that cloak of familiarity with which we are accustomed to see them, and which is, therefore, already a "construction." This is what he attempts to do in order to achieve—by a "radical reduction" Husserl would say—an insight into the "pre-objective" world of our primary experience.[22]

The eidetic reduction is, for Merleau-Ponty, the attempt to make the world appear before me as it is before I ponder on how it should be. It is not the negation of reflection, but the decision to reflect in another way. If I ask myself

---
[20] (Bibliothèque de Philosophie Contemporaine. Paris: Presses Universitaires de France, quatrième édition, 1960). Introduction, pp. 1-3. Cited hereafter as *S.C.*
[21] *S. C.*, Introduction. pp. 1-3.
[22] Cf. Taylor and Kullman, "The Pre-objective". We will return to the subject later.

whether I am perceiving or dreaming I have already forfeited the genuine phenomena of the world. The fact that I can ask the question at all simply means that I have already a foundation for my questions, the perceived world which I can distinguish from an illusion. The real problem is to "make explicit the primordial knowledge of the 'real', to describe the perception of the world as that on which our idea of truth is always founded."[23] Spiegelberg calls Merleau-Ponty's phenomenological reduction "the device which permits us to discover the spontaneous surge of the life world." This reduction, taken from Husserl, will be used by Merleau-Ponty for a refutation of phenomenological idealism. In fact, he attempts to use phenomenology as a means of discovering existences, rather than essences; he wants to be an existential phenomenologist.[24]

This reduction, therefore, of itself dispels all doubt with regard to the truth value of our experience. It is not a question of asking whether our evidences are truths, or whether such evidences might not be illusory as compared to some "truth in itself." If we ask the question about illusion it is because we have recognized illusion, but this is only possible on the testimony of some perceptions which are indubitable—that is, which are their own assurance of truth. The very fear of error, of deception, "is but another affirmation of our power to discover error—and this could not tear us away from the truth. We are in the truth and evidence is the experience of truth."[25] Perception is to be accepted without reflective analysis, as the first and fundamental presence to the world, as the *sine qua non* of our experience of truth. Perception cannot be questioned, for to do so we would have to regress to a more primary experi-

---

[23] *P. P.*, p. XI.
[24] Spiegelberg, Herbert, *The Phenomenological Movement, a Historical Introduction*. (The Hague: Nijhoff, 1960, 2 vol.), Vol. II, pp. 534-35. Cited hereafter as *Phenomenological* . . .
[25] *P. P.*, p. XI.

ence; but is there a stage prior to perception? "To look for the essence of perception is to declare that perception is not presumed to be true, but is defined for us as access to the truth."[26] That means simply this: I would seek a definition of perception, in an idealistic sense, by trying to find in my own thoughts a clear conception of what perception ought to be—but then I would by that very fact be unfaithful to my own experience of the world as given to me, and "I would seek what makes this world possible rather than what this world is."[27] This is, however, for Merleau-Ponty, already secondary reflection upon the given, and not the lived experience phenomenologically described. True, the evidence of perception is not exhaustive of the richness of the world; but it is a lived communication with the world, by which I am open to it without taking possession of it or comprehending it fully.[28] I will never be able to grasp such fullness and richness; my knowledge of the world as it is—not as I may theoretically think it to be—will always be somewhat ambiguous, never complete, always implying a "beyond" and a "more" which I may never possess fully, of which I can never give complete reason.[29] For Merleau-Ponty, nothing is to be supposed, invented, constituted; the presuppositions of science, of common sense "doxa," the constructions of idealism have no place in Merleau-Ponty's approach to reality because they all build a possible apart from the real, or they posit a "possibility" without any ground in that "reality [which] is a solid tissue."

Thus eidetic reduction, which for Husserl marked the way from existence to essence, for Merleau-Ponty becomes the means by which he attempts to catch things and facts in their uniqueness. Thus his approach is well characterized by him in the Preface when he states that the eidetic method is really

---
[26]*P. P.* p. XI.
[27]*P. P.*, p. XI.
[28]This is arrived at by means of reflection.
[29]*P. P.*, p. XII.

a "phenomenological positivism which grounds the possible on the real"[30], that is, by this method Merleau-Ponty aims at avoiding "construction" of essences (in the idealistic sense) and accepts as valid only the structures derived from lived experience.

The discussion of reduction and its function in the phenomenological investigation prepares the way for a consideration of the notion of intentionality (often cited as the most important discovery of phenomenology). Intentionality can be understood only in the light of the reductions.

Merleau-Ponty declares at the outset that there is actually nothing new in the assertion that "consciousness is the consciousness of something." What seems worthy of note in Husserl, he declares, is the fact that the latter distinguishes the intentionality of the act from the operational intentionality.[31] The intentionality of our act is that of our judgments and of our voluntary adoption of a position in any given case; the operational intentionality is that which establishes our union with the world previous to any pre-predicative and objective knowledge; it is evident in our thoughts and

---

[30] *P. P.*, p. XII. It has been suggested that Merleau-Ponty's philosophy is, in some respects, scholastic. This would be an instance to prove the point—if we could attribute to Merleau-Ponty's terminology the scholastic meaning.

[31] Spiegelberg, *Phenomenological* . . . , p. 110: "I might sum up the account of Husserl's 'intention' by describing it as that component of any act which is responsible not only for its pointing at an object but also for (a) interpreting pre-given materials in such a way that a full object is presented to our consciousness, (b) establishing the identity between the referents of several intentional acts, (c) connecting the various stages of intuitive fulfillment, and (d) 'constituting' the object meant."

For a detailed description of intentionality, see Lauer, *Triumph* . . . , Ch. 3, wherein the author observes that Husserl was not followed to the end even by his closest disciples, among whom Merleau-Ponty— that is to say, to the point of refusing to accept anything which is not "constituted in consciousness"—and the "constitution" is of course, "intentional"; but for Husserl this penetrating grasp of intentionality leads to the knowledge of the transcendental ego, which becomes, at the very end of the Husserlian reductions "a pure flow of consciousness." (Ch. 3, pp. 46-64).

in our evaluation of behaviors; it is found chiefly in our sentient life and "it furnished the theme which our knowledge will try to express in accurate terminology."[32]

As he sees it, the task of philosophy is not to render clear—by analysis—that rapport with the world which expresses itself indefatigably in us; philosophy can only place that expression before us again and again, and exhibit it for our acknowledgement such as it is. Philosophy is not intended to "explain" reality, but simply to present it to us descriptively.[33]

Yet, the situation of consciousness is quite strange for Merleau-Ponty: on the one hand, the imperious unity of the pre-objective world imposes itself on it; on the other, consciousness has the power to take such "given" from the viewpoint it chooses; such a viewpoint will recall another, it will complement it and thus enlarge the horizon of the whole. The enlarged notion of intentionality which he maintains makes it possible for phenomenology to go beyond the "intellection" of unchanging natures—Husserl's essences—and to become truly a phenomenology of genesis. This was also, it is true, the aim of Husserl, but Merleau-Ponty wants it to take on a much wider meaning.[34] (Later discussion will make clear just how far this intention is carried out by Merleau-Ponty.) Perhaps one could liken this grasp to the totality of vision of Hegel. "To understand" means to recover again the total intention, whether it be question of a thing perceived, or of an historical event or of a doctrine.[35] This implies to grasp not only the properties of the object perceived, the historical facts, or the ideas embodied in the doctrine in question; it means most of all to grasp the very manner of existing of the thing, of the historical event, of the intention in the mind of the thinker. This is a way of

---
[32] *P. P.*, p. XIII.
[33] *P. P.*, p. XIII.
[34] *P. P.*, p. XIII.
[35] *P. P.*, p. XIII.

being in the world, a way which makes the world to be in a certain manner and in which everything becomes meaningful—even the least human act, be it ever so half-hearted or habitual. The historian must be able to take up and assume this manner of expressing the world if he is to grasp the dimension of history.[36]

The above assertion stems from the fact that, for Merleau-Ponty, my behavior is always the taking of a position—no matter how inconsequential my act may be. Even my lack of action is not without consequence, for it will still be the taking of a position—that of indifference—and as such it will have an effect on the rest of the world: it modifies the total situation.[37] "Chance happenings" compensate each other and the "dust of facts" makes an agglomeration which forms a design delineating the human situation in a certain manner, thus making it possible for me to see it and to speak of it.

However, a question presents itself: how am I to understand the events of history? From the economic point of view? From the standpoint of ideologies, of politics, or of religion? Again, should I judge a doctrine from its intrinsic content or through the psychology of its author and the events of his [the author's] life? Holding again to the superiority of—or perhaps to the necessity of—a total viewpoint, Merleau-Ponty insists that I have to consider events and doctrines from all points of view at once, because only therein do I grasp the true and existential meaning of the facts in question. Every approach is indeed true, but *only* insofar as it is not taken by itself to the exclusion of, or in isolation from the other viewpoints. Each perspective presents to us an explicit existential meaning, but to have the

---

[36]Merleau-Ponty's insistence on the all-pervading influence of the pre-personal and pre-objective puts in question—to say the least—this assertion. It will be seen that the personal plays a minor role in the intersubjective and cultural relations. Much is left to the ego-consciousness which for Merleau-Ponty needs not be at the personal level.

[37]*P. P.*, p. XIV.

total picture we must grasp each and every view.[38] Herein, the influence of the "Hegelian truth" as a totality is clearly seen. Also, we can see the application of Merleau-Ponty's analysis of perception of reality as "profiles."[39] In this case each approach would be for us one of the existential profiles of the fact in question, just as in the perception of a solid we are presented one view of the thing at a time. Moreover, just as in perception the thing is seen against the background of the perceptive field, so the facts must be seen against the background of concrete existence which is the foundation of history.

Man can only think in terms of what he is; hence the psychological, as well as the economic explanations of a doctrine, are true; but no reflection on a doctrine will be adequate if it remains divorced from existential experience. The expression "existential experience" is not a tautology. If it is true that every experience is existential insofar as only an existing being can have an experience, yet not all experience is existential. All experience is existential in the very special sense in which Existentialism uses the term. Thus, for instance, the original experience of a scientist is a true experience, but it is not existential, that is to say, total and immediate, and pre-scientific. Existential experience *is* the "being-to-the-world" of man himself, his belonging to the world, his being comitted to his situation. Therefore, I cannot really reflect on a doctrine—and make it mine by assimilating its meaning—unless I "live it" in some way. As Husserl said, the meaning of a doctrine can only be learned by grasping its "genesis," the "genesis of meaning"; this means that our attempt at an understanding is successful only if we extend our investigation to the very foundation of a doctrine, to all the aspects which it embodies. History is indivisible and all the happenings are a manifesta-

---

[38]*P. P.*, p. XIV.
[39]Cf. *S. C.*, Ch. IV, pp. 200-41.

tion of the existential drama of life. To grasp the meaning of a doctrine is to grasp its full implications under all aspects: the life of the author, the historical moment of beginning and development of a doctrine, the influences of said doctrine on others—in a word, the totality of events which cradled it and either fostered or hindered its growth. Events also will determine its future, still unknown to the witness: "because we are in the world, we are condemned to meaning [condamnés au sens] and we can do or say nothing which does not assume a significance in history."[40]

The objection may arise that this insistence of Merleau-Ponty on the lived experience of the pre-objective world may, after all, be motivated by a purely subjective experience hardly worthy of the name of philosophical method and still less of philosophy. This objection has some weight in that Merleau-Ponty merely asserts—does not prove or demonstrate—the validity of his assertions. In fact, he *tells* us that phenomenology is not just a method, but this "all-embracing phenomenology" commits us to a certain conception of being and to an entire philosophy. Spiegelberg quotes Merleau-Ponty as disavowing any distinction between phenomenological description and phenomenological system: "I have never thought that phenomenology was nothing but an introduction to philosophy, I believe that it *is* philosophy." Merleau-Ponty rejects the assumption that phenomenology is a mere vestibule or introduction to philosophy, but denies, on the other hand, that phenomenology is empowered to go beyond description to "explanations." If then phenomenology is description and offers no explanation of the reality it describes, wherein is it rational, philosophical?

Merleau-Ponty answers:

> The most important accomplishment of phenomenology is, without a doubt, to have joined extreme subjectiv-

---

[40] *P. P.,* pp. XIV-XV.

ism and extreme objectivism in the notion of the world or of rationality. Rationality is exactly measured in terms of the experiences in which it reveals itself. There is rationality: that is to say, perspectives overlap, perceptions confirm each other, and thus meaning emerges.[41]

The philosopher therefore finds his rationality in his own world, as perceived and lived. But his meditation on the world—which is intended to clarify his relations to both the world and to the others—does not give his findings a reality which they do not yet possess. Nor can rationality be transformed either into an Absolute Spirit or into a world of the "realist" type. "The phenomenological world is not the explicitation of a more primary being, but the foundation of being; philosophy is not the reflection of a more primary truth, but like art, the realization of a truth."[42]

In other words, the philosopher is not to seek for a Rationality pre-existing in things; "the only Logos which pre-exists is the world itself"[43]: it is therefore the task of the philosopher to make this Logos manifest, even if incompletely (there is no thought which embraces all thought). But the philosophy which undertakes this explicitation is not at first a possibility which in the course of the reflection becomes real: it is real to begin with, as real as the world of which it is a part. Reason is not a problem; it is not a mysterious entity which we must discover or deduce; rather, it is a mystery, whose prodigious workings, however, are well-known to us because rationality is at the very root of all our relations. We cannot fathom its mysterious depth, and we should not attempt to do so, for the dissipation of this mystery would be tantamount to destroying both rationality and the world—further, this could not

---
[41] *P. P.*, p. XV.
[42] *P. P.*, p. XV.
[43] *P. P.*, p. XV.

The Philosophy of Merleau-Ponty

be done for this mystery is beyond reach of any solution.[44] There is here a note of profound respect, awe and astonishment before the world—an attitude which Merleau-Ponty expresses again and again, thus making it quite clear that the philosopher's approach to the world cannot be that of the objective scientist seeking to dominate, but rather that of the lover engaged in dialogue.

For him genuine philosophizing is a relearning to see the world. Now, since he made phenomenology synonymous with philosophy, does this mean that philosophy is its own ground, just as phenomenology rests on its own basis as revelation of the world (the pre-objective world)? This seems to follow logically. Yet, what Merleau-Ponty has to say at the close of his Preface seems to point in another direction:

> All knowledge is rooted in a ground of postulates and finally in our communication with the world as the prime foundation of rationality. Philosophy, as radical reflection, is deprived, in principle, of this resource.[45]

Thus philosophy would have to reflect indefinitely upon itself, meditate, remain in the state of questioning, even in a state of ignorance of its destiny. This then accounts for the incompletion of phenomenology and the perennial beginning of the phenomenological method. Far from being a fault, this incompleteness, this lack of direction so to speak, is the guarantee of a genuine philosophy; if it is the task of phenomenology to reveal the mystery of the world and the mystery of reason, these will remain always in process, in the making, so that the last word can never be said about either. Nor can the mystery be revealed, hence the conscious ambiguity of thought is somewhat justified.[46]

---
[44] *P. P.*, p. XVI.
[45] *P. P.*, p. XVI.
[46] "Il fraudra donc qu'elle s'adresse à elle-même l'interrogation qu'elle adresse à toutes les connaissances, elle se redoublera donc indéfiniment, elle sera, comme dit Husserl, un dialogue ou une méditation infinie, et, dans la mesure même où elle reste fidèle à son intention elle ne saura jamais où elle va." *P. P.*, p. XVI.

This also explains the slow march of phenomenology; it is a laborious work, demanding an engagement, even violence sometimes;

> because of the same type of attention and wonderment, the same exigencies of consciousness, the same will to grasp the meaning of the world or the history in its emergence,

it is not second to the great labors which produced the masterpieces of our literature and art.[47]

2. Scope of His Phenomenology

The question may be asked, how does Merleau-Ponty's own discussion of phenomenology actually give us a clear picture of the meaning and scope of phenomenology "for him"—for it is clear that he intended to develop his own phenomenology even if he did acknowledge Husserl as his master.

The key to his position with regard to phenomenology, as well as to his existentialism, is found in the first sentences of the Preface. After having described phenomenology as the study of essences and the treatment of every problem with a view to discover these essences, he adds:

> But phenomenology is likewise a philosophy which replaces essences in existence, and does not think that man can understand man or the world in any other way than on the basis of their "facticity."[48]

If it is a transcendental philosophy which suspends our natural affirmations in order to understand them, it is how-

---

[47] *P. P.*, p. XVI. Merleau-Ponty, *Éloge de la philosophie*. Leçon inaugurale faite au Collège de France, le jeudi 5 janvier 1953. (3rd ed.; Paris: Gallimard [1953]) especially pp. 79-86, is an elaboration of the above. Cited hereafter as *Éloge*.
[48] *P. P.*, p. I.

ever, a philosophy for which the world is already given as an inalienable presence, before any kind of reflection; the whole concern of this philosophy is to recapture the naive contact with the world in order to give it a philosophical status. The original notion—from Husserl—is here modified to consider the world as given in a way which does not deny the transcendence, but which, at the same time, implies a commitment proper to an existential philosophy.

If Merleau-Ponty thinks of phenomenology as capable of becoming an exact science (Husserl) he also takes into account space, time, and the world as lived[49] in order to describe these, our experiences, without any psychological or scientific "prejudgment," without any presupposition, whether causal, historical or sociological.

Merleau-Ponty has doubtlessly shifted the central meaning of phenomenology: he does not appeal merely to subjectivity, but rather attempts to combine the subjective with the objective approach through what one might call a "bipolar phenomenology." Moreover, though he finds himself in agreement with Husserl in the emphasis he puts on rationality, he reserves to himself the right to describe it differently: for Merleau-Ponty rationality is a mystery closely linked with the mystery of the world itself—should we say an "ambiguous rationality"?

Further, he agrees with Husserl in pointing out the inadequacies of the Kantian reflexive analysis which, moving from our experience of the world to the subject as a condition of the possibility of the experience, but as distinct from it, ceases to be—by that very fact—steeped in experience, and substitutes a reconstruction for an account of the same.

Spiegelberg observes that it is doubtful whether Merleau-Ponty could "go so far as to subscribe to Husserl's ideal of phenomenology as a pure science"; for he has much more

---

[49]Merleau-Ponty develops these themes in *Phénoménologie de la perception*.

the sense of the ambiguous, the relative and the tentative than Husserl had at the beginning of his philosophizing. Merleau-Ponty holds to the notion of a truth still in process, and essentially historical.[50]

Clearly then, Merleau-Ponty has gone beyond Husserl and has developed his own kind of phenomenology. He also maintains that there is no philosophy beyond phenomenology, that is, there is no "movement to a transphenomenal level" as John Bannan observes.[51] But, while in some respects Merleau-Ponty has gone beyond Husserl's own declarations, he has remained behind him in the expectation of positive results. This may be ascribed to his existentialism. It makes a lot of difference whether one is concerned above all with essences rather than existence.

3. Existential Phenomenology

De Waehlens states that Merleau-Ponty's total effort is towards the elaboration of a true existentialism, that is to say, a doctrine of a committed consciousness (conscience engagée). This is the fundamental position which Merleau-Ponty defends at two different levels in *La structure du comportement* and in *Phénoménologie de la perception*. The same idea is developed in his various articles, in his philosophy of history and in his interpretation of Marxism. De Waehlens admits that in the latter works there is more evident the influence of Hegel, but he sees no contradiction between Merleau-Ponty's existentialism and the profound inspiration which animated Hegel, particularly in his *Phänomenologie des Geistes*.[52]

Jules Chaix-Ruy looks at Merleau-Ponty's existentialism from the viewpoint of human freedom. Commenting on

---
[50] Spiegelberg, *Phenomenological* . . . , p. 539.
[51] J. F. Bannan, "Philosophical Reflection and the Phenomenology of Merleau-Ponty," *The Review of Metaphysics*, Vol. VIII, No. 3, Issue No. 31 (March 1955, pp. 418-42), pp. 430-31.
[52] A. De Waehlense, *Une philosophie* pp. 8-9.

Humanisme et terreur[53] he affirms that in refusing inevitability to the dialectic Merleau-Ponty intends to preserve a liberty, more complex than that of Sartre, although quite as real. With regard to his ontology, he says that Merleau-Ponty intends to show us that an existential ontology, if it is to be more than a subjective meditation—"un journal intime"—must appeal to a psychology on which to ground its conclusions.[54] This Merleau-Ponty has certainly attempted on a broad scale. But his notion of liberty is very definitely linked to the notion of engagement, the necessity of implementing one's decisions by action.[55]

Thus there are some good reasons for Spiegelberg's assertion that Merleau-Ponty is an "avowed existentialist" whose philosophy is "engaged," that is, involved in or committed to action. Still, Merleau-Ponty maintains that philosophy, though committed as deeply as man, because just as fully immersed in the world, must maintain a certain "detachment" necessary to "think about" the world. Likewise, his ambivalence in his view of communism—a position between Marxist action and Hegelian contemplation—stems from the same source of existential, yet reserved, commitment.[56] Still this new "existentialized rationalism" is not sufficient to account for Merleau-Ponty's philosophy. His profound knowledge of man, particularly through the science of psychology, makes his philosophy something more than a new version of existentialism. "The relation between science, especially the anthropological sciences, and philosophy provides one with the pervading theme of Merleau-Ponty's philosophy."[57]

---

[53] Merleau-Ponty, *Humanisme et terreur*, Les Essais XXVII, (Paris: Gallimard [1947]). Cited hereafter as *H.T.*
[54] *Les grands courants de la pensée mondiale contemporaine*, Ed. M. F. Sciacca, Panoramas Nationaux, Vol. I (Milan: Marzorati [1958]), pp. 600-602. Cited hereafter as *Les grands courants* . . .
[55] *Les grands courants* . . . , p. 602.
[56] Cf. Merleau-Ponty, *H.T.* and *Les aventures de la dialectique* (Paris: Gallimard [1955]). Cited hereafter as *A. D.*
[57] Spiegelberg, *Phenomenological* . . . , pp. 526-27.

Merleau-Ponty

Again, his existentialism may be viewed in the light of a re-examination of Descartes' "Cogito." According to Raymond Bayer, Merleau-Ponty has placed the "cogito" in an existential context while trying to deal adequately with the problems of classical philosophic systems. As a system, the Cartesian philosophy is a cultural entity; the "Cogito," however, is an existential experience—not as Descartes intended it, but

> in virtue of all the implications which Descartes himself excluded. At the root of all our experiences, we find a being which knows itself immediately because it is its own knowledge of self and of all things and knows its own existence not by inference or evidence, but by direct contact with self . . . Self-consciousness is the very being of spirit in operation.[58]

Herein is the existential significance of the "Cogito" for Merleau-Ponty: not a mere "cogito," but a "cogitatum"; that is to say, the intentional being of my consciousness is rooted in the world and in my being in the world.[59] It is not my existence which is validated by the consciousness I have of it but, on the contrary, consciousness is validated by existence.[60] For Merleau-Ponty, what Descartes really meant by "I think, therefore I am" is this: "something has happened to me."[61] It may be said then, that the most primary truth is indeed Descartes' "Cogito" but only amended to include the presupposition, the "I" which thinks is inseparable from his body and his lived situation.[62]

---

[58] R. Bayer, *Merleau-Ponty's Existentialism*, The University of Buffalo Studies, Monographs in Philosophy, Vol. 19, No. 3 (Buffalo: The University of Buffalo, Sept. 1951), p. 99. Cited hereafter as *Existentialism*.
[59] Bayer actually uses the expression "ontological status"—that could hardly be justified in the case of Merleau-Ponty. Cf. later discussion on the "Cogito."
[60] Bayer, *Existentialism* . . . , p. 102.
[61] Bayer, *Existentialism* . . . , p. 102.
[62] Bayer, *Existentialism*, p. 103.

The Philosophy of Merleau-Ponty

The relative merits of both phenomenology and existentialism are dependent on this: they make possible a more accurate analysis of our resources. The phenomenologist's description must converge into the philosopher's system, and human situations must approach a limit where they meet in some common world of mind.[63]

Merleau-Ponty has at least initiated such a move when he has declared that phenomenology is not just a method, but a philosophy. Further, he has also detached himself from other phenomenologists and existentialists in that he has given his philosophy a decidedly new direction: he has built his own investigation on the central theme of the body-subject. This is an altogether new approach:[64] for him man is not either a seat of sensations or an intellectual interiority, or a union of two different powers or types of beings; rather, man is a unity, difficult to understand and more difficult still to analyse and describe, yet so fundamental that neither man or the world can be understood unless seen in this perspective of unity rather than union.

Kwant expresses very clearly the meaning of Merleau-Ponty's "body-subject":

> Merleau-Ponty speaks about the *body itself*. Many have attributed to bodily beings a personal, subjective character, but the reason was that they considered the body inhabited or animated by an indwelling spirit, a spiritual soul, i.e., by a principle of a different order which is more intimately connected with the body. Merleau-Ponty does not at all mean this. . . . The body *itself* precisely as body, is an existence and therefore of a subjective nature. The body *itself* is a subject and there-

---

[63] Bayer, *Existentialism*, p. 104.
[64] Although there are unmistakable and significant similarities between the philosophies of Merleau-Ponty and those of J. P. Sartre and Gabriel Marcel in their respective view of the body, Merleau-Ponty's treatment is original enough to be considered new and, possibly, an advance over the others.

fore does not derive its subjective character from a principle distinct from itself.[65]

The key words are *existence* and *subject*. Merleau-Ponty wants to underline the fact that the existence of man is not like that of any other being—specifically, like any "thing." Man's existence is precisely to be man, that is, to be this body-subject which is in the world and yet not merely a part of nature, nor just one kind of "body" like many others in the physical realm. The body of which Merleau-Ponty speaks is the sole capable of giving meaning to the world—precisely because it is a human body. Kwant observes:

> That the body is a subject, a meaning-giving existence is deduced by Merleau-Ponty from the fact that there are many forms of meaning which, on the one hand do not have the character of a reality existing independently of us but, on the other hand, do not result from a free and conscious giving of meaning. It follows therefore that man must already be a meaning-giving existence on the pre-conscious and not-yet-free level, on the level of bodily existence.[66]

It is thus that existential phenomenology has for Merleau-Ponty its essential grounding in the human body; not only must I *be a body* to exist, but I must be precisely *this body,* such as it is, human and living (a dead body is no longer a body), with all that it entails, that is, all of its possibilities and activities. Moreover, "the effective existence of my body is indispensable to the existence of my consciousness."[67] From this view of the body as subject the step to the inten-

---
[65] Kwant, R. C. *The Phenomenological Philosophy of Merleau-Ponty*, Duquesne Studies: Philosophical Series, 15. Pittsburgh: Duquesne University Press, 1963, pp. 14-15. Cited hereafter as *Phenomenological Philosophy* . . .
[66] Kwant, *Phenomenological Philosophy*, p. 21. In the course of this work we will return on this point when considering Merleau-Ponty's examples of pre-conscious subjective existence.
[67] *P. P.*, p. 493.

tionality which reveals to me the world is easy: the body-subject knows itself as body only in the encounter with the world (and this includes the other body-subjects). That is why Merleau-Ponty says that we discover at the heart of the subject the ontological world as well as the ontological body: the ontological body-subject—a knowing subject—grasps, in a comprehensive view, the world itself.[68] Thus a dialogue ensues and the phenomenal world "becomes" in virtue of the presence of a subject, for the world *is* only for a subject. This dialogue is often deepened to a still more fundamental level—or heightened to a more exalted level—when in life this meeting of the body-subject and the world not only ends in a fusion of the philosopher and the consciousness of a thing, but in the consciousness of a remarkable accord between the subject and the phenomena themselves.[69] Here phenomenology is concerned with conscious life, because the subject is already aware of his lived experience; therefore the meanings which arise at this "knot of relations" can become a version of the world.[70]

Kwant observes that this meaning-giving power resides in the body-subject and is activated in the dialectical process of which the subject is the center:

The meaning makes the subject be, and the subject constitutes the meaning. The subject then, forms part of the

---

[68]*P. P.*, p. 467. This passage shows that *Phénoménologie de la perception* is not just a treatise on phenomenological psychology, but a fundamental ontology dealing with perception only. Dr. Kockelmans sees Merleau-Ponty's phenomenology as a method of Fundamental-Ontology and Metaphysics not unlike Heidegger's. (Personal Correspondence)

[69]*Eloge*, p. 40.

[70]In the Preface to *In Praise of Philosophy* J. Wild observes that it is precisely the task Merleau-Ponty assigns to philosophy to encourage a "living communication" between the various versions of the world and those of the past—a task which may well result in new and lasting meanings, in "a new approach to the life-world" being formed as a result of this renewal of philosophy. Northwestern University Study in Phenomenology and Existential Philosophy [Northwestern University Press (Evanston, Ill.): 1953], p. xxi.

circular causality, for it is through the other and makes the other meaningful. But the subject is a privileged point in the circular causality, for it is, as it were, the heart of the whole of meanings and centers everything around itself as meaning-for-itself.[71]

Luijpen looks at the dialogue between the body-subject and the world from another viewpoint. He raises the question of the reality of things, or of the existence of things and of the world as "brute matter"; but, he says, there is meaning in the world only if a subject is present—a subject *ex-isting* in the world:

> The real world in which man exists as a subject is not a world-without-man, a "brute reality," a world in itself. The idea of existence as expressing the essence of man, makes a contradiction of the thought construct "a world-without-man." As existence man is attached to the world, so that reversely also the world is attached to man. . . . A world-without-man simply cannot be thought, for it presupposes that it is possible to think a world without the thinking presence of an existing subject.[72]

It is now possible to specify in what sense Merleau-Ponty's phenomenology is existential: it is not so in the sense in which existential philosophers are said to disregard the essence of man on the grounds that beings gifted with consciousness make themselves what they are—that is, they create their own values, their own essence.[73] For Merleau-Ponty man does have an essence, which, however, is not

---
[71] Kwant, *Phenomenological Philosophy*, pp. 19-20.
[72] Luijpen, *Phenomenology*, p. 28.
[73] However, Merleau-Ponty's claim for the absoluteness of the subject is not unqualified: he admits that man is man—that is, subject— only in relation to the world and to other subjects; thus he actually depends on others and on his human condition for being what he is; as a center of meaning, though, man can be said to be absolute. Cf. *P.P.*, p. III, ff.

The Philosophy of Merleau-Ponty

distinct from his body as being-in-the-world: man's essence is precisely his "ex-istence"[74] in the world. Thus the phenomenon of man—the appearing of man in the world—is a "standing-out" as subject, and it is an affirmation of both the self and the world. This world and this subject, far from being mere phenomena manifesting some hidden reality, are *the* reality of which the philosopher speaks—no less than the real world of which the scientist speaks. It remains true then that there could not be a world without man; at any scientific or cultural level, the world *is* only for *a subject*, humanist or scientist, learned or illiterate. The marvel of the world consists precisely in this: meaning and existence are one.[75] Hence Kwant can well say:

> All meaning is connected with man. There is intelligibility because man, as dialog with the world, has risen to the level of rationality. Our existence, as giver of meaning, is the center of Merleau-Ponty's philosophy.[76]

However, this does not mean that once Merleau-Ponty has established that man is the center of intelligibility, he has explained everything, that is, man and the world. On the contrary, he has left the most important thing unexplained: man's contingency as well as the world's. But, within Merleau-Ponty's thought one could hardly expect to find anything else: if all meaning begins and rests with man, and if there is no other being than being-for-me,[77] a justification

---

[74] It is obvious that "existence" for Merleau-Ponty does not mean the "act of being" as it is understood by Scholastic philosophy. To exist for Merleau-Ponty (as for other existentialists) actually means to ex-ist, to stand out from the world; it means openness, intentionality, freedom, project, being-in-the-world, dialectical relation of man with the world.

[75] *P. P.*, p. 374. Cf. also the excellent analysis of Luijpen, in *Phenomonology*, pp. 22-24.

[76] Kwant, *Phenomenological Philosophy*, p. 124.

[77] "Notre expérience est nôtre, cela signifie deux choses: qu'elle n'est pas la mesure de tout être en soi imaginable,— et qu'elle est cependant coextensive à tout être dont nous puissions avoir notion." *Sens et non-sens*, (Collection Pensée, 3rd ed.; Paris: Nagel [°1948]), pp. 163-64. Cited hereafter as *S.N.S.*

of man's existence or of the world's in the light of a being other than the meaning-giving subject would not be possible. This therefore rules out the appeal to an Absolute which, in Merleau-Ponty's terms, could not co-exist with man without depriving the latter of his existence as absolute subject.

Thus, although the insight of our author into the human condition is most fruitful, it lacks the basis for the fundamental question of origin, and for the attainment of absolute truth.

Precisely because his phenomenology is existential, it will allow for novelty and process, hence, the impossibility of attaining absolute truth is understandable. That, however, does not make truth less "genuine" for Merleau-Ponty: it merely makes it contingent, as everything else is in his world. Does it mean then, that the basic tenet of phenomenology as the study of essences is disregarded by Merleau-Ponty? No, but it simply means that essences are not considered immutable or eternal, precisely because man as a contingent meaning-giving subject could not transcend his condition of being-in-the-world and attain absolute knowledge. The beings themselves of which man grasps the essence are subject to variations and changes, determined by their respective structuration,[78] and therefore knowledge about them could never be fossilized into static formulas. Besides, knowledge about essences is first and foremost based on perception; therefore, whether it be question of space-time relations, sexual encounters, aesthetic experience, the body subject is always involved and ambiguity will prevail. Speaking about aesthetics in Merleau-Ponty, E. Kaelin observes:

> If it seems absurd that the world is understood by the body because to understand is to subsume a particular

---

[78]The notion of structure will be discussed in detail later.

set of impressions under a general concept, then in the face of the evidence, we must either re-examine our notion of "understand" or our notion of "the body." And this is precisely what Merleau-Ponty has done.

According to Merleau-Ponty's philosophy of ambiguity, it is the body which through its dynamic relations to a lived situation constitutes the first meanings an intellect may grasp, as if by proxy, in any later attempt to codify the experience in smybols.[79]

Kaelin refutes the charge of irrationalism levelled at Merleau-Ponty by claiming that "anti-scientism would better describe our author's position: "This property [anti-scientism], perhaps more than any others—including its inception in phenomenology—is the mark of an existential philosophy."[80]

In his last article, "L'oeil et l'esprit" Merleau-Ponty gives perhaps the best summation of his existential phenomenology when he so strongly asserts the unicity of body and spirit. Commenting on the fact that the painter uses his body, he observes that it is hard to see how a spirit could paint. But it is by the use of his body—by lending his body—that the painter transforms the world into painting. However, this body must be recognized as operative not merely as a passive bundle of functions, or as a fragment of space: it must be seen as an interaction of vision and movement, if we are to understand this "transubstantiation."[81]

Merleau-Ponty never ceases to wonder at what he calls the singular power of the body to be at one and the same time both sensible and sensing: "It sees itself seeing, it

---
[79] Eugene F. Kaelin, *An Existential Aesthetic: the Theories of Sartre and Merleau-Ponty*. Madison, Wis.: The University of Wisconsin Press. 1962, pp. 245-246. Quoted hereafter as *Aesthetic*.
[80] Kaelin, *Aesthetic*, pp. 328-329.
[81] "L'oeil et l'esprit," *Les Temps Modernes*, 1961, nos. 184-185, pp. 193-227, p. 196. Cited hereafter as "L'oeil."

touches itself touching, it is visible and sensible to its very self."[82]

Yet the body-subject in discovering the visible world, does not appropriate things, but rather approaches them, and thereby opens itself to the world. There is really no clear distinction between the things seen and the body-subject seeing—this somehow explains the ambiguity of the situation. In this context the implication is, furthermore, that the vision of the eyes is analogous to the spiritual vision, but one cannot ever tell if, and at which point, there is a line of demarcation:

> That which we call inspiration must indeed be taken literally: there is truly inspiration and expiration of Being, respiration in Being, action and passion so little discernible that one does not know any longer who sees and who is seen, who paints and that which is painted.[83]

In the course of this study it will become clear, we hope, just how much the "existential" affects the "phenomenological" in Merleau-Ponty—in particular, how great a part the preconscious plays in our conscious or personal life. The analysis which Kwant makes of Merleau-Ponty's method of phenomenology quite accurately describes the attempt at penetrating the obscure and ambiguous reality of the body-subject in its pre-conscious mode of being. This is probably the most original contribution of Merleau-Ponty. The fact that his phenomenological investigation so often leaves us with an ambiguous result is no indication that the method is inadequate: on the contrary, it is a proof that we have not departed from reality—for, reality is indeed mysterious; a clear and distinct description would soon betray itself as a pure construct of the mind.

---

[82] "L'oeil," p. 197.
[83] Merleau-Ponty, "L'oeil," p. 202.

Merleau-Ponty, as an existential phenomenologist, wonders at the world he contemplates, admits that his knowledge is limited; he almost declines to look for absolute truth, because he knows that—within his human condition—he will not find it as a light dispelling all darkness, but only as light tempered by much shadow.

4. Existential Dialectic

However, Merleau-Ponty himself gives us the best characterization of his own existentialism. In his article, "Existence et dialectique"[84] Merleau-Ponty gives us a brief, yet very significant exposé of existentialism as he sees it. In designating as essential, in the past half century, the themes of "existence" and "dialectique," he refers to that which this generation has read into philosophy and not that which the contemporary philosophers are conscious of saying. The philosophy of existence is not only the philosophy which puts in man liberty before essence. It also maintains that such liberty is not liberty except as incorporated in the world, as a labor accomplished in a situation. Then even for Sartre, to exist is not just an anthropomorphic term: it is revealed existence, confronting a whole new figure of the world—of the world as promise and danger—which tends to ensnare liberty, seduce it or surrender to it, "no longer the flat world of Kant's objects of science," but a whole "panorama" of obstacles and ways, "a world in which we 'exist' and not merely the theater of our knowledge and of our free choice."[85]

However, Merleau-Ponty's concern is not so much to convince the readers that this century is going towards existentialism, but rather that it is also going towards a dialectic, although it may seem difficult to assign a place to dialectic in a philosophy of existence.

---

[84]*Signes* (Paris: Gallimard [1960]), p. 194. Cited hereafter as *S*.
[85]*S*., p. 196.

Merleau-Ponty

Leaving aside the numerous references of the author to contemporary thinkers who have seen the same thing, we will consider only the observations of those whose position, according to Merleau-Ponty, is not consonant with his. It is evident, he says, that Bergson and Husserl seek intuition, but for them dialectic is the philosophy of the rationalists. Merleau-Ponty asks:

> What is there in common among these philosphers dedicated to the [things] perceived, the positive, the methodically naive, and the artful philosophers who always dig into one intuition in order to find another?

To answer the question, he asserts, we must go back to the Hegelian dialectic:

> The dialectic which our contemporaries are rediscovering . . . is the dialectic of the real. The Hegel which they have reinstated . . . is the one who did not want to choose between logic and anthropology, the one who made dialectic emerge from human experience, but defined man as the bearer of the Logos, [the one] who situated in the heart of philosophy these two perspectives [dialectic and intuition] and the reversal [of the same] which transforms the one into the other. That dialectic and that institution are not only compatible: there is a moment when dialectic and intuition unite.[86]

Obviously then, for Merleau-Ponty the Hegelian dialetic is far from being an abstract elaboration of a system of thought divorced from reality. On the contrary, he considers it as a fruitful approach to the existential problem. His point of departure is what he calls a "crisis in philosophy," a crisis which is at once crisis of the science of man, and of science in general from which we have not yet emerged.[87]

---
[86] *S.*, pp. 196-97.
[87] *Les sciences de l'homme et la phénoménologie,* intr. Part 1: Le problème des sciences de l'homme selon Husserl (Paris: Tournier et Constance [1953]). Cited hereafter as *S. H. P.*

This, he thinks, has its foundation in the philosophical effort of Husserl, and he looks to him for inspiration in the attempt to solve that which he believes to be the crisis of the century. So he goes to Husserl for his phenomenological insight; but he does not remain in the Husserlian realm of essences. He asserts that one can follow through the Bergsonian as well as the Husserlian philosophy the struggle by which intuition changed the positive notion of "immediately given" into a dialectic of time, the vision of essences into a "phenomenology of genesis," tying by a living bond the opposed dimensions of time which he asserts, doubtless on the strength of his having described being as essentially temporal, "is finally coextensive with being."[88]

He is aware of the fact that dialectic presents a difficulty to modern thinkers because it requires a sort of detachment at the moment when reflection begins; but this is necessary, for as he has already made clear, consciousness cannot contemplate being without separating itself from it: "to possess oneself, one must go out of oneself; in order to see the world, one must withdraw from it."[89]

Yet this detachment has no resemblance to the scientific or positivistic attitude. It is still a commitment, and the reflecting consciousness does not seek a transparent intellectual grasp of the world. On the contrary, it is concerned with a lived experience, which, precisely because an experience involving space and time, is not clear, but ambiguous. In other words, the philosophical reflection of the existentialist, far from being just another kind of empiricism, must "return to each experience *the* ontological chiffre with which it is interiorly marked.[90] This is a reaffirmation of Merleau-

---

[88] *S.*, p. 197.
[89] *S.*, p. 197.
[90] *S.*, p. 198. It is not clear whether Merleau-Ponty uses "chiffre" in the same sense in which Jaspers uses it, but it is clear enough, it seems, that he means by it that which we would call the "ontological reality"—presumably the pre-objective world.

Ponty's effort to replace essences in existence; the ontological *chiffre* does not signify a pure essence, or an essence bare of all existential events: it signifies—or rather points to—existence itself. Empiricism is not enough; but evidently neither is essentialism: the first, because it cannot dispose of any but exterior connections and can only juxtapose states of consciousness;[91] the second, essentialism, stemming as it does from a consciousness which "constitutes" everything, at least in the Husserlian type of essentialism, has nothing to return to the experience because it took nothing from it— nothing in the ontological sense.

Looking towards the future, Merleau-Ponty sees two possibilities (not necessarily exclusive of each other): philosophy will never again pretend to know and express the meaning of nature or history simply by its own concepts; secondly, it will not desist from its radicalism, in the search for the true presuppositions and foundations which have produced the great philosopher. He sees it in today's literature, so frankly philosophical, in its reflections on language and truth; also in the fact that politics has become critical of its own tenets, its grounds, its certitudes and its projects. Because of all this existential turning towards philosophy, it would be disastrous if philosophy were to fail.

Merleau-Ponty has no doubts about what the heart of philosophy really is. He maintains that should philosophy lose its "a priori" its system or its construction, there would be practically *everything left,* because system, interpretation, and deduction have never been the essentials of philosophy. These are merely an arrangement for the sake of communication; they are a way of expressing a relation with being, with others, with the world. The system has never had other purpose than to express a certain thought— Descartes', or Spinoza's, or any other—in such a way as to

---

[91]*P.P.*, pp. 34-35.

establish a philosophical exchange. Such systems have lasted as long as the rapport lasted.[92]

Today, *such relation is attempted directly;* herein Merleau-Ponty gives us his deepest view of existentialism: because this rapport is not clothed in a system, this philosophy is not restricted to some specified field, but is present even in the testimony of an ignorant person who has loved and has seen reality in his own way, in the newest findings of science, in literature, in the sophistications of life, "even in the discussions of substance and attribute. Humanity [instituée] knows itself as problematic and the most immediate life has become 'philosophical.' "[93] The reality of today's world would leave no room for the rationality of former systems; there is rather a new way of answering the ageless questions of life and philosophy—the existential way; such a way is perhaps less elaborate, much more abrupt than the former, but it is the only answer that this century can give. "True philosophy is re-learning to see the world and in this sense a story told can be as profoundly significant of the world as a philosophical treatise."[94]

This open avowal of existential directness and almost disregard for the strict rationality of the systems, seems a little in contradiction with Merleau-Ponty's own approach to the world as "rational though a mystery," as well as to the rather systematic expression of his own philosophy. Yet, this is not contradictory: Merleau-Ponty is well aware of the fact that the knowledge of the world is at best ambiguous and incomplete, because the world is ever in the process of development, and therefore never expressible in terms of complete and definite statements. By world he means the world proper and man as being-in-the-world. If then, existentialism is a philosophy embracing both the world and man

---

[92] *S.*, p. 199.
[93] *S.*, p. 199.
[94] *P.P.*, p. XVI.

in their existential reality, this philosophy will never be a strict science in the sense of Husserl.[95] It does not follow, however, that the world is wholly absurd and that therefore nothing can be said about it in a rational way. There is rationality, in spite of ambiguity: being cannot be contained in a few simple concepts, yet, from the "profiles"[96] which are revealed to us in perception, presumably, we can "reconstruct" the world of our experience in consciousness and have the assurance of its truth.[97]

5. *Critique of Existentialism*

Merleau-Ponty is aware that other existential approaches different from his own are nevertheless valid—at least to a certain point. In his criticism of Sartres' *L'Être et le néant* Merleau-Ponty expresses even more clearly his own view of existentialism; hence a survey of this criticism will be most enlightening. He defends the existentialism of Sartre from the accusation—which is often leveled at all existentialism— that this philosophy is a poison to be shunned rather than a way of philosophizing to be discussed. Insofar as Sartre's work is an attempt to clarify the relation of man and his natural and social environment, his work deserves study. It is a merit of existential philosophy to seek in the notion of existence the ground for thought. Sartre has tried to do this. However, Merleau-Ponty adds that he has not com-

---

[95] Cf. Lauer, *Philosophie* . . . , Introduction, p. 7: "Quant à l'idéal scientifique, par lequel la philosophie n'est philosophie que dans la mesure où elle est scientifique, c'est là une idée, au sens kantien du terme, qui restée juqu'à la fin présente à la pensée de Husserl, une idée qu'il ne voulait pas abandonner. C'est un Leitmotiv qui se retrouve tout au long de sa philosophie, qui en détermine le développement en lui donnant son caractère distinctif dans l'histoire de la pensée. Cet idéal donne à cette philosophie sa force et sa fermeté, mais constitue en même temps la faiblesse qui lui est inséparable."

[96] Merleau-Ponty explains "profiles" in *S.C.*, particularly in Chapter IV—which will be considered later.

[97] Merleau-Ponty assumes that this can be done—still on the pre-objective level. The theory is doubtful: Merleau-Ponty offers, as usual, no demonstration; he merely asserts this.

pletely elucidated the point. His book is too antithetic: for Sartre, my view of myself and the view of others of me, are in a relation of opposition, of negation each of the other, instead of being described as the living bond of one of the terms to the other, and as their communication with each other.

For what concerns liberty, Sartre seeks to present it completely outside of all compromise with things; the subject is liberty, absence, negativity; therefore "nothingness" *is*. Actually, he sees the "realization" of the "néant" out of being which is action and which renders morality possible. But this also means that the subject is simply "nothing" and that "it needs to be brought within 'being,' that therefore the subject is not thinkable on the foundation of the world"; rather it "feeds on being as the shadows in Homer fed on the blood of the living."[98] Merleau-Ponty evidently does not find in the existentialism of Sartre the characteristics which are proper to this philosophical approach; existentialism maintains that existence is the movement by which man *"is* to the world—physical and social—and is engaged in a situation which becomes his point of view on the world";[99] secondly, existentialism holds that this situation is ambiguous, being at once an affirmation of and a restriction on liberty; thirdly, this engagement is, for the existentialist, a free decision and at the same time, a limitation of his view in regard to the world, of his manner of approaching it and of his way of learning and of doing.

Merleau-Ponty however, admits that the descriptions of Sartre have a profundity and a value which cannot be disregarded if one wants to understand the problems of philosophy in this century. After the Cartesian revolution existence as consciousness is certainly sharply distinct from existence as a thing, and the relation of one to the other is

---

[98] *S. N. S.*, pp. 125-26.
[99] *S. N. S.*, p. 125.

that of the empty to the full.[100] Sartre has well exemplified this in his philosophy; the emptiness of the *en-soi* await to be filled by the *pour-soi*. Likewise, we find the same theme, expressed in different fashion, in all existentialist philosophies. We cannot ignore the problem: the two aspects of being must be taken together, must be understood at the same time. Our being in the world, our being in a situation, our historicity are themes which demand our attention. Among the themes proposed by Existentialism, that of the intuition of being-in-itself is most often questioned. We are in the world, hence our consciousness turns necessarily to things. But these exhibit to us a permanence we lack. The very knowledge of our self is dependent on the relation we have to exterior things, on our actions in the milieu we have constructed for ourselves; in a sense, we see our own reflections in things. But if this is so, then our being-in-the-world is already conditioned by the things which have existed before us, and certainly do not depend on us for their being what they are. In a way, we are usurpers in this world. This is the impression we may have if we consider the stability of nature, and that order in the material world which we can never duplicate in our human world. Yet all this is fallacious reasoning for Merleau-Ponty,

> for being without any witnesses is inconceivable [because there would be no conceiving?]. Yet this is truly our point of departure: we see ourselves as the indispensable correlatives of a being which is, nevertheless, in itself. Such is the contradiction which ties us to the object.[101]

Commenting on Marcel's remarks[102] about the prevalence of material conception of the world, Merleau-Ponty asks

---

[100] *S. N. S.*, p. 126.
[101] *S. N. S.*, p. 127.
[102] *S. N. S.*, p. 127. Cf. Gabriel Marcel, *Homo Viator*, trans. E. Crawford (Chicago: Regnery, 1951).

whether "a religion which affirms the Incarnation and the resurrection of the body" could be astonished at the fact that consciousness adheres to the world and considers material being as "the" type of being itself. Dondeyne answers the question by pointing out that the problem is not the recognition of the materiality of the body, but rather the fact that for existentialism, this material being, man, is in a way his own maker. It is because of man that there is meaning in the world: man gives meaning to the world, and because he is part of that world, what he is depends entirely on him. His nature becomes only a sort of "possibility-in-general to bestow meaning." It is in this sense that the intuition of the *en-soi* is rejected, be it that of Sartre or of anyone else: it deprives life of any "a priori meaning, and value is simply the meaning one choses."[103]

Merleau-Ponty's position is not as radical as that of Sartre in many respects.[104] For instance he does not accept the dichotomy of the *en-soi—pour-soi*. His idea of embodiment—incarnate spirit—gives his existentialism a different viewpoint; still, it is in a way open to the same objections: does it allow for transcendence? It seems that it does not. However, further study is necessary before a position may be taken on this question.

He also questions Sartre with regard to the intuition of being and nothingness. Sartre has defined liberty as "noth-

---

[103] Albert Dondeyne, *Contemporary European Thought and Christian Faith*, Duquesne Studies, Philosophical Series, 8, Pittsburgh: Duquesne University Press, 2nd impr., 1963, p. 62. Cited hereafter as *Contemporary* . . .

[104] For a study of Merleau-Ponty in relation to Sartre see Kwant's *Phenomenological Philosophy*, ch. XII. Kwant's analysis singles out the philosophical, personal, and social likenesses and differences between the two philosophies, with a view to point out Sartre's influence on Merleau-Ponty. Actually, we are not too sure as Kwant claims (p. 211), that Merleau-Ponty's lack of analysis of the "cogito" and of freedom is to be attributed to his preoccupation with Sartre's position. Could it not be a consequence of his basic conviction that an investigation of human existence, based as it is on the pre-conscious, cannot but be ambiguous?

ing" and yet "everything," because it is the source of all human greatness. Liberty enters into all that which man does. The ambiguity of his conduct proceeds from this. Bad faith is inescapable in man and even the good is vitiated by the will to be good. "The principle of good and the principle of evil are then one. Man's misery is visible in his greatness and his greatness in his misery."[105] This does not show that Sartre's philosophy has extinguished the spirit in man, maintains Merleau-Ponty, "on the contrary, it has put spirit all over, because we are not spirit *and* body, not consciousness *facing* the world, but incarnate spirit, being-in-the-world."[106]

The expression "incarnate spirit" recurs again and again in Merleau-Ponty's works, but is it equally applicable to Sartre? Is not Merleau-Ponty describing his own existential view while giving a critique of Sartre's?

A further question Merleau-Ponty asks regards finality. If, he says, we deny man unhampered liberty—the kind the existentialists claim man has—and if man tends to his end necessarily, then, he is no better than a plant. However, the problem cannot be solved on the basis of philosophy alone; most certainly there is ambiguity here: what is the mean between man's avowed freedom and his natural tendency towards his ultimate good? Even for theology this is a difficult problem and the answer will at best be ambiguous, for mystery is involved here. But Merleau-Ponty pursues the question further and asks: "Can it not be, perhaps, that the religion of a God made man may end up, by an inevitable dialectic, in an anthropology rather than a theology?[107] This—a humanism without transcendence—is precisely that to which Merleau-Ponty's existential phenomenology seems to lead; at least, the judgment of the critics, thus far, implies

---
[105] S. N. S., p. 131.
[106] S. N. S., p. 129.
[107] S. N. S., p. 131.

as much.[108] It is premature, at this point, to say whether it is justified under all aspects.

He further points out the disagreement in debate and agreement in principle between Sartre and Marcel. They agree on the question of man's being: original integration is unthinkable: only an act of faith without notional content can affirm it.[109] Merleau-Ponty maintains that the Christian has really no choice: on the one hand he is confronted with a man who has to realize a certain pre-established nature; on the other, he has to admit that such a man can choose to neglect his goal. If one can say yes or no to his destiny, does he not have the liberty to choose—a liberty, in a sense, equal to God's?[110]

Clearly then, the author seems to believe that Sartre's notion of liberty is not incompatible with a Christian philosophy of man. Yet he himself does not subscribe to a theory of freedom unlimited. In fact, he observes:

> What is then liberty? To be born is at once to be born in the world and to the world. The world is already constituted, but never completely. Under the first rapport, we are solicited, under the second, we are open to

---

[108]Dondeyne, *Contemporary* . . ., pp. 62-64. The author says that there is no transcendence for some of the existentialists; for the "atheist," "man is the only measure of intelligibility and value. Man's historical character is so emphasized that eventually it swamps him altogether. Because of this, it would seem that the myst_ry of man automatically loses its profundity, its proper metaphysical dimension."

[109]*S. N. S.*, p. 132. "Sartre disait que la conscience qui, par le mouvement constant de l'intentionnalité, tend à être comme une chose sans jamais y parvenir, semblait témoigner d'une synthèse idéale entre elle-même et l'être, 'non que l'intégration ait jamais eu lieu, mais précisément au contraire parce qu'elle est toujours indiquée et toujours impossible.' . . . quand . . . Marcel donne sa propre solution, elle consiste à dire que la conscience est amenée, en réfléchissant sur soi, à se regarder elle-même comme dégradée, sans qu'il lui soit d'alleurs possible de penser concrètement le monde d'avant la chute.' . . . les deux conclusions ne se distinguent en somme que parce que M. Marcel, au lieu de constater la dialectique du pour soi et de l'en soi, la déclare intolérable et veut passer outre par l'action."

[110]*S. N. S.*, p. 133.

> an infinity of possibilities. But this analysis is still abstract, because we exist under these two relations at once. There is therefore never determinism and never absolute choice; I am never a thing and never naked consciousness.[111]

From the above passage it is clear that Merleau-Ponty's notion of liberty, is not precisely that of Sartre. Yet Merleau-Ponty vouches for the Sartrean notion of freedom unlimited; why? Is it to undermine the Christian notion of finality and limitation? Or is it to show that if Existentialism is materialistic then Christianity is also? Perhaps this is what prompted G. Morra to state that Merleau-Ponty's aim is to eliminate from existentialism all traces of religious nostalgia and to develop his philosophy as a positive humanism.

> Man must avoid the useless search for the Absolute, for the very existence of the Absolute would render human action useless and impossible. Before God as Infinite, —Beauty, Truth, Good, men would have nothing more to do, could not accomplish anything true, or beautiful, or good. Theology does not allow man any liberty. The negation of the Absolute Norm instead . . . allows the founding of a social anthropology which will seek to realize in the world that perfection, which, not existing as a datum, will be an effect of the free will of man.[112]

6. *Marxist Leanings*

The existentialism of Merleau-Ponty has another aspect, very pronounced, which is revealed quite clearly in the same criticism of Sartre's existentialism, his Marxism. Merleau-Ponty reveals his Marxist leaning insofar as he agrees with Marxism in denouncing idealistic philosophies. For Marx-

---
[111] *P. P.*, p. 517.
[112] *Enciclopedia filosofica*, Vol. III, Col. 522: "Merleau-Ponty" by G. Morra. [Translation mine.]

ism, he says, all philosophy is idealistic because it supposes reflection, that is, a rupture with the immediate—it is a particular case of alienation, a rejection of being. The very idea of speculative philosophy is the existential refusal to labor to transform the world. "The only way to obtain what philosophy seeks—the complete grasp of the world—is to enter into history instead of contemplating it."[113] It is clear that the strongest Marxist argument against a philosophy of the subject is "existential." Instead of transforming history as the philosopher should by his action, reflection does nothing but *interpret* the world, and this is inadequate from the very fact that it is already a kind of existing aside from the world and from history. It is then quite understandable that Merleau-Ponty should have been attracted by Marxism. Although for different reasons, both are engaged in action, existentialism because man is a being in the world, already committed to existence, Marxism because it is engaged in transforming the world by action. Both see men in history, as makers of history in fact; Marxism, however, is dominated by a partial view of the human situation, the economic, while existentialism embraces the whole of human situation, individual, social, cultural, without however excluding the economic. Merleau-Ponty sees therefore a common ground between Marx and Marcel insofar as both appeal to action to surpass the unauthentic condition of man and to renew man's engagement in the world. This would be a means to surpass the dialectic opposition (deplored by Marcel in Sartre's philosophy) of being and nothingness. However, it is all very well to be invited to join the movement of history: we must also know what this movement is and by what means we can make ourselves part of it; this is in substance Merleau-Ponty's observation, which seems to call for a kind of finality. But we look in vain for this sort of development: all that this means for Merleau-Ponty is that

---

[113] *S. N. S.*, p. 136.

man must decide for himself, make his own history, give history a meaning,—his own. One's decisions then are final: man makes himself whatever he wants to be.[114]

Merleau-Ponty sees the dialectic of being and nothingness, not just as an account of reality in terms of Sartre's existendialism—perhaps nothing more than a novel theory— but as a very real occurrence in the life of common people such as laborers struggling against discouragement and defeat. Referring no doubt to Marxist ideology, he maintains that the notion of "class" cannot inspire a man to die cheerfully, even if he could be convinced that thereby he would benefit mankind. Only the personal element of solidarity, the choice of each man to become part of an historical movement can make a man loyal to another man or to a movement. Marx attempted to achieve the personal engagement of the individual in his cause, but, Merleau-Ponty observed, without success.

In the same line of thought, Merleau-Ponty continues, Sartre attempted to develop a social theory on the Marxist plan, but he also did not succeed. An analysis of the subjective engagement at the moment wherein subjective and objective conditions of history meet, will discover the deficiencies—a consequence, perhaps, of the same Marxist failure. However, Sartre at least sharply outlines the problem of the reciprocal relation between consciousness and the social world—a problem rendered more difficult to solve by the negativistic approach of Sartrean thought.[115]

Marxism does tolerate liberty and the individual, but, precisely because it is a materialism, it charges man with a vertiginous responsibility. Hegel, on the contrary, insofar as he remains faithful to the history of spirit, finds in his consciousness to have entirely understood history and offers a guarantee of final synthesis. This is Merleau-Ponty's inter-

---
[114] *S.N.S.*, p. 138.
[115] *S.N.S.*, p. 140.

pretation (though he admits it could be interpreted differently) and it is significant for it shows that Merleau-Ponty's philosophy is not a materialism a la Marx, but a humanism which has not renounced the spirit. In fact, he says that a philosophy which renounces the spirit cannot affirm the possibility of man as integrated, nor postulate a final synthesis wherein all contradictions are done away with, nor affirm an inevitable realization. He would apply this test to any philosophy, whether it bore the name of Marx or Hegel. Merleau-Ponty admits there are fundamental differences between Marx and Hegel,[116] especially in the grounding of their philosophy: Hegel has a theology, whereas Marx's praxis has no other support than the coexistence of men.

This last observation introduces a fundamental question with regard to Merleau-Ponty's philosophy—a question which it may be difficult to answer even at the end of our study—just what is spirit for Merleau-Ponty? If he refuses a theology, if he denies the need for an Absolute, is he not at one with Marxism or with Sartrean atheism? These questions need much further investigation—they are merely indicated here—but one is tempted to ask Merleau-Ponty whether he ought not question his own philosophy on the same lines.

Conscious of his own Marxist existentialism, he asks however, why should existentialism tend to approach Marxism; not—he observes rather ironically—in order to be able to devour it[117] nor for the reasons advanced by some of Marx's critics. It is his contention that "a living Marxism must 'save' the existentialist's search and then integrate it, rather than reject it."[118]

---

[116] *S.N.S.*, pp. 142-43. "Si la synthèse est de droit chez Hegel, elle ne saurait être que de fait dans le marxisme. S'il y a un quiétisme hégélien, il y a nécessairement une inquiétude marxiste. Si Hegel peut s'en remettre aveuglement au cours des choses, parce qu'il reste chez lui un fond de théologie, la praxis marxiste n'a pas la même ressource, elle n'a pas d'autre support que la coexistence des hommes."
[117] *S.N.S.*, p. 142.
[118] *S.N.S.*, p. 143.

Merleau-Ponty

It is quite understandable, in view of his own existential position, why Merleau-Ponty has been so sympathetic to Marxism.[119] However, it is licit to doubt whether Marxism is really such as Merleau-Ponty describes it; or did he describe it as he would like it to be? After all, *if* he had approached Marxism phenomenologically he could only have come up with *his own* subjective finding; but this means also to have incorporated it in some way in his own thought. Did he not say in his "Preface," which is really his "Manifesto" on Phenomenology, that "reflection upon a doctrine will be total only if it succeeds in relating itself to the history of the doctrine . . . in an existential relation"?[120]

And it may again be by virtue of the same reflection that his view of existential Marxism changes, to the extent that his own development, social and political, as well as philosophical, leads him to new vistas in the perceptual field of his phenomenological milieu.

---

[119] His position on this point underwent a considerable change. Cf. *Humanisme et terreur* and compare with *Les aventures de la dialectique*.
[120] *P.P.*, p. XIV.

CHAPTER THREE
THE REALITY OF MAN AS A BODY
THE NOTION OF STRUCTURE AND FORM

Merleau-Ponty has pointed out that "genuine philosophy is a relearning to see the world"[1] and he claims to do just that in his two major works, *La structure du comportement* and *Phénoménologie de la perception*. His aim is to make a phenomenological study of man, of the world, and of man-in-the-world. This seems, at first, to present no particular problem, for, our experience is precisely *of the world* and we find ourselves *in the world*. However, since description is so basic to phenomenological reflection, we are bound to encounter some difficulties when we come to man who is at once subject and object of this phenomenological analysis. Man is in the world, part of the world, yet he is also the one who experiences this same world and describes it in all its multiform manifestations. Alquié comments on the extraordinary characteristics of this experience:

> The richness of the concrete description is admirable. Perception, dialogue, the revolutionary "elan," all the irreflexive life of consciousness about which we think so little, (which is ourselves) is given back to us new [comme lavée et mise à neuf]. Here we have the world of the infancy of man, free at once from the rigidity of law, the impersonality of metaphysical abstractions, of arbitrary theological interpretations; the world which understanding has not yet constructed, the ambiguous world wherein we and the other are at once subject and object, or neither, rather, pure existence.[2]

He then adds, comparing the analysis of Sartre to that of Merleau-Ponty, that the world of the latter is far more cheerful and simple than that of Sartre, wherein struggle between the Ego and the Other largely prevails. In Merleau-

---
[1] *P.P.*, p. XVI.
[2] Alquié, "Une philosophie . . .," p. 59.

Ponty one can enjoy the simple beauty of the child's world wherein there are no problems; this vision should make the philosopher aware of reality as it is in its primordial manifestation; it should lead him to the root of his thoughts—a root which goes back to childhood. However, one must not think that Merleau-Ponty's approach is merely a confusion of the orders of reason and of emotion; on the contrary, while he admits the relation of the two in the ambiguity of the body, he is very much concerned with the basic problems of philosophy, i.e., the true foundations of knowledge and of values. His phenomenological investigation is not aiming at a pure and simple description of the given, without qualifications or without further reflection, but at discovering in the immediate, such as it offers itself to consciousness, "the reason of all that which will follow. His return to the immediately given is always accompanied by the cares of problem solving."[3]

Merleau-Ponty's critics often question him on this point: it seems to imply that there is nothing further to explore once one has described the phenomenon, so that phenomenology becomes de facto "philosophy"; and yet, if one does not want to make of philosophy a purely constructive discipline, an abstraction, one is compelled to seek in the giving of experience the reason for its being—or its being there. If we do not discover the true nature of reality by a direct reflection on the phenomena given in experience, what else is there to reveal it to us?

Roland Caillois goes to the heart of the question when he affirms that "it is not possible to begin philosophizing by a pure description of being as it appears without asking at the same time the meaning which such enterprise would have. All phenomenology is at the same time a "critique."[4] A

---

[3] Alquié, "Une philosophie . . .," p. 61.
[4] Roland Caillois, "Notes sur l'analyse réflexive et la réflection phénoménologique: A propos de la *Phénoménologie de la perception* de Maurice Merleau-Ponty," *Deucalion I,* 1946, p. 127. Cited hereafter as "Notes . . ."

further consideration will disclose that the critical question must be directed to the fact itself of the philosophical question, rather than to the content of the question itself. This is understandable in terms of phenomenological investigation: that which appears in consciousness is the phenomenon. Reflection on the phenomenon is really a question posed to the conscious subject who, questioning himself on reflection, really is not distinguished from the being which is questioned (he himself). Philosophical knowledge is altogether different from other types of knowledge, because it does not pose the question outside the questioner himself—and, obviously, it does not attain an objective answer such as scientific knowledge could achieve.

Reflection is a human act: it clarifies the irreflexive, which however, has already in some way, a meaning before consciousness. The irreflexive becomes the foundation for reflection, insofar as reflection depends on it. At the same time, this reflection "can modify the structure of the given and that of the operation of my consciousness."[5]

It must not be thought, however, that for Merleau-Ponty reflection be defined as an activity of the intellect, as a pure "cogito." Nothing would be further from his thought. Reflection comprises life, because it is contained in it. Merleau-Ponty refuses all idealistic construction and maintains that my experience involves my body as well as my spirit, and therefore no reflection is divorced from the materiality of the world, or from the existential condition of man.[6]

Hence, to understand the philosophy of Merleau-Ponty we must first of all grasp the meaning he gives to the body

---

[5] Caillois, "Notes . . . ," p. 129.
[6] Cf. Roland Caillois, "De la perception à l'histoire: la philosophie de Maurice Merleau-Ponty," *Deucalion II*, 1947, pp. 57-85; he shows how man's existence is not merely natural; human existence is also historical existence; to be in the world is to be inserted in the becoming of history by a conscious awareness of our unique existence. Cited hereafter as "De la perception . . ."

as body-subject and to the world as horizon of our perception, and primordial data of phenomenological reflection. The body plays an important role in the dialectical relation between the self and the world, and between the Ego-subject and the Other. That which reveals subjects to each other is their appearance as "behaviors." In order to clarify this unique role of the body in behavior, Merleau-Ponty studies in detail the phenomena which disclose a body to another; he investigates the findings of psychology.

In the introduction to *La structure du comportement* he indicates his aim: he wants to show the relation of nature to consciousness, by investigating structure or form.

With regard to physics, he affirms that we see this science apply indifferently mechanical, dynamic psychological patterns as if "free from ontological pretensions, it had become indifferent to the classical antinomies of mechanism and dynamism which suppose a nature in itself."

In biology, he observes, the mechanistic and vitalistic theories remain open—chiefly because our image of the organism is still largely that of a material mass consisting of parts outside parts.

Then he proceeds to outline the various psychological approaches with a special attention to contemporary advances in this field which is really Merleau-Ponty's own.[7] But before considering his observations on the matter, it is necessary to establish the cultural background against which all of Merleau-Ponty's investigations are carried out. By this is not meant that he begins with a presupposition—at least not consciously—but it is meant that he has in mind certain modes of philosophizing against which he constantly directs his attacks to show their inadequacies to cope with experience as he sees it.

---

[7] *S. C.*, pp. 1-3.

The Reality of Man as a Body

The two modes of philosophizing which Merleau-Ponty has taken into consideration as—presumably—the two positions to which any philosophizing will eventually revert, are empiricism and intellectualism.

For him, empiricism is a prolongation of the naive, realistic approach to reality, a sort of systematization of that external reality which the common man asserts, with which one can communicate only through the senses, exteriorly. No matter under which heading and with what kind of refinements an empiricist position be expressed (whether it be that of the English Empiricists or that of modern positivists) the position is ultimately the same: the world is a reality in itself, ruled by certain laws, having certain properties independent of the subject experiencing it. In this context, perception is pure exterior receptivity by the subject; hence there is no place here for subjectivity. Therefore, to empiricism the fundamental element for the description of the phenomena is lacking: that of the indissoluble union between subject and the world from which meaning derives.[8] Empiricism cannot even be refuted completely, because it ignores its own origin; it cannot be refuted with "empirical" proofs because it refuses description and reflection. Instead, it reconstructs a world by positivistic methods, according to "laws," and refuses the testimony of subjective consciousness. In psychology, empiricism actually destroys both subject and object by attempting to reduce both to a sum of stimuli-responses according to fixed laws.

The style of thought which Merleau-Ponty calls "intellectualism" represents the opposite extreme of empiricism. Intellectualism and empiricism form the two poles between which

---

[8]Cf. *P. P.*, pp. 30; 33; 69; 134-39; *S. C.*, pp. 200ff; 210-17; 240. "Sur ce plan l'empirisme n'est pas réfutable. Puisqu'il refuse le témoignage de la réflexion et qu'il engendre, en associant des impressions extérieures, les structures que nous avons conscience de comprendre en allant du tout aux parties, il n'y a aucun phénomène que l'on puisse citer comme une preuve cruciale contre lui." *P. P.*, p. 31.

Merleau-Ponty's own thought moves. His aim is actually a synthesis of the two. Unfortunately, he puts together all types of intellectualism, be it question of rationalism, critical thought, idealism, or, in other words, be it Cartesian, Kantian, or Hegelian the fundamental tenets of the position are the same: the subject is accorded an ontological precedence, it has a privileged place for the very possibility of experience due to its immanent transparence which will be, eventually, criterion of certitude. All this is achieved by intellectual analysis. At this level of intellectual knowledge the "thing" is understood by means of its adequate idea, it is conceptualized and identified with its intellectual definition or meaning.

It matters little whether the end result of this be absolute idealism (immanent representations) or Platonism (the world finds its prototype in the ideas); the end result is the same in as much as the "real" is made immanent to consciousness (although the "intelligible thing-idea" maintains in its immanence the character of exteriority and "represents" an element of experience and not the "universal fact" which consciousness is).[9] Further, since the world will thus have been reduced to clear ideas, it will always be possible to reconstruct, intellectually, the whole of human experience, temporal as well as a-temporal or eternal. Naturally, the role of perception is here very reduced. Thus also the empirical subject will be surpassed by the "transcendental" (here meaning a-temporal or universal) or absolute subject within which the activity of pure rationality will take place, and all contradictions will then be resolved. Therefore, not in perception which is at best ambiguous and a mere approximation to knowledge, do we have the truth, but in the contact with a "disincarnate" subjectivity which makes the same truth immanent to us.

---

[9] *P. P.*, pp. 455ff.

The Reality of Man as a Body

It is almost impossible to single out all of Merleau-Ponty's references to the above, for his whole exposition of phenomenology is made against such a background. His most vigorous criticism is found in his major works, particularly in *Phénoménologie de la perception.*

At the level of irreflexive experience it is impossible to separate definitively consciousness from the lived body and from the lived world, for none of these elements of man's experience exists in isolation; the very diversity of the senses and their unity of operation suggests an interrelation between them and the living body in the world.[10] But even at the reflexive intellectual level one cannot separate the consciousness from the body, first of all because the reflexive is resting on the irreflexive; secondly, because the subject is never perfectly transparent to itself; lived experience is not without ambiguity.[11] Moreover, intellectualism—as seen by Merleau-Ponty—implies the hypothesis of a transcendent subject which is incompatible with the finiteness and passivity of knowledge and makes it necessary to identify man with God. It would also make it impossible for many "selves" to exist as independent and autonomous, hence the danger of solipsism would appear.[12] Actually, if there are empirical subjects, then the transcendental is a useless duplication—because, according to Merleau-Ponty it is this empirical subject which knows, and loves, and is known.[13]

In short, intellectualism forgets the interrelatedness of consciousness with the body, of the body with the world, of reflexion with the irreflexive in a temporality which is ambiguous because it is multiform and always new—always in process and in a dialectical relation—without transcendence. Needless to say, for different reasons, empiricism falls into

---
[10]*P. P.*, Parts I-II; pp. 172; 231; 241ff; 418.
[11]Cf. *P. P.*, Part III, Ch. I, pp. 424-68.
[12]*P. P.*, p. 427.
[13]*P. P.*, p. 150.

the same contradictory position, equally unjustifiable, according to Merleau-Ponty.[14]

In his criticism Merleau-Ponty does not intend to detract from philosophical reflection which he undoubtedly considers superior to any other form of reflection; nor does he intend to minimize the importance of empirical investigation. But in his attempt at an evaluation of the merits and of the shortcomings of both positions, in his attempt at a phenomenological investigation, he falls quite easily into a kind of unqualified criticism. To establish his phenomenological existentialism, he neglects philosophical positions quite relevant to the inquiry precisely because, in his haste, he has simplified the opposing positions in thus reducing them. His own critique is therefore weakened.[15]

---

[14] Cf. *S. C.*, pp. 210ff; 222ff. "Empirisme et intellectualisme transportent dans les modes primitifs du comportement des structures qui appartiennent à un niveau très supérieur: structure de pure juxtaposition—l'atome—ou structure de pure intériorité—la relation. On dira peut-être qu'en refusant de construire le comportement à partir de ces notions, qui sont constitutives de ce que nous entendons par nature, en les récusant comme anthropomorphiques, nous nous référons implicitement à quelque réalité en soi, à quelque *Grund* d'où l'intelligence émerge et par rapport auquel elle puisse être dite superficielle. Or cette réalité même, ajoutera-t-on, ne peut être nommée ni pensée que par l'intelligence. Nous aurons à distinguer l'intelligence et l'intellectualisme, et peut-être à reconnaitre l'existence de significations qui ne sont pas de l'ordre logique. Il ne peut s'agir ici que d'une description préalable qui ne résout pas les problèmes transcendentaux de la 'pensée confuse', mais qui contribue à les poser." *S. C.*, p. 135.

Cf. also, *P. P.*, pp. IV, VI; 35; 43-77; 150; 231-33; 247; 274; 340; 423-68. This extensive reference to the topic discussed does not really cover Merleau-Ponty's treatment of the same; it must be remembered that his whole philosophy is presented against the background of the two main positions he considers; hence no consideration of his thought can be dissociated from the views of empiricism and intellectualism.

[15] This is also the opinion of Franco Sandrini, who in his unpublished dissertation, studies in detail the consequences of this limited vision of other philosophical positions by Merleau-Ponty. Cf. Sandrini, *La fenomenologia di Merleau-Ponty e il rapporto dialettico* (Unpublished dissertation, Louvain: 1957), pp. 164; 382 ff. Cited hereafter as *La fenomenologia*. . . .

The Reality of Man as a Body

Merleau-Ponty considers the various psychological approaches to consciousness, both classical and current, without finding in any a suitable point of departure for a genuine account of experience. He then asks himself whether any solution will be found—will it be necessary to revert to criticism or should one turn to transcendental philosophy?

He will try to answer the question by beginning from an analysis of the notion of behavior. To him, this notion is all important because it is, in itself, indifferent to the classical distinctions of "psychic" and "physiological", hence it can be redefined. In his description of behavior, Merleau-Ponty will follow neither the interpretation of Watson, nor that of American psychology. In fact, he criticizes Watson for denying consciousness as interior reality in favor of physiology, and for reducing behavior to reflexes and conditioned reflexes, without admitting intrinsic relations. Merleau-Ponty introduces consciousness not as a psychic reality, not as a cause, but as a structure—which is given in its appearance—and inquires into the mode of existence of such a structure. This is the burden of *La structure du comportment,* in the words of Merleau-Ponty himself.[16]

1. Investigation of Behavior: Reflexes or Structures?

In accord with his plan, Merleau-Ponty begins by examining the notion of behavior according to scientific definition. He admits that the scientific analysis has defined itself in opposition to that of a naive consciousness. Thus from the viewpoint of the scientific study of behavior one ought to reject as purely subjective all notions of intention, utility or value. If behavior seems intentional, it is because it is regulated by certain pre-established nervous circuits of such a kind as, in fact, to obtain satisfaction. For instance, referring to the absent-minded reaching for a fruit while one is absorbed in work, Merleau-Ponty maintains that, according

---
[16] *S. C.,* p. 3.

to science, even a second attempt to reach the object (after the first has failed) is deprived of intention.[17]

The burden of the investigation will then be this: is human behavior the result of responses to certain physical stimuli, or is it the carrying out of intentions? Is it perhaps a combination of the two? What is the role of consciousness in the implementation of physical activity, whether reflex or intentional?

In his attempt to understand the relation of nature to consciousness, Merleau-Ponty touches on various possible approaches, none of which, he finds, is adequate to the task. Going back to the type of psychology prevalent today, he sets out to study in detail the various steps leading to what is supposed to be a conclusive analysis of the workings of the reflexes in man's conscious activity.

After studying with an almost clinical eye the various workings of man's physical makeup from the viewpoint of the psychology of "reflexes" and the resulting behavior under every aspect, he comes to the conclusion that the findings do not explain the relation of consciousness to nature. It is not that the reflexes do not exist; they do, but it is not through them that one understands the rest. The reflexes are not the principal object of psychology; they only represent a very particular case of behavior, observable under determined conditions. The object of biology is to discover life "in act" as it were, not by superposition of reflexes or by postulating a "vital" force; rather, the object is to find life as it is in an indecomposable structure.[18]

---
[17] *S. C.*, p. 7.
[18] "On ne saurait considérer comme une *réalité biologique* toute réaction obtenue au laboratoire en interrogeant un organisme malade ou dans des conditions artificielles. . . . L'objet de la biologie est de saisir ce qui fait d'un vivant un vivant, c'est-à-dire non pas—selon le postulat réaliste commun au mécanisme et au vitalisme,—la superposition de réflexes élémentaires ou l'intervention d'une 'force vitale', mais une structure indécomposable des comportements. C'est par les réactions ordonnées que nous pouvons comprendre, à titre de dégradations, les réactions automatiques." *S. C.*, p. 48.

The Reality of Man as a Body

The above disposes of the notion that we can explain the higher by the lower; "indecomposable structure" means something over and above that which is structured. Merleau-Ponty does not admit a one-to-one relation of stimulus to response; rather, response must be conditioned by structure. It has been proven, in fact, that the same stimulus may provoke no response or a different response depending on the organism which receives the stimulus—for Merleau-Ponty a change may mean a new structuration. (More will be said on this later.) This makes more intelligible the assertion, by Merleau-Ponty, that if a law of behavior will be found, it will depend on the total nervous system and on those active interventions which are needed for the conservation of the organism—and which are its structural modification—rather than on reactions to local arrangement (i.e., isolated stimuli-responses).

But how can one understand this dependence of the parts from the whole, asks Merleau-Ponty. Certainly, if one wants to refute finalism, one cannot do so by ignoring the facts on which it bases its arguments, one must face these facts and endeavor to understand them.[19] Merleau-Ponty finds that all of the psychological explanations based on experimentation are insufficient to explain human conduct.[20] One of the reasons why such observable data are insufficient for Merleau-Ponty is that the experiments are conducted in a way which is not "lived experience" but a "contrived situation" which would simulate life. Hence, the data gathered are not the genuine sort of behavior which would be

---

[19] *S. C.*, pp. 25-26.
[20] *S. C.*, p. 47: "Ici la variation de la réponse en présence de stimuli analogues est en rapport avec le sens des situations où ils apparaissent; inversement il pourra se faire que des situations, qui paraissent différentes si on les analyse en termes de stimuli physico-chimiques, provoquent des réactions analogues. Les réflexes du laboratoire ressemblent aux mouvement d'un homme qui marche dans la nuit et dont les organes tactiles, les pieds, les jambes fonctionnent, pour ainsi dire, isolément." [This passage is attributed by Merleau-Ponty to Goldstein's *Der Aufbau des Organismus*, p. 111.]

the result of a spontaneous life situation as lived by a conscious body. Behaviorism then, is found sadly wanting. Therefore, from the examination of "reflex behavior" he goes on to study what he calls "superior behavior," that is to say, "reflexive" behavior.

The difference between reflex and superior (reflexive) behavior lies basically in this: the first is essentially dependent on nervous excitations and conditioning; the second implies elements of intention and is based, at least for man, on symbolic forms. Now, judgment is required to understand symbols. Therefore, at this level, we already have an element clearly apart from and superior to the physico-chemical apparatus involved in the "reflex" behavior.

It is precisely the notion of form which can supersede the atomistic conception of nervous functioning. Yet, it will not reduce the activity to an undifferentiated function, nor will it reject psychological empiricism by embracing the spiritualist antithesis.

> The analysis of perception will lead us to reestablish a break: not between sensation and perception, nor between sensibility and intelligence, nor, more generally, between a chaos of elements and a superior function which will organize them, but between different types or levels of organization.[21]

According to Merleau-Ponty, the notion of form does not represent a static substance, defined once and for all, but one whose relation to that which it informs or structures will be determined in each case by the level of organization at which it is operative. Therefore, since it is no longer necessary to classify behavior as simple or complex, it will be fitting to define it according to structure or form. One can distinguish "syncretic forms" (formes syncrétiques), "revocable or variable forms" (formes amovibles) and

---
[21] *S. C.*, p. 100.

The Reality of Man as a Body

"symbolic forms" (formes symboliques)[22] corresponding, not indeed to three types of souls, but to three types of behavior—for there is no type of animal (Merleau-Ponty evidently includes man here) whose behavior is such that it never surpasses the syncretic level, nor that it does not at times descend from the symbolic. Nevertheless, animals can be classified according to the type of behavior which is most familiar to them—for man, the symbolic.

What are the characteristics of each type of forms? Briefly, at the level of the "syncretic forms" behavior is tied either to certain abstract aspects of the situation (as in the case of conditioning carried out, for instance, in laboratory experiments)[23] or to certain complexes of very special stimuli. In any event, it is imprisoned in the frame of natural conditions and it does not easily adapt to uncommon situations. In this case the behavior has more of the instinctive than of the intelligent—the latter is hardly discernible. This type of form still remains engaged in matter.

The "revocable or removable" forms, on the contrary, have a certain independence: when there appear in behavior "signs" which are not determined by instinctive releasing

---

[22] *S. C.*, pp. 113-14. Merleau-Ponty uses the term *syncretic* to signify a union of two or more original reflexes—or stimuli—response ensemble. Form *syncrétique* is that by which the animal responds literally to a complex of stimuli, rather than to certain traits essential to the situation in question.

Forms *amovibles*—revocable or removable forms—are forms which are not tied strictly to instinctive movements, but to signs—this therefore implies at least the capability of learning conditioned responses. At this level there can be a sort of *end* in view, be it ever so elementary.

Formes symboliques—symbolic forms—refer to the level wherein the sign becomes symbol; this is specifically the human level. Man is neither bound by pure matter, nor by instinctive or conditioned types of acts. He can see the signification of a sign; set himself an end, choose a kind of response rather than another. It is in this sense that for man the "sign" becomes the "symbol." In other words, man can create meaning and find meaning in those situations wherein inferior types of behavior simply follow a "sign" without distinguishing—intellectually—its signification.

[23] Cf. *S. C.*, pp. 114-15.

mechanisms, one is brought to think that such signs are the result of structures relatively independent from the matter within which they are realized. Herein is involved the adaptation of the organism to contiguity, spatial and temporal, not however, an adaptation relying merely on conditioned stimuli, but on a structured whole to which a meaning is given. Thus the objective description of behavior discovers in it certain structures, more or less specified, a signification more or less rich, and a reference to situations which are sometimes personal, sometimes abstract and sometimes "essential." Further, whenever the stimulus, conditioned or not, is such that it entails, besides contiguity, a logical or objective relation, then there are special reactions which come close to what we may call "end," or in human language, means to end.[24]

The symbolic form, which is proper to man, is that wherein the "sign" becomes "symbol." This never happens at the animal level. The symbolic form is characterized by the introduction of novelty—a piano player can improvise. It does not matter if the "stimuli" here are themselves manmade; all aptitude acquired with regard to the manipulation of an object is acquired by taking possession, with our body, of a type of "artificial behavior" imaging the given object. It is really an adaptation to the human structure of that object itself. It will be seen that symbolic behavior is the condition of all creativity and of all novelties in the ends of conduct or behavior. It is therefore not astonishing that it manifests itself first by adaptation to objects which do not exist in nature.[25]

---

[24] *S. C.*, p. 133.
[25] *S. C.*, p. 131, Note (2). Kwant has this to say: "According to his [Merleau-Ponty's] point of view, we become familiar with the world by discovering and analysing the potentialities of the "ego-body." The world in which we live is designed by and for man. It is adapted, adjusted to his fundamental possibilities. Whoever apprehends the meaning of a chair sees the structure of the human body. . . . A world beyond the possibilities of man would no longer be a human world.

The Reality of Man as a Body

All genuine aptitude results from an impulse from within, whose efficacy is not due to some exterior stimulus, but is rather a property of its own interior structure; the meaning likewise, is immanent and the response is symbolic. The symbolic dimension is precisely that which is lacking to the animal; it is instead, that which distinguishes man, since it is a possibility which implies novelty and creativity: man can express in a variety of manners the same theme, and by this a cognitive and free type of behavior is actualized.

> With the symbolic forms there appears a behavior which expresses the stimulus for itself, which opens itself to the truth and to the proper value of things, which tends to adequate the signifying and the signified, the intention and that which it intends. Herein behavior has no longer only a signification, it *is* itself signification.[26]

From the above discussion Merleau-Ponty draws the conclusion that the conditioned reflex is either a pathological phenomenon or a superior behavior: it is only at the level of a symbolic behavior that one encounters an activity regulated by objective stimuli, while vital behavior is governed by syncretic ensembles. The above discussion also shows that for Merleau-Ponty we cannot explain the higher by the lower nor the lower by the higher. Behavior, inasmuch as it is a structure, does not depend on either of the two orders

---

Merleau-Ponty's vision is valuable, but it does not suffice to explain the human realm of meaning. It is not possible to deduct the world of meaning from the potentialities of the "ego-body", because a possibility is not knowable to us but is recognized only in its actualization. We know, in fact, more about the human possibilities than the caveman, because we have *realized* them to a greater extent. *Encounter* (Duquesne Studies, Philosophical Series, 11; Pittsburgh: Duquesne University Press, 1950), p. 30. Cited hereafter as *Encounter*. It may be observed here, in passing, that Merleau-Ponty does not in principle admit that we may take a possibility as the basis for an actuality. Cf. Preface to *Phénoménologie de la perception*. This point will be discussed further.

[26] *S. C.*, p. 133.

traditionally understood to be responsible for activity: the interior order of reflexive thought or the exterior order of physical events. Insofar as it does not remain within the confines of space and time as objective, behavior transforms the experience in a typical situation and the reaction in an aptitude; it therefore detaches itself from the order of the "in-itself" and projects a possibility which is interior to itself. The movements of behavior do not, it is true, point to a being which is completely conscious; its intentions do not reveal to the animal pure being, but they do reveal being-for-the-animal; that is to say, only a certain manner of being or existing which does not yet reveal a consciousness.[27] However, the animal is not wholly deprived of interiority even if the latter cannot be called pure consciousness; depending on the degree of integration which the animal possesses, he is a "certain manner of being to the world" or of existing. Very significantly Merleau-Ponty refers here to Hegel's words: "A consciousness is . . . a 'hole through being' but we have here [Merleau-Ponty refers to the animal] only a hollow."[28]

Summing up, for Merleau-Ponty the structure of behavior as it is offered to our perceptive experience, is neither thing, nor consciousness—and this is precisely why it is opaque to the intellect. The fact that behavior is not reducible to its supposed parts is not the whole meaning of Merleau-Ponty's lengthy study. An instant of reflection, he declares, must certainly have made clear to us that we cannot have knowledge of anything at all without knowing our own thoughts; that is, we cannot either confront the world or refuse it without becoming conscious, and without admitting a pre-objective existence—a being for itself.

---

[27] *S. C.*, pp. 135-36.
[28] *S. C.*, pp. 136-37: "Une conscience est, selon le mot de Hegel, un 'trou dans l'être' et nous n'avons encore ici qu'un creux. Le chimpanzé qui peut physiquement se lever, mais reprend dans tous les cas urgents la posture animale, qui peut assembler les caisses, mais ne leur donne qu'un équilibre tactile, traduit par là une sorte d'adhérence à l'actuel, une manière courte et pesante d'exister."

Behavior is then made up of relations; it is "thought" and not merely an in-itself as any other object (thing) would be—this we easily learn from reflexion. But the insight we have through reflection, for Merleau-Ponty, is lacking the essential contact with the phenomenon—which is constitutive of behavior:

> behavior is not a thing, nor an idea; it is not the shroud of a pure consciousness; as a witness of another behavior I am not pure consciousness. This is just what we mean when we say that behavior is a form.[29]

With this Merleau-Ponty thinks to have found a way out of the dichotomy "intellectualism versus empiricism": the notion of form, with its ambivalence, seems to him the appropriate means for avoiding the classical antithesis between the analysis of the central factors of behavior and its exterior manifestations, or between a philosophical position which maintains a juxtaposition of exterior relations and that which finds thought as the intrinsic relation of all phenomena. He admits the notion of form, as he understands it, is ambiguous. It is now necessary, he maintains, to understand it, and not merely to be satisfied with the descriptions heretofore given of it (i.e., the examples given from physics and the definition of its characters useful to resolve the problems of physiology and psychology) for "without an understanding of the notion of form the philosophical meaning of the foregoing discussion will remain equivocal."[30]

2. Levels of Structuration

As is apparent, at this point Merleau-Ponty has not yet found a satisfactory explanation of the relation of consciousness to nature. Even "superior behavior" does not offer a

---
[29] *S. C.*, p. 138.
[30] *S. C.*, p. 138.

sufficient and convincing explanation of the relation of consciousness to nature, because it does not account for the total experience or the total activity involved. Neither can he find a more complete answer when he examines the workings of the three levels of life, physical, vital, human; for "the reactions of an organism are not edifices of elementary movements, but gestures resulting from an interior unity."[31] How to define this unity is the burden of his inquiry. This will involve him, ultimately, in the study of man as *incarnate spirit*, whose conscious activities cannot be explained by any partial account of physical, biological, or psychological events, but rather by a view of the dialectical relation of his three levels of life. The notion of "structured form" will be the key to an understanding of man's activities, an understanding which will not be in any way exhaustive, or even clear, because there is an intrinsic ambiguity in the workings of consciousness. To attempt to do away with this ambiguity is tantamount to depriving man of his richer self; to attempt to understand one level of life apart from another is like attempting to understand the parts aside from the whole in Hegelian terms—the moments of the dialectic independently of the synthesis. The categories describing these three levels must therefore be universalized, says Merleau-Ponty:

> It is here that the notion of form will warrant a truly new solution. Quantity, order, value or signification, which pass respectively as properties of matter, life and

---

[31] *S. C.*, p. 140. Merleau-Ponty describes at great lengths the levels which he calls "physical," "vital," and "human"; but these are not powers of being, or distinguished levels either completely independent one from the other or casually related; they are rather three dialectics. It is important to note, from the very beginning, that the labels "physical," "vital," and "human" do not connote as they seem to, material reality, living beings, and men, respectively; obviously this would be too simple—and there would hardly be a reason for such a lengthy discussion by Merleau-Ponty. It will be seen that these three dialectics are the ground of the integration of existents.

spirit, would no longer be more than the dominant characteristics of the orders in question, and would become universally applicable categories. Quantity is not a negation of quality as if the equation of the circle were to deny the circular form of which on the contrary it is meant to be a rigorous expression.[32]

Merleau-Ponty sees no reason why an objective value should be denied those phenomena which pertain to the levels of life or of the moral—human—realm, because they too have their place in the physical order. If knowledge of physics, insofar as it has something to do with structures, admits the categories previously reserved for the kind of knowledge proper to life and spirit, then perhaps biology and psychology should not avoid the mathematical and causal explanations. He is aware of the direction this new order will take: a philosophy of forms will be substituted for the philosophy of substance. (This declaration will prove useful in determining his meaning of "incarnate spirit"—not an easy task to accomplish.) In all this however, there is a saving aspect: a philosophy of structure which maintains the original characters of the three orders (described above) and holds to the universality of quantity, order and signification in forms, will ultimately preserve the distinctions of the physical, vital and human orders: it is precisely by their structuration that they are distinct from one another. This simply means that matter, life and spirit participate differently in the nature of *form* "represent different degrees of integration and constitute a hierarchy wherein the individuality is further realized."[33] Merleau-Ponty further asserts that it would be by definition impossible to conceive a physical form having the same properties of a physiological one, or a physiological form equivalent to a psychic

---
[32] *S. C.*, p. 141.
[33] *S. C.*, pp. 142-43.

one. It is therefore clear that he does not see a chain of continuity of physical action between stimuli and responses. On the contrary, behavior will have to be viewed as a mediation of physiological and psychical relations. In other words, for him, the physic, the vital and the psychic do not represent three powers of being, but three dialectics. This dialectic relation is precisely the point he wants to make; all of his efforts are bent to show that this is the relation attaining between man and things, man and the world, man and others at the human cultural level.

3. Body-Soul Dialectic

When Merleau-Ponty comes to the relation of body and soul,[34] which involves besides the theory of form, the problem of perceptive consciousness, he has evidently hit the center of the mystery of man. In this study he gives the fundamental reasons for his notion of "incarnate spirit" rather than "soul using a body."[35] He does not accept the materialists' models and rejects the spiritualists' as well.

As usual, Merleau-Ponty does not try to *explain* the relation. Rather, he tells us what the relation could *not* be, and then describes the phenomena he observes. The relation of body and soul is obscure if, by an abstraction, we consider the body as a mere fragment of matter (here the soul would be an entity in itself), but it is quite clear if we view the body as the bearer of a dialectic; the latter approach would be the only legitimate theme for philosophical reflec-

---

[34] *S. C.*, Chapter IV, pp. 200-41.

[35] *S. C.*, p. 225: "L'esprit n'utilise pas le corps, mais se fait à travers lui tout en le transférant hors de l'espace physique. Quand nous décrivions les structures du comportement, c'était bien pour montrer qu'elles sont irréductibles à la dialectique du stimulus physique et de la contraction musculaire, et qu'en ce sens le comportement, loin d'être une chose qui existe en soi, est un ensemble significatif pour une conscience qui le considère; mais c'était du même coup et réciproquement pour faire voir dans la 'conduite de l'expression' le *spectacle d'une conscience* sous nos yeux, celui d'un esprit qui *vient au monde.*"

tion.³⁶ Going therefore beyond the study of structures—which are not reducible to a dialectic of physical stimuli and corresponding movements—he points to the surprising phenomenon of a consciousness coming into its own, of a spirit opening to the world.³⁷

From this we can see clearly why we cannot posit between soul and body a relation similar to that of concept to word, define soul as the "sense of the body," or the body as the "manifestation of the soul." Metaphors which have been used by philosophers to express the independence or priority of the soul as an entity such as that of the artisan and its tools (Cartesian) for instance, cannot be accepted for they usually involve a purely exterior relation.

There is nothing very revolutionary in the rejection of those types of relations of soul to body; the theory of hylemorphism does as much; the criticism often leveled at the Platonic theory of soul shows that others before Merleau-Ponty had seen the problem.

Referring to the theory of "the artisan and its tools" he says that "there is no reason to speak of a perfection of the spirit in itself."³⁸ The body is implied in the accomplishment of the spirit: if one can speak of the body as preventing the accomplishment or perfecting of the spirit, then certainly one can also say that the body is implied when the spirit is perfected; this is so simply because body and soul are interdependent. This is perhaps one of Merleau-Ponty's very valuable insights. It is true, asceticism often speaks of

---

[36] Merleau-Ponty describes the relation between the epistemological subject and his object: "Puisque le monde physique et l'organisme ne peuvent être pensés que comme des objets de conscience ou des significations, le problème des rapports de la conscience et de ses 'conditions' physiques ou organiques n'existerait qu'au niveau d'une pensée confuse qui s'attache à des abstractions, il disparaitrait dans le domaine de la vérité où seul subsiste à titre original le rapport du sujet épistémologique et de son objet. Ce serait là le seul thème légitime de la réflexion philosophique." *S. C.*, p. 220. However, Merleau-Ponty fails to specify how this relation between an epistemological subject and his object is established.
[37] *S. C.*, p. 225.
[38] *S. C.*, p. 225, Note (1).

the role of the body in the perfecting of the soul, but what is really meant is that the body is an "instrument" which may be rendered docile to the directions of the soul in the performance of good acts. Basically therefore, it is always the body under the directing influence of the soul which is a "means" to the perfecting of the soul itself—actually, the perfection of the soul is presupposed—the very thing Merleau-Ponty denies it is possible to assume.

Just what does he mean by the body being responsible for the "accomplishment" of the soul? To understand his meaning, we must follow closely the steps by which he arrives at that which he calls the dialectic of soul and body, a dialectic of a unique kind, because it never implies just one body, nor just one relation. This observation gives us an insight into the kind of dialectic he will postulate; it also explains why he has rejected those types of definition and description of body-soul relation discussed above: they are external to each other and represent a constant relation between two invariable components, the body, a physical entity, and the soul, a spiritual substance.

It will become clear that for Merleau-Ponty the terms "body" and "soul" do not have the classical connotation (discussed above) although he does not deny outright these connotations. However, as a phenomenologist, he is concerned with describing the immediate data of his experience, an experience which is always *in* the world, hence contingent and temporal.

Making use of the notion of behavior, he approaches the relation of body and soul from the viewpoint of perception: the body appears as a phenomenon with which we are familiar; we perceive human behavior through the body. As he has said in dealing with the three levels of life,[39] the body is not merely a physical entity closed within itself upon which the soul may act by an exterior causality. It is

---

[39] *S.C.*, p. 139. Cf. Chapter III.

The Reality of Man as a Body

more correct to say that the body, having a higher degree of integration by reason of its structuration as a *human* body, is the visible expression of meaningful behavior, communicable to other "ego-bodies" which are, likewise, centers of meaning and points of mutual encounters. This already implies an intersubjectivity—to be discussed later—but actually it will be seen that the encounter is necessary for the very "realization" of the subject.

Merleau-Ponty doubtlessly takes his point of departure from the classical notions of body and soul, otherwise he could not postulate a "soul"—however, he does not begin with an a priori definition of what the soul must be. There is in his description a genuine attempt at a phenomenological investigation free from "presuppositions." His chief concern is to show, against the inadequacies of the empirical as well as of the intellectualistic approach, that there is between body and soul a dialectical relation, an interplay at the various levels of structuration, and that it is only by the acceptance of this existential and therefore ambiguous relation that one can have an insight into man's behavior.[40]

As is customary with him, he draws heavily on observation of abnormal phenomena in human behavior. It is precisely by comparing and contrasting the findings of psychology in both normal and abnormal behavior that he claims to show that which constitutes the essential relation at each level of "reality"—in this case he claims to find the essential relation of spirit and matter.[41]

---

[40] We will not dwell on his critique of empiricism and intellectualism. At the end of our discussion, it will probably be possible to see the relation among the various types of dialectic Merleau-Ponty singles out in his investigation of behavor—e.g., reflex, superior, symbolic; physical, vital, human; body and soul; figure and background, etc. But it will not be easy—perhaps not even possible—to attempt a synthesis which Merleau-Ponty himself has declined to make.

[41] What does Merleau-Ponty mean by spirit? Spirit is for him simply that by which man transcends matter, or the conditions of pure matter. He does not admit this term in an historical traditional sense. (Dr. Joseph Kockelmans' personal correspondence.)

For the normal, the body will not be a mere object of which he is conscious as he is of every other "thing" in the world. If the body becomes for him a mere object of his consciousness, then he has not achieved the dialectic relation—rather he has embraced the position of the "pure subject" who is a *spectator* before the world and also before his own body which he considers as part of the world of objects. For Merleau-Ponty then, the body is rather the mediator between the ego-consciousness and the world in such a way that I can say "I am my body," I am a point of view on the world;[42] my existence is a behavior capable of intuitions, of expressions, of liberty and of thought; but these are tied inseparably to my body, which [body] conditions and manifests my activities.[43]

However, this conditioning of my activities on the part of my body is not to be taken as a causal action. In fact, Merleau-Ponty goes to great lengths of analysis to show that it is not by a causality of stimuli and reflexes that behavior can be explained—or understood—but rather that there is a certain ambiguity in the corporeal nature; we can see that there is interaction at the various levels—physical, psychological, etc.—but we can only assign meaning to the global activity as a whole. If we attempt to localize and sectionalize the various activities which manifest themselves at the bodily level, we lose the signification of the action itself—we lose sight of the structure of behavior itself.[44]

Just what is the presence of the body to consciousness? It is not, says Merleau-Ponty, of a body-in-itself over against a consciousness (also an "in itself"); on the contrary, consciousness experiences at every moment its inherence to an organism, but in such a way that it is not a presence before a material object, but rather a presence of its own history

---
[42]*P.P.*, p. 175: "Mais je ne suis pas devant mon corps, je suis dans mon corps, ou plutôt je suis mon corps."
[43]Cf. *P. P.*, pp. 101-103; 493-95.
[44]*P.P.;* Cf. *S.C.*, pp. 218-23.

and of the dialectical development of which it is aware. The spirit does not "utilize" the body, but *is* through the body. (Briefly, Merleau-Ponty wants to do away with the dichotomy of matter and spirit as was so often pointed out.)[45]

Now, whether our body be manifesting a dialectic far superior to the purely biological, or whether it be reduced (because of sickness) to mimic intentions which it no longer possesses

> whatever be the case, the relation of body and soul, as well as the meaning of the terms themselves, will be modified accordingly, that is, the putting into action of the intentions succeeds or fails depending on whether the subordinated dialectics are overcome or not.[46]

This is the first hint at relativization which Merleau-Ponty gives us with regard to the notions of body and soul. Already we can see that the meanings assigned to these terms are very flexible. It is almost as if he were saying, depending on the materials we have to deal with, the dialectical interaction will result in a synthesis of one kind rather than another. Therefore it is certainly not a question of a physical structure—homogeneous perhaps—in a dialectical relation with a spiritual or vital entity which also could be always identified. The relation is quite different: each body-soul relation is in a sense unique as to kind and as to degree, because, if we want to look back at his notion of form, every change in an organism means a new structuration.

Thus, in reference to sensation for instance, he will say that since we do not always have sensations (presumably he means that different organisms will have varying degrees of alertness and of sensitivity or that in sickness and near death we lose the power of sensation) our thoughts do not

---
[45] *S.C.*, pp. 224-25.
[46] *S.C.*, p. 226.

always find in the body the plenitude of their vital expression. In such cases of disintegration, soul and body are apparently distinct—and this is the truth of the duality.

> But the soul, if it does not dispose of any means of expression—or rather, of any means of effectuating itself—ceases likewise to be that which it is, ceases to be soul.[47]

The body which loses its senses ceases immediately to be a living body and becomes a heap of chemicals (when it dies). Body and soul, can never be absolutely distinguished without ceasing to be; consequently, their empirical connection is founded on their very structuration by which meaning appears and the organism is no longer just a fragment of matter. "Thus, considering such a *structure* the true foundation of reality, we reveal at once the distinction and the unity of soul and body."[48] Yet, a duality reappears, at one level or at another, when physical conditions affect the intellectual functions, as for instance, when bodily needs prevent our thoughts or feelings; the sexual dialectic itself, which is not just a physical function, usually manifests itself by a passion; "integration is never absolute and forever breaks down . . . There is a moment in which we divest ourselves of a passion because of fatigue or of self-love."[49]

In all the foregoing examples, Merleau-Ponty shows clearly the interdependence or rather the interplay of soul and body which results in a living organism. He further considers the character of this relation which is far from simple. It is founded on the principle that all integration supposes the normal functioning of the subordinate structures which, likewise, seek their own good. However, there is not for Merleau-Ponty a duality of substances: the no-

---
[47] *S.C.*, p. 226.
[48] *S.C.*, p. 226.
[49] *S.C.*, p. 226.

tions of body and soul must be made relative; the following is perhaps the most difficult passage to interpret relative to the topic:

> There is the body as a mass of chemical components in interaction; the body as a dialectic of the living and of its biological medium; the body as dialectic of the social subject and its group; and, likewise, all our habits form an impalpable body for the self of each instant. Each of these stages [degrees, steps] is soul with regard to the preceding stage, body with regard to the one following. The body in general is an ensemble of ways already indicated, of powers already constituted; [it is] the already attained dialectic foundation [ground] on which a superior form is actualized, and the soul is the sense [meaning] which is then established.[50]

The above is doubtlessly a new interpretation and one worthy of study: there is really no simple relation between soul and body; matter and spirit are not two single powers which may be subsumed into a synthesis. There is instead, a whole complex of dialectical developments, never the same, wherein the relation is never constant; moreover, each is to be determined by the previous developments and in relation to a further one. Is this an attempt at achieving a dialectic within the individual? The intricacies of the dialectic of *body* at the different levels and of *soul* in the relation which *is not* but *becomes* at each new stage, make it indeed impossible to frame a philosophy once and for all, with definite principles and fixed axioms. The philosophy which Merleau-Ponty is trying to present to us, as a living thing, cannot be captured and stabilized into a static framework.

Contrary to what he had said previously, Merleau-Ponty now grants that the body-soul relation can be compared to

---
[50] *S.C.*, p. 227.

that of concept to word, but the relation must be seen analogically—that is, if we perceive a unifying constituting action of language operations, and if we consider language as that wherein the living word (as expressive of original meaning) is preserved and made available.[51]

The whole discussion leads Merleau-Ponty to the assertion which is particularly worthy of note: "Our analysis then leads us to the ideality of the body, but it is an idea which utters itself and likewise 'becomes' in the chance of existence."[52]

Can we say that this ideality is the end result of a Husserlian ideation? As far as ideality is concerned, yes; but when Merleau-Ponty adds that this idea *utters* itself and *becomes* in the hazard or chance of existence, we are beyond Husserl. It is not a question of a constituted essence, but of an essence revealed in existence. Herein Merleau-Ponty is trying to show that phenomenology is the replacing of essences in existence: the essence of the body is revealed but not in an abstract manner, rather in a concrete, lived situation. How this is done, however, Merleau-Ponty does not say. At this point one can see the Hegelian influence on Merleau-Ponty. He affirms that the notion of Gestalt will bring us, by a natural development, to the Hegelian concept before it has become conscious of itself. The concept as concept has no exteriority, even if Nature can, in a sense, be called the "exteriority of a concept." The Gestalt dwells on the unity

---

[51] *S.C.*, p. 227. Merleau-Ponty will often use the term "disponible" meaning available or "being placed at the service of."—Because of its specific, existential connotations, we will retain the original in most cases. "On peut bien comparer les relations de l'âme et du corps à celle du concept et du mot, mais à condition d'apercevoir sous les produits séparés l'opération constituante qui les joint et le retrouver sous les langages empiriques, accompagnement extérieur ou vêtement contigent de la pensée, la *parole* vivant qui en est la seule effectuation, où le sens se formule pour la première fois, se fonde ainsi comme sens et devient disponible pour des opérations ultérieures."
[52] *S.C.*, p. 227.

of the interior and the exterior, of nature and thought; yet, the consciousness for which Gestalt exists "is not intellectual consciousness, but perceptive experience." In fact, intellectual consciousness must question perceptive consciousness in order to find a definitive clarification of essences. He further indicates that the status of the object, the relation of form to matter and of body to soul, individuality and plurality of consciousness are founded on perceptual experience.[53]

From all this can we conclude that for Merleau-Ponty the intellectual is subordinate to the perceptual and that the concept as a means of communication is of little value apart from perceptual consciousness? There is no pre-eminence of one over the other: relations are intended to be dialectical; hence the perceptual is considered as a moment in the total movement just as much as the intellectual. There is an interplay of relations wherein the perceptual plays the basic role, but is hardly dissociated from the intellectual; in fact, it is quite evident that in Merleau-Ponty the existential approach does not in any way deny the need for, or the value of the conceptual expression.

According to his observations, I really have no way of knowing whether my perception of anything is like that of another; the fact that others use the same words to indicate the same thing is no guarantee that they experience the same impression. Therefore he must say that perception, as knowledge of individual things, is an individual consciousness and not consciousness in general. That which I perceive without attempting to recognize, the "this" which my consciousness experiences without words is neither signification nor idea, though it could serve as the basis for either. When however, I name or recognize something I perceive, I substitute for the experience of a fleeting reality that of a concept; "when I pronounce the word 'this' I relate a

---

[53] *S.C.*, pp. 227-28.

singular and lived experience to the essence of lived experience,"[54] whatever that essence may be.

This is the way Merleau-Ponty sees the relation which essences have to the existing world and their function in the apprehension of such a world. Knowledge of the essence, for him, is not the end but a means to grasp the meaning of the world and of man in the world. Our philosophical endeavors cannot be fruitful without the knowledge of essences, but these must be *discovered* in the existents themselves, not merely *constituted*.[55] This is important: a phenomenologist may very well look upon the essence as constituted in consciousness, but this is not to be a constitution in the absolute sense; there is a way of re-constituting that reality which one has encountered in the first naive, pre-philosophical contact, which is, however, without reflection, as Merleau-Ponty sees it. According to Professor Lauer, this reconstitution would follow a re-examination of all problems by a return to the fundamental data of the problems themselves; their solution should result from essential insights. But this reflection is already secondary, because even a first contact with the world implies reflection.[56]

The foregoing remarks seem to have strayed from the consideration of body-soul relation, but that is not really the case. For Merleau-Ponty, perception is the necessary activity of the incarnate spirit; that is why a discussion of the body involves us in a study of the perceptual field in all its

---

[54] *S.C.*, p. 228. Cf. also Taylor, "The Pre-objective . . ." pp. 108ff.
[55] Professor Lauer questions the suitableness of phenomenology for "a movement from the abstract to the concrete"; he admits that Merleau-Ponty's intent to reinsert essences into existence is laudable and "the results in Merleau-Ponty's case are brilliant." Yet, Professor Lauer adds, "I see primarily [in phenomenology] a movement from the concrete to the abstract, from fact to essence. In such a framework the historical may function 'by way of example' (as it does for Husserl), but scarcely as integral to the very structure of reality." "Questioning the Phenomenologist," *Journal of Philosophy*, Vol. LVIII, No. 21 (Oct. 12, 1961, pp. 633-40), p. 639.
[56] Lauer, *Triumph* . . . , p. 16.

manifestations. Again and again, he refers to the partial view we have of objects we perceive; he calls this profiles. Referring to the perceptive experience of the same object by two subjects, he remarks that if each were to have the full "vision" of the object—for instance of a cube—all at once, they would not be perceiving a thing, but grasping an idea. Material things reveal themselves to us by degrees, but ideas are grasped by the spirit at once. Knowing about the world is different from perceiving this or that fragment of it—the only way we can perceive is within the near horizon. A perception which is coextensive with the thing perceived is inconceivable, and not just physically, but logically impossible, because perception is by definition, of the existent and not of signification. Neither the relations of things in their original and characteristic properties of existent nor the relation of the aspects of the thing to the total object are logical relations corresponding to those of *sign to the signification*: when I speak of "side" of a chair I mean just "side" and not "sign" of something belonging to the chair.[57]

4. *My Body Perceived and Experienced*

My body must likewise be distinguished from all other objects of perception, for the perception of my body has characteristics which are unique: I can never perceive my body completely, nor place it in a position which will permit me to see it from all sides—unless I view it in a mirror. I really view only its reflection and have not a direct perception of it, or of any of its parts. Still less do I know, experientially, that within my body there are certain organs, which perform certain functions—only science can tell me that. Therefore, certain parts of my body will always remain for me only significations. Can I ever see, directly, my eyes or their living expression? My retina is for me an absolutely

---

[57] *S.C.*, p. 230.

unknowable thing; all this simply shows that all perception is by perspectives—and these perspectives are, of course, partial views of the objects involved. Merleau-Ponty sums up his discussion thus:

> To say that I have a body is simply another way of saying that my knowledge is an individual dialectic wherein intersubjective objects appear, that these objects, when given in their actual existence, present themselves by successive aspects which could not coexist; that finally one of these [objects—my body] offers itself obstinately 'on the same side' and I am unable to turn around it.[58]

This does not mean that the body is "enigmatic" but, rather, that whatever we know about the body is not the pure result of perception; it is by way of signification that we fill the "lacunae" in our perceptive grasp. It is true, Merleau-Ponty admits, that we transform in significations even the lived perceptions we have of our body—which by definition are not significations but direct grasp of the object. We do this by our descriptions; but we can always clarify the point by recalling that whenever we speak of something perceived we already imply its being given by profiles and therefore not something which we did actually grasp at once as we would grasp an idea. We do not explain perception as related to individual consciousness "by the body" in terms of causality. However, we must distinguish between individual perspectives and those of intersubjective

---

[58]"Sans que j'en puisse faire le tour." *S.C.*, p. 230. He also goes on to say that with the exception of the image which the mirror gives me (which image at any rate is not stable [cette image bouge] and therefore it is not a real thing, my body as I know it is truncated at the shoulders and ends with an object which I can touch—and which others tell me is visible [my head] and which further, science tells me contains certain organs. But of all these I will never see anything directly. p. 231.

The Reality of Man as a Body

significance, if we want to account for the fact that others perceive things which we do not.[59]

He introduces here a new distinction: not the classical one of sensibility and intelligence, but of "the lived" and "the known." Hence, for him, the body-soul problem is transformed instead of disappearing: the problem will be "the relation of consciousness as flux of individual events, of concrete and resistant structures, to consciousness as a tissue of ideal significations."[60] As a result of this first phase of reflection, Merleau-Ponty sees therefore the acquisition of the idea of a transcendental philosophy, that is, that of a consciousness constituting the universe and knowing the objects by an exterior, indubitable experience (the Husserlian type of transcendental consciousness). But, at once he springs back to his existential point of view: is one not then obliged to re-establish within consciousness a duality which one does not admit exists? For, the objects, both as unities and as significations, are known through individual perspectives. Just how do I equate the incarnate "rectangularity" (of this rectangular thing) with the signification of it, which I explicitate by a logical act?[61] He has not solved the problem at this point.

Merleau-Ponty admits that all theories of perception fall into the same dilemma: how to explain, on the one hand, consciousness as a function of the body and therefore interior but depending on certain exterior events, and, on the

---

[59] *S.C.*, pp. 231-32: "Mais s'il n'est toujours pas question de relier extérieurement ma conscience à un corps dont elle adopterait le point de vue d'une manière inexplicable, et si tout revient en somme à admettre que certains *hommes voient des choses que je ne vois pas*, pour rester fidèle à ce phénomène, il faut distinguer dans ma connaissance la zone des perspectives individuelles et celle des significations intersubjectives."
[60] *S. C.*, p. 232.
[61] *S. C.*, p. 232. "Quand je regarde un livre placé devant moi, sa forme rectangulaire est une structure concrète et incarnée. Quel est le rapport de cette 'physionomie' rectangulaire et de la signification 'rectangle' que je peux expliciter par un acte logique?"

other hand, the fact that such exterior events influencing the body are only known through consciousness; consciousness is therefore both a part of the world and coextensive with it.

Now there would be no dilemma, he says, if one were to consider purely the realm of signification; therefore a transcendental consciousness would not have to face this problem. But he comes to grips with an existential experience which perception cannot explain. For instance, a little reflection reveals that the experience of passivity is really a construct of the spirit. Also, contrary to what realism would have to say, to the degree to which one comes to know the body scientifically, to that precise degree one makes it impossible to

> give a coherent sense to the supposed action of the world upon the body and of the body upon the soul. The body and the soul are significations and have therefore no meaning except in relation to a consciousness. From our point of view, therefore, the realist thesis of common sense disappears at the level of reflexive thought which is confronted by significations only. The experience of passivity is not explained by an effective passivity. But it [the experience of passivity] must have a meaning and be able to be understood. Realism as a philosophy is an error, because it transposes into a dogmatic thesis an experience which it deforms or makes impossible thereby [by this very transposition].[62]

This passage contains some very important references to the body-soul dialectic, in particular the concept of matter influencing spirit—or the causality of body on soul. Just what does Merleau-Ponty mean by the "action of body on

---

[62] *S. C.*, p. 233.

soul"? To understand his meaning it is necessary to refer again to the passage in which he defines the various "degrees" of body-soul relation mentioned above: the notions of body and soul have to be relativized so that at each succeeding stage "that which was soul with regard to the preceding one becomes body with regard to the one following"[63] thus recognizing a dialectical process. Yet, even the notion of interaction is difficult to understand without admitting that the higher is influenced by the lower; if we merely say that the new "soul" is what it is because of the pre-conditioning of the body by the soul then, it would appear, the formative process is still on the part of the soul—but is this Merleau-Ponty's meaning? The crux of the matter is perhaps the signification which he gives to "soul"—is it merely a figurative way of expressing a vital activity going on at different levels? But then what would be the meaning of "spirit" as he uses it? Can it be that he merely uses the term to mean a form in the Aristotelian sense of form—which may very well be material? If that were so, then the philosophy of Merleau-Ponty would not be more than a new kind of materialism, and the charge of some contemporaries that in his philosophy there is no place for transcendence would be justified.

Moreover, what does he precisely mean when he says that body and soul are "significations which make no sense except in relation to a consciousness"?[64] Does he mean that what I actually experience is the total psycho-physical being (the person—though at this point he does not go that far) and that only reflexively do I distinguish the significations "body-soul"? This would vouch for the basic integration of the human conscious individual; it might also imply that I only "know" the relation of body and soul but I do not "experience" body and soul apart from the total human be-

---

[63]Cf. *supra*, p. 114; *S. C.*, p. 227.
[64]*S. C.*, p. 233.

ing. In this case, "signification" would be the result of a reflexive act by which I determine that a dialectical tension attains between two different aspects of the "behavior" I experience or "know."

In all previous discussions Merleau-Ponty has pointed out again and again that I experience my body—in fact, he also pointed out in what way the experience of it is different from the experience I have of other objects. If I experience my body, if body is "spirit incarnate" then body and soul are not just significations or meanings which I assign to certain structurations of my behavior. The expression "spirit incarnate" if taken literally, would seem to indicate that some kind of an entity in its own right and specifically different from the body—that is the spirit—has become incarnate, has entered into a relation so intimate with an organism as to make of the related entities one being. Again, still pursuing the line of thought above, "significations" could be accepted in this context to mean that the unity of the spirit and body is such that we can only distinguish spirit and body as significations, but not as realities, for apart from each other neither *could be*.

There is still room for another interpretation: if body and soul are to be relativized as he says that they should be, then truly they are nothing more than significations, because in that case there would really not be any such thing as a body—with a certain physical nature—any more than there would be a "soul" of a certain spiritual or immaterial nature. In this case we would well say that these significations make sense only in relation to a consciousness. But then we could also say, "Would anything make sense without a consciousness?"

But the most crucial problem seems to be this: what is this "undefinable" body-and-soul? Does it imply a sort of evolutionary development restricted here to the personal subject, and having a starting point in man rather than in

The Reality of Man as a Body

lower forms of life? And just what is "spirit" (to ask the question again) if soul is developmental to such an extent that it does evolve from that which in the lower estate was termed "body"?[65]

5. *Directness and Unity of Perception*

Merleau-Ponty, however, does not seem to be concerned with the problems he raises as he continues his study of perception. The error of realism, he says, is based on an authentic phenomenon which philosophy has to elucidate: the phenomenon of the proper structure of perceptive experience which refers the partial "profiles" to the total signification—the corporeal conditioning of perception demands nothing more nor less. Not being the result of cerebral functioning, but the signification of it, "the perceived" is therefore not an effect of the nervous system's workings. Now all "consciousnesses" (conscious beings) which we know present themselves to us through a body which is their perspective aspect. If to each individual dialectic correspond certain cerebral states, these are not present to consciousness. Philosophically, it would mean that each time I have a perception of some sensible phenomenon an observer, properly situated, could detect in my brain certain other phenomena which could never be given to me in actuality—to understand them I should have to recognize in them a signification corresponding to the content of my perception. On the other hand, I can represent to myself a certain phenomenon of my perceiving organs in a purely significative manner. The spectator and I are tied up by our corporeity so that the experiences given to me as concrete perspectives can be given to him only as significations, and vice versa. Merleau-Ponty thus expresses the exchange:

> My total being—psycho-physical—(that is, the experience I have of myself, that which the other has of me,

---
[65]Cf. *S. C.*, pp. 225-27; *P. P.*, p. 230.

and the scientific knowledge which he applies and I apply to the knowledge of myself) is, in the last analysis, an interlacing of significations such that, when some of them are perceived and pass to actuality, the others are only virtually intended. But this structure of experience resembles that of exterior objects. Further they [the significations] presuppose each other.[66]

The relations described above, continues our author, imply a point of view on my part—a being in situation—which, however, precludes me from seeing my point of view, except through virtual signification. "The existence of an exterior perception, that of my body, and 'in' this body, the phenomena imperceptible to me are therefore rigorously synonymous."[67] But—and this gives us Merleau-Ponty's view on a classical problem—between the two there is no relation of causality. These are *concordant phenomena*. His notion of structure as opposed to the various theories of perception examined in the preceding chapters, has here its stronger reiteration; man is a unity, and his acts are not the result of reflexes or conditionings. Perception is not the result of the functioning of the perceptive organs, but a vital, human act which the individual performs. My perceptive organs do not "cause" my perceptions, but "I" perceive through my organs of perception.

Merleau-Ponty looks at the problem from still another aspect: the access to the domain proper to perception has always been difficult to philosophers because of an illusion: it has always seemed possible to develop a geometry of perceived objects. The very perception of distance has always been confused with the estimation of science in that regard. In fact, all sciences consider the world as complete without reflecting that in such a world perception is constitutive. But we are in a world previous to number, space, time,

---
[66]*S. C.*, p. 234.
[67]*S. C.*, p. 234.

The Reality of Man as a Body

causality—a lived perception. "The problem confronting perception is precisely to find a way to cross this phenomenal field and seize the intersubjective world which science is attempting to determine."[68] The antimony referred to above—consciousness as function of my body, and consciousness as means by which I know—is founded on the ambiguity of this perceptive experience; thesis and antithesis express well its two aspects: on the one hand, my perception is radically contingent, always in a flux of individual events—hence the apparent realism; on the other hand my perception attains to the things themselves.

An access to the world is possible through an articulation of perspectives leading to individual significations.

> There are therefore things *exactly in the sense in which I see them,* in my history and outside of it, inseparable from this double relation. I perceive the things directly, without my body creating a screen between them and me; it [the body] is a phenomenon as they are, gifted however with an original structure, which justly presents it to me as an intermediary between the world and myself. . . .[69]

Merleau-Ponty stresses the fact that I see through my eyes as instruments of my "looking" and not as an ensemble of tissues and organs; the same could be said of all the organs by which I perceive the world. Recalling the "given" of the naive consciousness we can now say that the philosophy of perception is not derived entirely from life; according to our author, it is not surprising that consciousness should fail to recognize itself since it is consciousness of things. He affirms that one either confronts the constituted world by the perceptive experience of the world and engenders perception beginning from the world—as does real-

[68] *S. C.*, p. 236.
[69] *S. C.*, p. 236.

ism; or, one sees in it only a rough sketch of the science of the world as a critical approach would do—that is to say, the latter would strive to ascertain first whether the science of the world itself is possible given the means which man has of knowing exterior reality; it would try to answer the question, "Can man know—and if he can, how far can this knowledge be accepted as certain?"

However, Merleau-Ponty adds, one may invert the natural movement of consciousness in his study of perception. To consider perception as a type of original experience wherein the real world is constituted in its specific structures is one such inversion; it is in fact an imposition on the movement of consciousness itself. He claims to define the "phenomenological reduction" according to the meaning given it by Husserl in his later works. On the other hand one must not suppress every question for the sake of the reduction: rather it is necessary to understand the lived relation between the "profiles" of the things and the things themselves, which this relation presents; without any confusion with the logical aspect of the problem (of perception) one must strive to understand the relation of the perspectives to the significations which are intended through them. The notion of intentionality will be the key to an understanding of these relations.[70]

6. Genesis of Consciousness

The next task Merleau-Ponty sets himself is to examine what happens when we have consciousness not of truth but of illusion. Granting that the complex of consciousness is not an outside thing but an interior structure which will therefore tend to preserve itself, how can one understand the true significations of our life? It will be necessary to distinguish between the effective *structure* and the ideal

---

[70] *S. C.*, pp. 236-37.

signification of our psychic events. Likewise, it will be necessary to distinguish in our development an ideal liberation which does not transform us in our own being, but merely in the consciousness which we have of ourselves, and a real liberation which is a true "metamorphosis." Obviously, we do not reduce ourselves to our idealization of consciousness any more than we can reduce things to the signification by which we express them. In the same way we can show the sociologist that the supposed structures of consciousness he relates to certain supposed economic and social structures are only the consciousness of those structures or the object of a transcendental consciousness. But—and this needs to be underlined—"transcendental consciousness, the full consciousness of self, is not complete, it is yet to become, that is to say, it is yet to be realized in existence."[71]

With regard to the relation of self to others, Merleau-Ponty remarks that deception is possible if I take account only of the idealization of behavior, whether it be my behavior or that of others; in the latter case I would therefore know nothing but the exterior of his conduct.

> My perception of him is never, in case of pain or grief, equivalent to his of himself, unless indeed I were so close to him that our sentiment constituted together a sole "form" and that thus our lives would cease to flow separately. It is only by this commitment—rare and difficult—which I can truly join him, as I also can only know my natural movements and know myself sincerely by the decision to be myself.[72]

The meaning he gives to "form," "soul," and "spirit" seems important for the clarification of his previous discussion on the body-soul relation. Now we can find in the above discussion a help towards understanding—through his

---
[71] *S. C.*, p. 238.
[72] *S. C.*, pp. 238-39.

signfication of "form"—his ambiguous use of the terms mentioned. If two persons can participate *in* the same form, as he clearly seems to imply, then the term is used more in a metaphorical than in an ontological sense. But then what happens to the personal, substantial reality? If by soul—form—he means that complex of characteristics, that structuration which determines a being at any one time, then there is no question of supposing that when he speaks of "incarnate spirit" he intends a spiritual being in its own right—just what he means will remain very ambiguous; more ambiguous still will remain the fact of the spirit's own individual development and its relation to others. The passage referred to above also contains a very valuable insight into the possibility of interpersonal relations: though "rare and difficult" an intimate relation is possible. This means a great deal, since he maintains that the two cease to live their own lives separately. He admits however, that I have no innate power to know the other truly, but I only communicate with him by means of the signification of his behavior, that is, I can look at his structure and penetrate, under his words and actions, the locus wherein they arise—his real self. This means actually that the behavior I witness is a true revelation of the self from whom the actions arise. The other, as well as myself, expresses a manner of existing before expressing a manner of thinking. Accordingly, when I, through dialogue, come in contact with him and lay hold of my thoughts in order to respond to him, by that very fact "I am involved in a *coexistence* of which I am not the unique constituent, and which founds the phenomenon of social nature, as the perceptive experience founds that of physical nature."[73]

But this does not yet mean that I have a reflexive consciousness of my relation. According to Merleau-Ponty consciousness can be in the existing things, without reflecting,

[73] *S. C.*, pp. 239.

it can abandon itself to their concrete structure—not yet converted into signification. Certain episodes in the life of consciousness can by their very inertia imprison its liberty, limit its perception of the world, impose a stereotype behavior; yet, before thinking our class or our milieu, we *are* that class or that milieu.[74]

Does this mean then that I *am* with others, that I form a social or a community life even *before* being conscious of it? Probably not exactly so, since Merleau-Ponty speaks of "cultural objects" falling under my consideration, awakening my intentions and making themselves understood by me; yet, there may still be a consciousness of things apart from or previous to their signification *for* my consciousness. This is, it seems, another way of underlining what he calls "reality" of a pre-objective world—a notion which he has endeavored to discuss at every level, but which he has not succeeded in clarifying. In fact, he has not even justified his contention. But then, who has made clear just *what* "reality" is?

Further, one must admit that the "I think" does not necessarily possess its own object: one can be deluded about it.[75] Even if the "I think" did accompany all of our representations, as presumably it should according to critical philosophy, several problems would still remain unsolved: the approach which reduces "things" and experiences to a net of significations and transforms the life of consciousness into a pure dialectic of subject and object, does not reveal the process involved therein. Is it merely the revelation of something implicitly known, or does the experience bring about a new structuration of consciousness? Further, how does this separation of consciousness from the temporal involvement occur? Does it result in a clear vision of things

---

[74] *S. C.*, p. 239.
[75] *S. C.*, p. 239: "Le 'Je pense' peut donc être comme halluciné par ses objets."

and of consciousness itself, or merely in a superficial grasp of things? "Is the reflexive transition to intellectual consciousness an adequation of our knowing to our being, or only a manner by which consciousness creates for itself a separate existence—a quietism?"[76]

Merleau-Ponty does not answer his own questions, but points out that he does not intend thereby to close his eyes to the problems. He would like to "equate consciousness to the whole of experience," or assume the whole of the *"en-soi"* consciousness into the *"pour-soi"* consciousness.[77]

The meaning of the foregoing statement is a bit obscure. It seems that Merleau-Ponty wants to express once more, by it, his constant intention of making "the pre-objective" a foundation of philosophical reflection. He does not want to re-instate empiricism even if his insistence on the existent object seems to imply just that; nor does he want to excuse himself from the need of justifying phenomenological reflection on the ground that experience itself—perceptual—is direct and evident. What does he mean by the intention of equating the "in-itself" with the "for-itself" consciousnesses? (Just what he means by *"en-soi"* consciousness he does not say at this point.) To explain this—as well as to achieve it, as Merleau-Ponty is trying to do, is a serious undertaking; the position one takes on this point will decide one's view of man in relation to his human acts and his liberty as well.

Rather abruptly, Merleau-Ponty introduces the moral viewpoint in the current discussion: it will make a great difference for man's notion of morality whether he views reality from the phenomenological viewpoint or from the intellectualistic and critical one: a critical philosophy will, accordingly, base its notion of morality "on the reflection which finds behind every object the thinking subject and his

---

[76] *S. C.*, p. 240.
[77] *S. C.*, p. 240.

The Reality of Man as a Body

liberty."[78] But if one recognizes—be it as a phenomenon—an existent consciousness with its consistent structures, then the outlook on morality turns out to be quite different. Since our knowledge will then depend on what we are, and from this knowledge—which sociology and phychology will clarify and examine, in relation to the self—morality will take its cue. Man will thus not find a morality ready-made, nor will he find in himself the source of morality. Rather, the moral standpoint will have to be achieved by the elucidation of the consciousness of one's own concrete being, and will only be verified by the active integration of the dialectic of body and soul.[79]

Obviously, there is here an existential overtone in the rejection of dogmatic morality and of the certainties which accompany it. For Merleau-Ponty morality would then become a relative thing, that is, it would depend on the integration of the body-soul dialectic. Would this mean, perhaps, that morality is not possible for those who remain in the concrete experience, without reflection, without reaching the stage of signification? Is there no moral dimension after all? It would not be surprising, however, if it were so: if one equates the lack of reflection in a phenomenological milieu with a lack of understanding in an intellectualistic-critical philosophy, the results would be equivalent.

Finally (again an unprepared passage, in a sense) Merleau-Ponty declares that death is not left destitute of meaning, for, the lived experience is forever threatened by the contingency with which it is burdened; a continual menace is therefore present against the eternal signification which existence seems to express fully. It will then be necessary to specify that "the experience of eternity is not the unconsciousness of death"; it is also necessary to distinguish "love of life from the attachment to a purely bio-

---

[78] S. C., p. 240.
[79] S. C., p. 240.

logical existence. The sacrifice of life will then be philosophically impossible; it will only be possible to stake one's life, which is really a more profound way of living."[80] Again, this passage raises the question of the meaning of Merleau-Ponty's terms in his phenomenological context. "Life" here is a value rather than an existence of some sort—certainly not biological. Is this value in any way related to spirit, or is it another structural development—at a higher level—wherein the significations body and soul are "new" in the sense of a new "degree," or a higher synthesis in the dialectic? At present, the question cannot be answered. It is easy to answer it in the common sense view of the matter, according to which "life" in this context means the spiritual life of the self to which values are attached, which self can decide to "lose" his life (the biological) in order to "save" it (the spiritual).[81] For Merleau-Ponty the meaning is neither so simple nor so clear; the ambiguity attaching to "soul" makes one wonder.

7. *Limitations of Phenomenology*

Throughout his works, one of Merleau-Ponty's chief concerns is with the problem of perception. In concluding *La structure du comportement,* he says:

> If one understands by perception the act which makes us know existents, all the problems which one comes upon will be reduced to the problem of perception. It lies in the duality of the notions of structure and signification.[82]

This is really the burden of the whole book: to clarify the notion of form or structure, the ways in which perception takes place, and the meaning of signification in reference to

---
[80] *S. C.*, p. 240.
[81] *Matt.*, 16: 25-26.
[82] *S. C.*, p. 240.

consciousness. The notion of form is basic and dominates all of Merleau-Ponty's discussion:

> A form such as for example the structure "figure and background" is an ensemble which has a meaning and which offers therefore to intellectual analysis a point of support. But, at the same time, it is not an idea,—it constitutes itself, it alters or reorganizes itself before us as much as does a spectacle.[83]

Our access to eternal significations—ideas—is somewhat limited by the contingency of lived perspectives to which the supposed physical, social, and psychological "causalities" bring us back.

The structure, however, is the "truth" of both the naturalistic and the realistic philosophies. What are, really, the relations of passive consciousness to self? One cannot "think" perceptive consciousness without suppressing it as an original mode of being; likewise, can one maintain a signification without referring it to intellectual consciousness?

If the essential solution to the problems discussed above consists in rejecting existence to the limits of knowledge (this is the proposed solution of the intellectualist-critical philosophy) and in finding the intellectual meaning in the concrete structure, and if the fate of such critical philosophy is tied to an intellectualistic theory of perception, "it will be necessary to re-define transcendental philosophy in such a way that it may be possible to integrate therein even the phenomenon of the real."[84]

Quite in keeping with the "incompleteness" of phenomenology, "the real," remains ambiguous in this context.

---

[83] S. C., pp. 240-41.
[84] S. C., p. 241.

CHAPTER FOUR

CENTRAL ROLE OF THE BODY IN ITS RELATION TO SELF, OTHERS AND THE WORLD

At the end of *La structure du comportement* Merleau-Ponty leaves us somewhat in suspense: his investigation of the relation of body and soul, or perhaps more properly, of the body and its workings, ends in a series of questions concerning phenomena, the organism, perception, intentionality, intellection, signification, and behavior. He claims that the inquiry is far from finished at this point. We may reasonably expect then that the investigation be continued in *Phenomenologie de la perception,* Merleau-Ponty's other major work. In fact, there he takes up the study of perception in detail, always centering his attention on the role of the perceiving organism, the body.

Briefly, this is the order of investigation he follows. In the Introduction he focuses his attention on the phenomena of sensation, passing on to association, attention and judgment, to come finally in the concluding chapter to treat of that which he calls the phenomenal field wherein the various phenomena already examined take place. The phenomenal field is that horizon of relatedness within which I perceive the world; since my horizon cannot—at one and the same time—extend to everything, my position of relatedness is always more or less circumscribed: the visual field, wherein perception largely occurs (for there can be perception without sight, if we take perception in the widest meaning) is one such situation.

With 'the foregoing preparation, he continues in Part I the detailed study of the body: in Chapter I he studies the body as object in relation to mechanistic physiology; in the second, he describes the experience of one's body in the light of classical psychology; in the third, he examines the spatiality and motion of the body; at this point he comes to a certain generalization which he calls the synthesis of one's body.

In Chapter V, he resumes a detailed study of the body now as characterized by sexuality. Finally, he investigates gesture and language as "expressions." In these last two chapters we have some of the most significant considerations for the purpose of this study.

The second part of the book deals with the world as perceived: Merleau-Ponty's contention is that the theory of the body is already a theory of perception, since it is precisely through the body that we have access to the world: it is through this body that we have sensations whereby we experience the world. This needs clarification: he maintains that the theory of body he proposes is already a theory of perception because it would be impossible to explain, or rather to describe the body without becoming involved in a description of perception in its *actuality*. We use this term with caution, for, it is at least doubtful whether one may describe something "in process" without, by that very description, solidifying it into a static condition.

In the first chapter he discusses at great length the phenomena of sensation—always in opposition to the empiricist and intellectualistic viewpoints as he does throughout—and comes to the conclusion that perception is at first a pre-objective and pre-conscious experience. Only on this experience will later be founded reflexive thought properly so called, although the origin of this thought will hardly be known as having been a conscious experience.[1]

In the second chapter, Merleau-Ponty investigates space, in an endeavor to answer the question, puzzling to the phi-

---

[1] *P. P.*, p. 279. Further, he adds: "Reflection will therefore not know of itself its full significance unless it mentions the irreflexive foundation which it presupposes, from which it profits, and which constitutes for it an original past, a past which has never been a present." *P. P.*, p. 280.

losopher, "Is space a 'form' of knowledge?" The problem is not to find the relation of container to contained, for this obtains only in regard to objects; nor is it to find a logical relation such as that which exists between individuals and class, for space is anterior to every supposed part. He discounts all imaginary "space"—that is, having a connotation of materiality and definiteness—and asserts that space is not the real or logical milieu *in* which things are placed, but rather the means by which the position of things becomes possible.[2] His investigation of "high," "low," "depth," "movement," "lived space" seems to convince him that space is not understood either as involving an irreducible multiplicity—as when it is thought of as the "place" for things; or as a subjective unifying system of relations—always as thought, not as experienced. His investigation of experience brings him to affirm that a dialectic is here at work, an intermingling of relations—lived relations—which can only be grasped imperfectly by consciousness: there is much ambiguity, "There is the absolute certitude of the world in general, but not of anying in particular."[3]

In the third chapter we find Merleau-Ponty engaged in the study of the natural world and of the "thing"; he studies the constancies of perceptive experiences, the unity of the "thing" (which he seems to identify with the "real");[4] the natural world under various aspects, and finally hallucination which—to him—is a sort of confirmation of our perception of things and of the world.[5]

---

[2] *P. P.*, p. 281.
[3] *P. P.*, p. 344.
[4] Cf. *P. P.*, p. 396: "Se demander si le monde est réel, c'est ne pas entendre ce qu'on dit, puisque le monde est justement, non pas une somme de choses, que l'on pourrait toujours révoquer en doute, mais le réservoir inépuisable d'où les choses sont tirées."
[5] *P. P.*, p. 385: "Hallucination disintegrates the real before our eyes, and it substitutes for it a 'quasi-reality' . . . this phenomenon of hallucination takes us back to the pre-logical foundations of our knowledge and confirms that which one comes to say about things and about the world. The most important point is, that the patients for the most part distinguish their hallucinations from their perceptions."

Merleau-Ponty is very emphatic in denying that we can grasp the reality of the thing if we study its "constants," as if a thing had first its size and shape—unchanging—and then would appear under various perspectives to us, the latter being merely accidental to the thing.[6] The real question is not so much to determine what is the real shape or size of a thing, as to discover how there can be objectivity. The fact that I do come in contact with things through my body does not solve all problems. Although the thing is "for-me" it still remains an "in-itself" which escapes me to a certain extent.[7] However, these few considerations are a mere outline of the study Merleau-Ponty undertakes of the thing and the natural world—of the "real" which lends itself to an infinite exploration.[8] His conclusion, however, is that *ambiguity prevails*, both in my perception of things and in the knowledge I have of myself, for a temporal situation such as that in which I find myself is at best ambiguous.[9]

In the last chapter of Part II, he centers his attention on the human phase of the world;[10] thus he considers natural time and history, the relation of persons,[11] the co-existence

---

[6] *P. P.*, p. 345: "Que voulons-nous dire par là et sur quoi jugeons-nous donc qu'une forme ou une grandeur sont la forme et la grandeur *de l'objet?*"

[7] *P. P.*, pp. 372-74; cf. pp. 382-84. Cf. also Kwant, *Encounter*, Chapter III.

[8] *P. P.*, p. 374.

[9] *P. P.*, p. 397. This notion of ambiguity prevailing in human relations will be found to play a major role in Merleau-Ponty's discussion of all phases of his philosophy. The interplay of influences of things and of the world on man and man's active interchange and modification of such conditions as influence him make of the mutual relations a "dialectic," a tension wherein no force or influence can be said to dominate absolutely at any one time, but all contribute to the total effect.

[10] It is not to be inferred that Merleau-Ponty ever maintained that the world could make sense without consciousness, but in this chapter he considers more specifically the human and cultural factors in relation to the world. Cf. Kwant, *Encounter*, Chapter IV.

[11] On this point it will be seen that Merleau-Ponty's treatment is not as profound as it might be expected. He stresses so much the pre-personal in the relations of the body-subject that the personal does not appear in its full meaning.

of psychological subjects in a natural world and the relation of men in a cultural world. This involves him in the problem of communication and of truth. He explores, further, the possibility of coexistence and liberty, of social life and of transcendence. His investigation is always conducted from the viewpoint of perception, with the understanding that it is through the body as a body-subject that I make contact with other bodies and thus effectuate a relation at the conscious and cultural level.[12]

In the third part of the book Merleau-Ponty examines the Cogito, temporality and liberty. After having examined perception, that is, direct human experience, he turns his attention to the Cogito with a very specific intention, which he declares:

> To phenomenology understood as a direct description must be added a phenomenology of phenomenology. We must reconsider the *cogito* in order to find in it a more fundamental Logos that that of objective thought. . . . On the level of being one could never understand that the subject may be at once "naturant" and "naturé," infinite and finite. But if we recognize time as the subject, if we connect to the paradox of time that of the body, of the world, of the thing, and of the other we will realize that beyond these, there is nothing to understand.[13]

Does Merleau-Ponty refer, in this passage, to a new level of philosophical reflection? He has maintained that phenomenology is reflection on the pre-reflexive; here he seems to hint that a phenomenology of phenomenology might be a "reflection" on the phenomenological reflection which has

---

[12]This topic will be discussed further, especially in connection with communication and language.
[13]*P. P.*, p. 419.

thus far placed the phenomenologist in a position to know something about "reality." This further reflection then would examine the very activity of consciousness engaged in phenomenological investigation; it would be reflection on the "cogito" itself—could we call it a "second reflection"? It is difficult to say just what Merleau-Ponty had in mind when he wrote the above quoted words. Whatever it be, it must not be interpreted as the equivalent of an abstraction—or a formalization of concepts—but perhaps as a more concrete signification of the concepts themselves. Spiegelberg calls Merleau-Ponty's interpretation of the Cogito (he refers to the Cartesian Cogito) his most distinctive, if not his most convincing change in the pattern of phenomenology, "to use Merleau-Ponty's new and pointed expression, the new *cogito* is my being-present-within-the-world," not an illusion-proof Cogito, but a committed consciousness—the only indubitable consciousness.[14] From the few considerations proposed one could hardly imagine the "new" Cogito to be a new level of abstraction—this much seems clear.

In the chapter on Temporality, Merleau-Ponty does nothing but explicitate that which he has expressed again and again throughout his work: temporality is implied in subjectivity. Time is not an objective dimension of the world; past and future are dimensions of our own subjectivity: "Time is therefore not a real process, [or] an effective succession which I undertake to mark off in order to measure. It is rather born of my relation to things."[15] That which is past or future for me is actually present for the world. According to him, it is proper to the nature of past and future not to be except as supported by an effective presence. They can only occur in a subject which is temporal. He goes further when he characterizes the subject as

---

[14]Spiegelberg, *Phenomenological* . . . , p. 549. We will discuss the topic further.
[15]*P. P.*, p. 471.

time, and time as the subject.[16] The meaning of this is that the subject is not just *in* time, but is engaged in and lives time. He thus unites the signification of spatiality with that of temporality:

> It is by communicating with the world that we communicate doubtlessly with ourselves. We possess time completely and we are present to ourselves because we are present to the world.[17]

> The world is inseparable from the subject, but from a subject which is nothing other than a project of the world; the subject is inseparable from the world, but from a world which he himself projects. The subject is being-to-the-world and the world remains "subjective" because its texture and its articulations are designed by the movements of transcendence of the subject himself.[18]

There is therefore an interdependence between the subject and the world. It will become evident that this relation is—for Merleau-Ponty—a dialectic which will become the foundation of the existential doctrine of freedom.[19]

---

[16] *P. P.*, p. 483: "Il faut comprendre le temps comme sujet et le sujet comme temps."

[17] *P. P.*, p. 485.

[18] *P. P.*, pp. 491-92. "This interdependence is at the same time Merleau-Ponty's settlement of the perennial controversy over idealism and realism, which thus far even phenomenology has been unable to achieve. The recognition of the mutual dependence of subject and object allows us to pass beyond this stale and hopeless controversy; it seems almost too obvious to refer here to the pattern of the Hegelian synthesis, which Merleau-Ponty himself does not mention on this occasion. Instead, Merleau-Ponty calls subject and object two abstract elements of one single structure called 'presence' . . . in which the subject is essentially presence to the world and the world is 'subjective.' " Spiegelberg, *Phenomenological* . . . , p. 553. The question, however, is "Is the controversy really settled?" To affirm that it is, does not make it be.

[19] *P. P.*, p. 495.: "La solution de tous les problèmes de transcendance se trouve dans l'épaisseur du présent préobjectif, où nous trouvons notre corporéité, notre socialité, la préexistence du monde, c'est-à-dire le point d'amorçage des 'explications' dans ce qu'elles ont de légitime,—et en même temps le fondement de notre liberté."

Central Role of the Body

He deals with human freedom in the last chapter of *Phénoménologie de la perception*. His notion of liberty is somewhat different from that of Sartre. Merleau-Ponty admits that man, being in a situation, is never totally free; he is already committed to the human involvement in the world, hence his choice is within a milieu over which he has no power or control; further, man's choice is not totally conscious: it is rather pre-conscious.[20] Because of our interdependence with the world, it is never easy to distinguish that which is choice from that which is situation. However, it is quite true that I have always the freedom to stop one project and begin another, but I always choose from what is available so to speak. But one must choose, or rather he chooses even when he refuses to choose—in the sense that one always expresses something, since one cannot remain in the void—the choice, however, is not always an act: to remain what one is is to continue in a previous choice. It is not necessary (nor is it implied) that if I do not refuse I thereby choose incessantly. This is the notion of Sartre for whom without a continual choosing of oneself one is not—existence before essence.[21] It will be seen that Merleau-Ponty's treatment of liberty is somewhat disappointing.[22] But if one reads the last few lines of the *Phénoménologie de la perception* it will become apparent that he could not treat of liberty in any other way: "man is a knot of relations and relation alone counts for him." There is no theoretical

---

[20] *P. P.*, pp. 510-11.

[21] *P. P.*, pp. 515-16: "Que devient donc, de ce point de vue, la liberté dont nous parlions en commençant? Je ne peux plus feindre d'être un néant et de me choisir continuellement à partir de rien. Si c'est par la subjectivité que le néant apparait dans le monde, on peut dire aussi que c'est par le monde que le néant vient à être. Je suis un refus général d'être quoi que ce soit, accompagné en sous-main d'une acceptation continuelle de telle forme d'être qualifiée. *Car même ce refus général est encore au nombre des manières d'être et figure dans le monde.*"

[22] This only refers to *P. P.* as will appear; he develops the theme better in other writings.

answer to vitally important questions such as "Shall I make this promise?", "Shall I risk my life?", etc. There are things, and situations and persons which call for a response. Whatever be the case, it is the task of philosophy to make us learn again to see things clearly, and "it is true that philosophy realizes itself in destroying itself as separated philosophy. It is precisely here that philosophy remains silent,"[23] for at this point the hero takes over: he alone knows what the relation of man to man should be and no one else can speak for him. That man is a "knot of relations" becomes here very significant: he acts because of those relations, but the force of the relations also influences his choice.[24]

Now we might expect to find in this serious and comprehensive study of man-in-the-world some answers to the questions proposed at the end of *La structure du comportement*. Such expectation, however, is not fulfilled. In fact, even the last words of the *Phénoménologie de la perception* are hardly calculated to give us a sense of completeness, since relations are by their very nature subject to change and variation. Does then Merleau-Ponty's painstaking phenomenological investigation of perception give us no other light than that which we already had, perhaps, with regard to man's condition?—that is, that man is contingent and finite, that his being-in-the-world depends on his relations with others and that, finally, the workings of his intellect and his very thought depend on his materiality, on his body? If not new, his analysis is still very valuable—even if not conclusive—for having called to our attention certain aspects of man's relation to himself, to others, and to the world in relation to the dialectic of body and soul. However, the importance of his investigations, according to Professor Lauer

[23] *P. P.*, p. 520.
[24] *P. P.*, p. 520.

is the introduction of dialectic into transcendental phenomenology. Like Husserl, the experience he chooses to describe is primarily perception, but the mutual conditioning of world and perceptive consciousness is a far cry from Husserl's purely constitutive phenomenology. The advantage of this is that it enables Merleau-Ponty to describe man's body not as an object but as a condition for objectivity, as the point of contact between consciousness and the world. Meanings are contributed by consciousness, it is true, but these are based on a pre-given world, whose givenness is mediated by the body.[25]

If man is radically contingent, if he is immersed in materiality, if his consciousness is utterly dependent on his relations to others, and if his condition in the world is determined by the very structuration of his being, it is no wonder that man cannot ultimately be defined with any semblance of finality—and therefore no abstract and general notion can be applied to him absolutely and without qualifications. Notwithstanding the fact that Merleau-Ponty does not consider man as a pure possibility—as is the contention of other existentialists—and therefore recognizes in him a basic "essence," still this "essence" is not to be taken abstractly, nor as co-extensive with "man." Hence man can never be defined except in his milieu, that is to say, concretely, at a given moment of time, in a given spatial configuration, and in a concrete relational existence with other men. An examination of the *Phénoménologie de la perception* shows how Merleau-Ponty situates man through his body in the maze of intentions and relations which make up this universe. Moreau says that it is precisely the merit of the *Phénoménologie de la perception* to have contributed to the rehabilitation of the sensible in showing not only that it

---

[25] Lauer, *Triumph* . . . , p. 182.

is not reducible to a phantom, but that it is required to give meaning to scientific representation.[26]

As was pointed out before, Merleau-Ponty in describing the phenomena of perception gives us an insight into this "primary" mode of access to the world, prior to any scientific exploration. Now the body is a phenomenon of special importance. That is the reason why he investigates the body so thoroughly: we could almost say that his whole study is directed to clarify the significance of the body in relation to self, to the world, and to others. There is, in short, no relation and no aspect of his phenomenology which does not imply the body.

1. Prerequisites for an Investigation of the Body

In the introduction to the *Phénoménologie de la perception*, discussing sensation, attention, association, judgment, and the phenomenal field, Merleau-Ponty does nothing but consider the role of the body in these several functions. From a critique of the so-called (by him) "classical prejudices" about the true nature of perception, he gradually comes to show the necessity of a return to the phenomenon, and of course the phenomenon which stands out is the body. He considers the body as the vantage point of perception. He investigates sensation as impression, as quality, and as the consequence of an excitation. As he had already shown in *La structure du comportement* he maintains that none of the current theories of sensation adequately explains the phenomenon of sensation. All that which has been said on the subject of sensation has been, according to Merleau-Ponty, a "construction" of the sciences, not a description of the phenomenon as it occurs. However, to study phenomena

---

[26] Joseph Moreau, *L'horizon des esprits*, Bibliothèque de philosophie Contemporaine (Paris: Presses Universitaires de France, 1960), p. 44. Cited hereafter as *L'horizon* . . .

it is necessary to have recourse to psychology if we do not want to miss the real problems involved. It is necessary to resort to the phenomenal field[27] and become acquainted with the subjects of phenomena by means of psychological descriptions; otherwise we may fall into the position of that reflexive philosophy which pretends to begin with—or attain—a transcendental dimension. We should not however, fail to see that psychological description once purified of all psychologism, can become a philosophical method. It will also be necessary, besides presenting the descriptions, to fix by references and philosophical anticipations the points of view wherein the perceptive experiences may seem to be true.[28]

Hence, in his investigation of the body, Merleau-Ponty insists, we may not begin without psychology, nor with psychology alone. "Experience anticipates philosophy, as philosophy is nothing but elucidated experience." But, having sufficiently circumscribed the phenomenal field, we may enter the ambiguous domain of human experience with psychology as a guide to our investigation; an autocriticism by the psychologist himself may lead us, by a reflection of the second degree, to the phenomenon of phenomenon and thus convert the phenomenal field into a transcendental one.[29]

---

[27]By phenomenal field Merleau-Ponty means the locus of our direct experiences: "La critique de l'hypothèse de constance et plus généralement la réduction de l'idée de 'monde' ouvraient un *champ phénoménal* que nous devons maintenant mieux circonscrire, et nous invitaient à retrouver une expérience directe qu'il faut situer au moins provisoirement par rapport au savoir scientifique, à de réflexion psychologique et à la réflexion philosophique." P. P., p. 66.

[28]P. P., pp. 76-77. This is necessary if we do not want to place ourselves, at the very first, in a transcendental dimension which we suppose eternal and then actually miss the real problem of constitution. That is why it is so important for Merleau-Ponty that we resort to the phenomenal field. "Il nous fallait fréquenter le champ phénoménal et faire connaissance par des descriptions psychologiques avec le sujet des phénomènes." P. P., p. 77.

[29]P. P., p. 77.

2. The Body as Object

Having thus prepared the stage for his phenomenological investigation, he gives us first a perspective of the body in relation to the perceptual field. Among the other objects of our perception, our body can be considered just another object in the world. However, my body is that by which I am in contact with the world (my point of view of the world) hence it cannot be treated merely as an object among objects—rather, it can, but ought not. Yet I can either objectify my body or think of it abstractly as of a mere idea. This would be a departure from my very experience of my body as perceived stemming from the lifelong effort of my consciousness to posit objects, for it is not consciousness except insofar as it recovers and recollects itself in an identifiable object. And yet

> the absolute position of even a single object is death to consciousness, because it congeals all experience, much as the addition of a crystal to a solution makes the whole of it crystalize at once.[30]

Merleau-Ponty observes then, that since we cannot remain in the alternative of either not understanding the subject or of knowing nothing about the object, we must seek the object at the very heart of our experience. It is therefore necessary for us to describe the appearing of being and to understand the paradox involved here: there is a "for-us" of the "in-itself." That is to say, the being which appears to us is what it is itself, and yet it also is for us—that is, it reveals itself to us, it can be known by us. Now Merleau-Ponty plans to proceed, without any preconceptions, to question objective thought on its own ground: he will ask only those questions which objective thought itself would pose with regard to reality. The consideration of the

---
[30] *P. P.*, p. 86.

Central Role of the Body

constitution of the body as an object is therefore of great importance—it is a decisive moment in the genesis of the objective world. But one will thus see that the body even at the scientific level screens itself from the treatment to which science itself attempts to subject it. In fact the body will right then emerge not at all as a mere object, but as a relation to a subject, and its emergence will show that, as Merleau-Ponty has maintained, a study of the perceived reveals the subject perceiving it:

> As the genesis of the objective body is nothing but a moment in the constitution of the object, in withdrawing from the objective world, the body will draw to itself the intentional threads which bind it to its surroundings and finally will reveal to us the perceiving subject as the perceived world.[31]

It will now remain to be seen whether Merleau-Ponty's investigation does yield such results purely on a phenomenological basis. His study proceeds in the accustomed mode of description of the phenomena which are the object of psychological studies of the normal as well as of the abnormal. That he leans so heavily on data furnished by the psychology of the abnormal is perhaps due to the fact that he is very familiar with the field; perhaps also because he thinks that he can best show the relevance of a form by accentuating the visible results in behavior when it is lacking. At any rate, to understand the import of his conclusions, it is necessary to follow his investigation in detail.

Merleau-Ponty's contention that perception is the primary fact of our being-in-the-world immediately involves him in the consideration of the body as both perceived and perceiv-

---

[31] *P. P.*, p. 86. "... nous révélera le sujet percevant comme le monde perçu."

ing.[32] The body presents certain characteristics: it has a certain permanence—that is to say, it is constantly perceived by me, but this permanence does not mean that it can be explored indefinitely; rather that it offers me always the same side for observation. To say that my body is always present to me is not to say that it is before me, but that it is "with" me. When I say that I always perceive my body, I do not mean that I perceive it as an object, but that there is something about my body's presence to me which makes it unthinkable that my body be absent or even that it be changing in relation to me.

However, my body can be for me an object inasmuch as I can view it—as I am able to view the parts of my body which are far from my eyes. But (and here Merleau-Ponty describes in detail) as I come close to the area wherein my eyes are situated, the body detaches itself from that which is "object" and there is created a sort of neutral zone, a "quasi-space" wherein objects have no possibility of being, as far as sight is concerned, because my eyes have no access there.[33]

With regard to the possibility of sensing my body and of sensing other objects through my body, he has this to say:

> ... if I touch with my left hand my right hand while it [the right hand] touches an object, the right hand *object* is not the right hand *touching*: the first is an intertwining of bones, muscles and flesh bearing down on a point in space, the second traverses space as a rocket in order to discover the exterior object in its place.

Then he concludes:

> Insofar as I see or touch the world, my body cannot be either seen or touched. That which prevents my body

---

[32] Merleau-Ponty refers to the body as "our own proper body"—we will use simply "the body" or "our body."
[33] *P. P.*, p. 106-108.

from being an object, from being "completely constituted" is the fact that it has objects [i.e., my body itself is that by which objects are.] It is neither tangible nor visible in the measure in which it is that which sees and touches.[34]

The body is therefore not as any other object, but one which has the particularity of being always available to me—always present. Its permanency is absolute inasmuch as it serves as a foundation for the relative permanence of objects.

Another interesting characteristic of my body—Merleau-Ponty observes—is that by which my body is capable of a "double sensation," that is to say, "when I touch my right hand with my left hand, the object *right hand* has this singular power of sensing also"—this is not to say that the right hand (or both hands) is at once touching and touched; rather

> When I press my two hands one against the other, it is not two sensations which I experience together, as I perceive two objects juxtaposed, but an ambiguous organization where the two hands can alternate the function of "touching" and "touched."[35]

Thus "double sensation" means that in the passage from one function to the other (touching and being touched) I can recognize the hand being touched as the same which is just now touching. In a sense, when the body catches itself, so to speak, in the act of knowing—"touching itself in touching" other things it really comes up with a kind of "reflection" which at once marks off the body from all other objects; which [objects] can never be said to touch my body

---

[34] *P. P.*, p. 108.
[35] *P. P.*, p. 109.

except when it is inert—never when it is engaged in active exploration of the world or of itself.[36]

Another characteristic of the body is its affectivity. Exterior things are only represented to me; my body is felt by me. When I feel pain in any part of my body, the experience is from within; when I express the feeling of such pain, I do not express the thought of it, i.e., "I think that my foot is the cause of the pain," but "The pain comes from my foot." Hence, Merleau-Ponty asserts, we must recognize the whole field of affectivity as a background to the working of consciousness when it is question of experiencing one's own body. All this is not new to psychology; what is new, Merleau-Ponty asserts, is the philosophical consequences which we can draw from the same observations and which classical psychology has neglected on account of its impersonal framework—"it has believed it is possible to separate in its observations that which belongs to the situation of the observer from the properties of the absolute object"[37] and further, psychology has attempted to make of the experience of the living subject itself an object. But it takes little to see that the living subject will view its own body in a far different way than it is viewed by any science—psychology, biology, physics, as well as different from all other exterior objects, even if the knowledge of our own body is incomplete without the help of science. Merleau-Ponty mentions several times that from the shoulders up I cannot know myself experientially and hence science comes to fill the lacunae. However, even without scientific help, experience derived from the perception I have of others should make up for me what is missing by way of direct knowledge of my body. It is precisely here that the role of the "encoun-

---

[36]". . . dans ce paquet d'os et de muscle qu'est ma main droite pour ma main gauche, je devine un instant l'enveloppe ou l'incarnation de cette autre main droite, agile et vivante, que je lance vers les objets pour les explorer." *P. P.,* p. 109.
[37]*P. P.,* pp. 110-11.

ter" as viewed by Kwant becomes significant: if we do not come to know even "things" without a relation to the other, how much more so must the experiential knowledge of our own body-subject be linked with the experience of communion with the other.[38]

What are the philosophical consequences which we are to draw from psychological insights? Very briefly: consciousness is a way of being; to be conscious is to communicate with the world and with others, to be with and not merely alongside things or others as exterior objects. There is a relation which embraces both spatiality and time: our manner of sensing our body is always tied to a condition which situates the body-subject as well as the related exterior objects in a certain place and at a certain time. No one can avoid this situation—and even the psychologist who thinks of achieving a scientific objectivity will find himself in his

---

[38]Cf. Kwant, *Encounter*, p. 10: "Our familiarity with the things which surround us comes to us through our familiarity with our fellow men. This familiarity exists only for one who know how to behave in a certain way. It has no absolute character but is coherent with a pattern of behavior which we have learned from the society in which we were brought up. . . . Inter-human communication has made our environment something which appears quite natural and obvious to us."

Kwant also discusses Merleau-Ponty's treatment of consciousness under the heading of "metaphysical consciousness" (*Phenomenological Philosophy*, ch. VII, pp. 112ff). In it he emphasizes the role of consciousness in man's relations to his fellow men and to the world. He claims that the original situation of the subject in the world is basic and that "we arrive at metaphysical consciousness . . . when we reduce everything, including the knowing subject, to this original fact." (p. 119).

However, the author states on pp. 17-18 that Merleau-Ponty makes consciousness more or less marginal to subjectivity. In fact, he even expresses his idea thus: "While for many modern thinkers consciousness is the center of the many aspects proper to subjectivity the same cannot be asserted with respect to Merleau-Ponty. True, he does not quite deny consciousness to human subjectivity. . . . But . . . consciousness even in its depest level is so obscure that it cannot be verified." Hence it is no longer the central characteristic of subjectivity. It would be interesting to compare these two significant passages in Kwant's work. The assertion that consciousness is found at a deep and mysterious level does not seem to us to make it only marginal.

experiential milieu situated: he will find himself as an immediate presence "without distance to the past, to the world, to the body and to others."[39]

3. Spatiality of the Body

There is something to be said for the psychological contention that the body is an object among other objects if one considers the materiality of the body insofar as it is a spatial organism. But for Merleau-Ponty, the body is a space which is expressive (un espace expressif).[40] We may recall his observations about the spatial movement of the hand directed to the exploration of an object. Again he returns to the significance of the movement of the hand in the pursuit of an end. But because both the hand and the object which it seeks to reach are incarnate and therefore material the pursuing hand is involved in a spatial dimension. That which differentiates the mere object from the body is the fact that the body is in space in a quasi-intentional way: it carries out my intentions of motion.

The body is not spatial simply because it has parts outside of parts: Merleau-Ponty observes that I do not move my legs because they are at a certain distance from my head—in space—but because they carry out my motive power. But, more than this, the body is not constituted simply because of its significant participation in actions which have a value; it is also the source of the significance of all space. It is because of our body that the spatiality of other objects takes on a meaning, it is our body which makes things to be "things" as we touch them or see them. Although our body

---

[39] *P. P.*, p. 113. Cf. M. Merleau-Ponty, "Le primat de la perception et ses conséquences philosophiques," *Bulletin de la Société Française de Philosophie*, 4le année, No. 4 (Oct.-Dec. 1947), pp. 119-53: "If I consider how my knowledge of things is a relation to that of others, perception . . . appears as the paradoxical phenomenon which renders being accessible." p. 124. Cited hereafter as "Le primat . . ."
[40] *P. P.*, p. 171.

is not the passive exhibition of a neutral instinct, still it is our general way of life—our means "of having a world." Movements of the body are developed almost without conscious effort, in most cases. There seems to be a sort of intelligence of the body: a new dance is learned without analyzing the sequence of movements. Children learn dances very easily and well: the sequence of movements seems to come naturally. This is also the reason why habits can be formed: the body seems to have understood and retained the new meaning.[41] From his detailed study of the spatiality of the body, Merleau-Ponty concludes that

> the experience of the body makes us recognize an imposition of meaning which is not the work of a universal constituting consciousness, but a signification which clings to certain contents. My body is that significant core which behaves as a general function and which nevertheless exists and is liable to sickness. In it [our body] we learn to know that union of essence and existence which we will find in general in perception.[42]

From the results of the analysis of the body as a spatial organism, Merleau-Ponty comes to certain generalizations: what is true of all other things is also true of the body: perception of space and perception of the body, spatiality of body and its being "body" are not two distinct problems. The spatiality of the body is the manner in which it realizes itself as a body, it is its unfolding as a body. To be a body is to be in the world, related to the world in a certain way: "To be body is to be linked to a certain world ... and our body is not first in [dans] space: it is to [à] space.[43] Further, the relation of the different parts of the body to each other, the visual aspect of the body, the movements and the

---

[41] *P. P.*, Chapter III, Part II, especially pp. 165-72.
[42] *P. P.*, p. 172.
[43] *P. P.*, p. 173.

tactile powers of the body are not just coordinated: the whole ensemble is a signification and it is at our disposal as a common and general meaning. As we do not assemble the various experiences we have in perception, we do not likewise assemble the different parts of our body as if we were to achieve a "body" by accumulation. Our body is a unity and when we perceive it, when we live it, we have the experience of an organic whole which we have not constructed, but which was given to us as a whole in our lived experience. This is true also of our perceptions in general: we do not assemble our perceived world piece by piece, as it were. We perceive the whole of the world which presents itself to our view. Whatever is given to us at any time, is given as a whole in a field of perception in a manner which Merleau-Ponty describes as "figure-background"—that is to say, we always perceive things in relation to a general field which extends in space (and time)[44] and which forms as a background for the object or objects on which we happen to focus our attention. The important thing to note is that we do not assemble things according to an "a-priori" law: our first grasp of the object is a Gestalt, not an analysis of segments or elements which we then combine into a significant whole. The signification is given with and in the perception.

Once more Merleau-Ponty observes that I cannot place myself "before my body" to observe it as I would observe any other object for "I am my body."[45] The body cannot even be compared to a physical object: it could only be compared to a work of art. He examines in detail the various works of art, painting, poetry, music, novel, and points out how each of them, even though the creation of a mind, is actually expressed through matter and is, so to speak,

---

[44] Although Merleau-Ponty does not here explicitly refer to the twofold dimension of space and time, we can never think in terms of one of them alone. Temporality implies both space and time.

[45] "Mais je ne suis pas devant mon corps, je suis dans mon corps, ou plutôt je suis mon corps." P. P., p. 175. Cf. supra, p. 159.

incarnate. Thus the idea of the painter is communicated by means of canvas and colors, that of the musician by the sounds, that of the poet by the word.

Language is either incarnate in the sound of the voice expressing it, or in a written conventional form; in either case, it is committed to a material kind of medium for its preservation (even though the thought thus expressed be immortal). Prose literature depends just as much as poetry on material expression, though not to the same degree. Thus, for instance, a novel may be summarized—hence the very expression of the writer is not of the essence as it is for the poem—yet the content must be preserved intact in its characterization and temporality or the sense of the event is lost.

It can be said, therefore, that the signification of every work of literature, is neither free nor an eternal truth or an exemplary idea detached from materiality. Yet, the true work of art radiates its own signification without abandoning its spatial and temporal situation. "It is in this sense that our body can be compared to the work of art. It is a bond of living significations and not the function of a certain number of covariable terms."[46]

In a previous discussion on the topic of the spatiality of the body, Merleau-Ponty had pointed out that man "dwells in" space and time[47] and therefore all of his movements are a continual relation to both space and time: there is continuity between past, present and future as there is a development of a new movement from the previous one.

---

[46]*P. P.*, p. 177. "Une certaine expérience tactile du bras signifie une certaine expérience tactile de l'avant bras et de l'épaule, un certain aspect visuel du même bras, non que les différentes perceptions tactiles, les perceptions tactiles et les perceptions visuelles participent toutes à un même bras intelligible, comme les vues perspectives d'un cube à l'idée du cube, mais parce que le bras vu et le bras touché, comme les différents segments du bras *font* tous ensemble un même geste."

[47]*P. P.*, p. 162: "Il ne faut donc pas dire que notre corps est *dans* l'espace ni d'ailleurs qu'il est *dans* le temps. Il *habite* l'espace et le temps."

Merleau-Ponty

Again, one should say with Merleau-Ponty that, precisely, the body "knows" without analysis what its posture and movements are to be in any given action.[48] Motion is an intentional activity, but this intentionality is derived from the consciousness of a body-subject; it is not yet an intentionality at the intellectual level. Still it is significant: the body manifests itself through its expressive actions; it also understands meanings related to motion and transforms the grasp of these significations into habit. The body thus elucidates the nature of spatiality by its motor habits; this gives us an aspect of the body's relation to the world.

Now Merleau-Ponty maintains that the general habits of the body can be meaningfully related to the motor habits; and if we understand these, then we can elucidate the general synthesis of the body, for in a very general sense any activity of the body could be viewed as a motion—that is, even perception is a sort of movement towards the object; further, it is often followed by the spatial movement towards the object perceived. It is for this reason that Merleau-Ponty affirms that all habits are at once perceptive and motor. But there is another way of viewing habits as at once motor and perceptive; or, rather, of viewing the perceived and the perceiver in a different relation. He explains it thus: If I were to become accustomed to use a stick to explore objects,[49] then the stick itself would cease to be an instrument for me, and it would become a sort of prolongation of my sense organs. Then the world of objects with which I come in contact by touch would no longer become present to me at the contact of my hand, but rather at the point of my stick, so that the stick would become a prolongation of my arm. The result of all this—Merleau-Ponty points out—is that the stick has become a means of perception rather than an object among other objects, be it

---
[48] *P. P.*, pp. 160-61.
[49] And this would be an example of motor habit.

an instrument-object. It is no longer an object which the eye can perceive, but an instrument *with which* I perceive. Thus, if we were to consider the body as a whole, the stick would figure as a true appendix of the body. Thus also the exterior object in relation to the stick would become not a mere object but a thing towards which the stick would lead us, following perspectives which are then not mere signs but aspects of the thing.[50]

The above discussion—the experience of spatial perspectives—raises the question of the things perceived. How is the passage effected from the signification to the signified? Merleau-Ponty maintains that the position of intellectualism conceives such passage as merely an intentional one. The sensibly given and the various perspectives—at any level—will be considered as revelations of that core of intellligibility which the thing must possess if it can be known at all. But this does not do justice to either the perceived thing or the perceiving subject, because it separates the one from the other. Further, it does not admit the existential relation of the subject perceiving with the thing perceived, and it postulates a transcendental construction. Instead it should admit the active relation of a transcendent consciousness with the things and with the world by means of a body whose organs are capable of receiving an impression, as well as of achieving a dialectic.

The analysis of motor habits "as extension of existence prolongs itself into an analysis of perceptive habits as acquisition of the world. Reciprocally, all perceptive habits are both motor habits and the grasp of a signification through the body."[51] To learn to see colors, Merleau-Ponty affirms, is to acquire a certain style of vision, a new usage of the

---

[50] " On est tenté de dire qu'à travers les sensations produites par la pression du bâton sur la main, l'aveugle construit le bâton et ses différentes positions, puis que celles-ci, à leur tour, médiatisent un objet à la seconde puissance, l'objet externe." *P. P.*, p. 177.
[51] *P. P.*, p. 178.

body; it is to increase and reorganize the corporeal scheme. The same may be said of any and every corporeal activity which places us in a new relation with the world. (This applies particularly to the child who is learning to use his body in relation to things and to the world.)[52] Our body, as a system of motor and perceptive powers is not an object for an "I think"; rather, "it is an ensemble of lived significations tending to its own equilibrium. Occasionally, a new cluster of significations is formed; our old movements are integrated into a new motor entity while the first visual experience gives way to a new sensorial entity,"[53] and thus our natural powers suddenly acquire a richer and fuller expression than that implied by our perceptive fields, or by our practice; and the existential situation of the body is emphasized by its very relations to the world.

---

[52]Merleau-Ponty deals with this topic particularly in *Les relations avec autrui chez l'enfant*, Part I (Les Cours de Sorbonne) Autographié (Paris: Tournière et Constans [1953]). Cited hereafter as *R.A.E.*
[53]*P. P.*, p. 179.

CHAPTER FIVE

MAN: A SEXED BEING

The passage from the consideration of the body in general to the specified aspects of the body as characterized in its relation to others brings us first to a study of man as a "sexed" being.

Although in the *Phénoménologie de la perception* Merleau-Ponty does not develop the theme of the personal encounter to the fullest extent, but rather only indicates its possibilities still at the pre-personal level, a great insight is already contained therein. By defining man as a "sexed being" he implicitly emphasizes the role of the body in that which is the human relation in the fullest sense of the word, the sexual relation. But this relation, as will be seen, far from being purely a biological or instinctive function is characterized by a specifically human structure.

1. *Intersubjectivity*

Merleau-Ponty prefaces his investigation by reiterating his aims: first, to make evident the primordial function by which we appropriate[1] and thus assume, space, time, objects and instruments; second, to describe the body as the means of such appropriation. But it is not so easy—he maintains—so long as we revert to space or to things perceived, to rediscover the relation of the incarnate subject to his world, because the world, in its relation to the epistemological subject already transforms itself. In fact, the natural world is an existent in itself beyond its existence for me; because of the act of transcendence by which the object opens and surpasses itself

> we find ourselves in the presence of a nature which does not need to be perceived in order to exist. Hence,

---

[1] Merleau-Ponty's expression is, "make exist for ourselves."

> to make evident the genesis of "being-for-us," it is necessary to consider that sector of our experience which manifestly has no sense and no reality except for us, and *that is our affective milieu*. We must ask how an object or a being begins to exist for us by desire or through love, and we will thus understand better how objects and beings can exist in general.[2]

From the above declaration we gather that Merleau-Ponty wants to avoid the idealist "esse est percipi"; he likewise admits the possibility of a consciousness in the world which is not, however, consciousness of self. Most important of all is the insight into the unity of man, so clearly implied here: we really do not understand how things are made *for us* unless we grasp how we relate to them through love and desire. This means that human knowledge is not merely an intellectual affair, but rather an event involving the whole human person; thus the dichotomy between intellect and feelings is ruled out. This view implies more than it may seem at first sight: if true, it would mean that knowledge is always influenced by our affective states and that therefore there is little room for the so-called "objective knowledge"—that is, one uninfluenced by the subjective states of the knower. It is to be noted that Merleau-Ponty substitutes the term "intersubjective" for "objecive"; but for him "intersubjective" has a different meaning, or rather, it follows from what he means by body-subject: an object is intersubjective when it is known by me as others know it; that is to say, the perceived object is available to a number of subjects not as an idea but as a concrete thing. The relation here is directly between the body-subject and the object (thing) hence the term "intersubjective" means "common to body-subjects."

That which differentiates Merleau-Ponty's meaning from the classical connotation of "objective" as applied to any

---
[2] *P. P.*, p. 180.

thing known, or to any truth for that matter, is this: for Merleau-Ponty there is no such thing as matter or sensation without communication with other sensations and the sensation of others—this means that there is no such thing as an "objective" reality independent of subject or independent of relations to other "objects." Likewise, and for the very reason that there is not "just" matter or "just" sensation, there is also *not* just form, that is to say, there is not an understanding or an apperception intended to provide a meaning to that which is meaningless or insignificant and to make "certain" the a priori unity of my experience and of intersubjectivity, (that is, of mine and of the other's experience). That which makes an experience intersubjective is therefore not the intellectual understanding of the same thing, the grasp of the "form" of the thing (which, corresponding to the *essence* would be unchangeable and therefore "objective"), but the mutual experience of the "perceptively given" by myself and by the other.

In his article, "Le primat de la perception,"[3] Merleau-Ponty sums up his thought on intersubjectivity and makes clear the meaning it has for him in relation to objectivity:

> In the same way in which my body, as a system of my perceptions of the world, founds the unity of the object which I perceive, in the same manner, the body of others, insofar as it is a bearer of symbolic behavior . . . breaks away from the condition of one of my phenomena [ceases to be one of my phenomena], presents to me the task of a true communication, and bestows on

---

[3] This article is perhaps the most significant statement of Merleau-Ponty's understanding of the role of perception in human knowledge and intersubjective relations. It would warrant a great deal of study especially for the dialogue it involves with other philosophers whose position is not in harmony with that of Merleau-Ponty himself. The nature of this work does not permit us an explicitation of all its [the article's] valuable insights.

my objects *the new dimension of intersubjective being or of objectivity.*[4]

Merleau-Ponty could hardly have been more explicit in presenting his view on this matter. It is in no way similar to idealism which believes, as Merleau-Ponty observes, that it has achieved community of perception when it has merely reached a common intellectual definition of a thing. His insight is a direct step towards a theory of intersubjective relations, the real point at issue in this study. Intersubjectivity presents a problem precisely because it is not concerned with the purely intellectual notions so easily available to a mind dealing with abstractions. However, Merleau-Ponty's solution, as was pointed out, does not cover the full scope of intersubjective relations: it lacks the interpersonal. This will become apparent in Merleau-Ponty's detailed study of sexuality. It must be kept in mind to avoid unwarranted conclusions.[5]

2. Sexuality, an Original Form of Intentionality

In his discussion of sexuality, Merleau-Ponty is again concerned with description, rather than with any demonstration—the latter of course, is not within the province of phenomenology, hence one can hardly reproach him with failure here. However, one is not always justified in drawing sweeping conclusions and generalizations on the mere strength of the description of certain phenomena. According to Dr. Kockelmans, however, Merleau-Ponty does not reach his conclusions from the studies of abnormal behaviors which he cites; rather, having already his theory in mind, he merely uses these examples from psychotherapy and psy-

---

[4] "Le primat . . . ," p. 125.
[5] Cf. Moreau, *L'horizon* . . . , p. 53; also *P. P.*, pp. 464-65 where Merleau-Ponty describes as intersubjective experience the perception of a "paysage."

Man: A Sexed Being

choanalysis to explicate and elucidate his basic insights into his philosophy of man, which, he maintains, is founded on existential experience.[6] His theory, based on the study of the normal as well as of the abnormal, is ultimately an affirmation that sexuality is an original form of intentionality, an openness of the ego-subject to the other and to the world, an intentionality irreducible to corporeal automatism or to mental representations and which operates according to a dialectical exchange. It is clear that for Merleau-Ponty sexuality is not a mere phase of man's relation to others, an occasional type of behavior arising from certain situations; man is a sexed being through and through; his sexuality is his very being as man, and as he says in various ways, sexuality permeates the whole of man's existence. On the one hand there are stimuli with sexual significance and an Eros which animates the natural world; on the other hand these same stimuli revert to and dialogue with "the mute and permanent question which is normal sexuality."[7] Thus sexuality results from the encounter of these two poles which both imply and transcend each other in a dialectical exchange, which is not however a "relation between thoughts, both inseparable and contradictory, but rather the tension of an existence towards another existence."[8]

How does Merleau-Ponty come to these conclusions? By plodding his way laboriously through the manifestations of man's affectivity from the most tenuous relation to the deepest and most intimate intersubjective exchange at the personal level, taking note of nuances of meaning and signification relevant to his investigation.

Thus he begins by considering the nature of affectivity through a consideration of affective states. He maintains that, ordinarily affective states are described as a sort of

---
[6] Personal correspondence.
[7] *P. P.*, p. 183. Cf. pp. 182-83.
[8] *P. P.*, p. 195.

mosaic: that is, as self-contained pleasures and sorrows and inexplicable in themselves. As usual, he undertakes to show that both intellectualism and empiricism do not give us the true picture. If one admits with the intellectualists, that in man such affective states are imbued with intelligence, then one also admits that simple representations of said pleasures and pains can be substituted for the actual experiences. For the intellectualists then, affective states are a sort of commentary on our thoughts resulting from an arbitrary interpretation of events to which we give our own subjective interpretation (subjective here is taken in the idealistic meaning of interior construction of consciousness) and not the intersubjective significance of the events themselves. Empiricists, instead, equate sentiment, mechanically, with corporeal facts. Since man can suffer, not only through the actual physical pain he experiences, but also through the recollection or the representation of it, it follows, for the behaviorist, that the qualities of pain or pleasure can be extended to the conditioned reflexes. Thus, representations, of which man is capable since his sentiments can be intellectualized, can play a role of *cause* in provoking sentiments. Therefore affectivity can be calculated since it can be derived from previous facts. But this then means that "affectivity is not granted the status of an original and independent mode of consciousness."[9]

That this is not so, according to Merleau-Ponty, becomes clear by the observation of the behavior of the abnormal. For, he says, if the assumption were correct then lack of sexuality would be the result of either a loss or a lack of certain representations of sexual nature; or it could be due to a lessening of or an incapability of experiencing pleasure. Studying a mental patient—a particular case history— Merleau-Ponty notes that such an individual never seeks the sexual act of his own initiative, nor is he affected by sug-

---

[9] *P P.*, pp. 180-81.

gestive images, conversations or even perception of a body (which would usually affect a normal person). None of the actions which would have a sexual appeal for a normal person has any effect on the abnormal, except in a very restricted sense and closely related to a definite physical contact; further, as soon as the direct contact ceases, whatever sexual feeling had been experienced by the patient ceases also. All indications in this case are, for Merleau-Ponty, that the patient is not moved by "sexual reflexes" nor by "pure states of pleasures." Further, if sexuality were for man an autonomous reflex apparatus, and if the sexual object were definitely linked with a certain organ anatomically defined, then the cerebral impairment of an individual would have no effect on the sexual behavior of the same; in fact, it might even free the individual for a more pronounced sexual activity for then the governing power of the intellect would be lacking.[10]

Again according to Merleau-Ponty's interpretation of the data gathered from the study he is quoting here—the abnormality in sexual behavior is rooted in the fact that it is the structure itself of perception and of the erotic experience which is altered in the case of the patient; hence his insensibility to the perception of an object which would otherwise arouse feelings is understandable.

For the normal person, instead, a body is not like any other perceived object. Besides the exterior perception—or rather, the perception of the exteriority of the body, there is a secret and more intimate perception which has the character of a sexual appeal, both personal and individual, which calls forth an affective response.

This kind of perception is different from the objective, yet it is a signification distinct from the intellectual; it is an intentionality which is not the "pure consciousness of a

---

[10] *P. P.*, pp. 181-82; Merleau-Ponty usually refers to Schneider (as noted on p. 181, Note 1).

thing." Neither is this erotic perception in the order of the understanding, for understanding is through ideas, while "desire understands blindly in binding a body to a body." Likewise, with sexuality we are not dealing with a type of corporeal function, "but with an intentionality which follows the general movement of existence and bends with it." Sexuality is therefore not an autonomous cycle. It is interiorly bound to the whole being, as knowing and acting, thus manifesting a sole structural, typical behavior wherein these sectors of life are in a relation of reciprocal expression.[11]

Even for Freud, Merleau-Ponty maintains, sexuality is not merely an organic function or an instinct, but rather a general power to orient oneself towards a certain structuration. Because of this structuration man has a history. If the history of man under the aspect of sexuality gives us the key to his life it is because sexuality is a manner of projecting oneself in relation to the world, that is, with regard to time and to other men. However, Merleau-Ponty observes, there is need to clarify the meaning of this generalized notion of sexuality: just what does one mean by the term? Merleau-Ponty disagrees with psychoanalysis when it maintains that either sexuality is within the structuration of life, or that it integrates the whole of life. Acually, it is a quesion of seeing whether one is more justified in saying that in the last analysis all existence has a sexual signification or that all sexual phenomena have an existential signification. In the first case, existence would be an abstraction; in the second, sexual life would only be a general way of projecting ourselves. But for Merleau-Ponty the problem is to determine why the sexual drama is more fundamental, more frequent and more severe than all others and "why sexuality is not only a sign, but a privileged one."[12]

As with all organs of perception, which never operate independently of the whole organism, sexuality is not inde-

---
[11]*P. P.*, p. 183.
[12]*P. P.*, p. 186.

pendent, but intimately connected with all other human functions—and this may explain why with the abnormal we find, usually, a foundation of the trouble in some drama relative to the affective life. Merleau-Ponty's theory of structuration and form is quite applicable also here: the body is not merely the instrument or the manifestation of personal existence; personal existence gathers in itself, not only the body, but also sight, hearing and sexuality in what is their annonymous existence in order to give them a signification. This signification, however, is not spiritual, for the body is not the transparent envelope of the soul—of the spirit—even if we admit that the life of the body and of the spirit have a relation of expression and that the signification of a physical event is always psychic.[13]

3. *Affectivity and the Incarnate Spirit*

Merleau-Ponty insists again that spirit is not something independent of and apart from the body. In his estimation, spirit *is* only insofar as it is incarnate. Therefore, strictly speaking, for him spiritualism or any theory of soul would have no meaning, because it would have no object.

Merleau-Ponty illustrates his meaning by a study of the abnormal. The functions of our body are so intimately correlated to one another that they can be called a common existence—co-existence. Thus the disturbance aroused by a problem in the affective life will have its repercussion in the physical, perceptive, expressive life of the person involved. Merleau-Ponty makes a particular study of the loss of speech and of memory. In each case the loss is directly related to some trouble in the affective life of the patient and affects the whole organism.

Discussing the case of a loss of memory, Merleau-Ponty maintains that this forgetfulness is not an accident: the object is lost because it belongs to a sector of the patient's life

---

[13]*P. P.*, pp. 186-87.

which he refuses (because of a rupture in affective relations with someone). It is as if the object did not exist any more. Thus, to forget is *an act*: the patient keeps the object at a distance as he keeps at a distance the person involved. The object, however, is not completely lost: simply, the patient does not know where it is—"intentionally." But when the trouble which caused the alienation is over, the object is "found" again. The reason why the "souvenir" is not really lost is this: our own acts as well as our own body, instead of being present to us in isolated and singular acts, are really present to us as a whole; thus an object which the patient refuses because of an affective distressing situation is not really lost to consciousness, but merely pushed in the background. We also discover that whatever we experience from sense perception we perceive through a general acceptance of our bodily condition and of our life. Therefore, our acceptance or our refusal of our body will be the determinant of our mental field, "just as the retention or the loss of a sense organ will either enlarge or delimit our direct perception of a certain portion of our physical field."[14]

The use of our bodily organs and powers, and as a result, communication with others, always implies a choice on our part—for Merleau-Ponty, not necessarily a conscious one (conscious is here taken as consciousness of self, at the intellectual level). To be able to act or to communicate with others presupposes the possibility of a choice: either I wish or do not wish to communicate. However, a person who is under the influence of a traumatic experience which reveals itself by loss of speech for instance, has no choice: he cannot choose to speak, for he has lost the possibility to do so. There is a reason perhaps for the condition of aphasia: since the word is, of all the functions of the body, the most intimately linked to co-existence, the inability to speak may clearly indicate a refusal to co-exist. The patient has thus

---
[14] *P. P.*, p. 189.

cut himself off from the other; the field of communication which was previously open to him is now non-existent.[15]

In connection with this aspect of our communication with others, Merleau-Ponty makes a distinction between psychological and metaphysical hypocrisy. By the first, one deceives others by hiding from them his consciously known thoughts; by the second, instead, one deceives himself and ends up in a situation over which he has no control precisely because it is neither willed nor consciously posited; although this latter condition is not absolutely inevitable, it may befall the most sincere and authentic person: this metaphysical hypocrisy is *part of the human condition*. It may become a way of existence, just as much as hysteria, sulkiness or aphasia. These existential situations become structures of the behaviors affected by them.

This seems a rather strong expression for a condition which is, after all, not a permanent change. We must recall the meaning Merleau-Ponty gives to the term "structure." By it he means a whole existential mode of organization by which a certain behavior manifests itself—a sort of Gestalt wherein both the world and the body are involved thereby exhibiting a meaning or signification. Merleau-Ponty calls a certain behavior a "structure"; he further asserts that such a structure is changeable, as he shows quite clearly by the examples of aphasia and hysteria: with a new experience, a new structuration occurs. That would make every experience, not just an accidental, but an essential change. The patient should not be identified with the person who was previously healthy and happy. This seems too daring a notion. At close scrutiny, would it not mean, perhaps, that the very identity of the person is in question? It seems clear from previous discussion that a new structuration for Merleau-Ponty literally means a new kind of being, so that the subject would be a fluid entity, never the same.

---

[15] *P. P.*, p. 187.

Merleau-Ponty

This "becoming" of structures, as pointed out previously, always implies the body; this holds true in any change for better or for worse. The cure from the trauma is effected by way of some physical contact rather than by revealing to the patient the origin of the trouble.[16] The will is not involved here. In fact, Merleau-Ponty observes, neither do the symptoms appear nor is the cure effected at the level of consciousness properly speaking, that is, at the level of intellectual awareness, and of willed actions. The analogy of sleep illustrates his meaning clearly. He maintains that sleep occurs when we have achieved a mimic of it. Our consciousness and our will can do no more than that.

Aphasia as a situation can be compared to sleep:

> I stretch myself on my bed, . . . I put my projects out of my mind. But the power of my will or of my consciousness stops here. As the faithful, in the dionysian mysteries invoked their god by mimicking the scenes of his life, I summon the visitation of sleep by imitating the breathing of the sleeper as well as his posture. The god is there when the faithful are no longer distinguished from the role which they play, when their body and their consciousness cease to oppose to him [the god] their particular opacity . . . and are entirely fused in the myth. There is a moment when sleep comes . . . I succeed in becoming that which I make believe I am.[17]

---

[16] *P. P.*, p. 190: ". . . la médecine psychologique n'agit pas sur le malade en lui faisant connaitre l'origine de sa maladie : un contact de la main met fin quelquefois aux contractures et rend la parole au malade, et la même maneuvre devenue rite, suffira . . . à maitriser de nouveaux accès."

[17] *P. P.*, p. 191. "Il y a un moment où le sommeil 'vient,' il se pose sur cette imitation de lui-même que je lui proposais, je réussis à devenir ce que je feignais d'être : cette masse sans regard et presque sans pensées, clouée en un point de l'espace, et qui n'est plus au monde que par la vigilance anonyme des sens. Sans doute ce dernier lien rend possible le réveil: par ces portes entr' ouvertes les choses rentreront ou le dormeur reviendra au monde."

Man: A Sexed Being

Merleau-Ponty does not fail to note that even though in sleep I become an unconscious "lump" there is still within me that which he calls "the anonymous vigilance of the senses" by which I am able to return to the world of consciousness. It is by the same means that the patient is enabled to return to the intersubjective world, for he is never wholly closed within himself; but it is through some impersonal functions of language and of the organs of sensation that he returns to the intersubjective world (and the sleeper to the full consciousness of wakefulness).[18] He further affirms that "we remain free with regard to sleep and sickness in the exact measure in which we are engaged in the state of waking and of health for our liberty rests on our being in situation, and, in fact, it is itself in situation."[19] Does Merleau-Ponty mean that not only with regard to sleep, but also with regard to sickness the state we are in is, in a way, induced? But, he says, wakefulness, sleep, sickness and health do not proceed from the will or from consciousness; they are existential. This notion would mean then that our existential condition does not result from a decision of the will, but rather, that the will is a result of our being in a certain situation; in other words, we will one thing rather than another because the existential circumstances we are in make us *be* a kind of person rather than another—and this is not to say that we are victims of environment.[20] This assertion could raise a number of questions which Merleau-Ponty does not mention, but which he implicitly answers by declaring that our existential circumstances arise in the last analysis from the body.[21]

Merleau-Ponty has thus prepared for the central point of his theory of body which he expresses thus:

---

[18] In what way the sense organs are impersonal is not clear. As to language, this topic will be discussed later.
[19] *P. P.*, p. 191.
[20] Cf. Preface to *Phénomélogie de la perception*, p. III.
[21] However, to say that is not to explain abnormality.

> It is precisely the role of the body to assure this metamorphosis: it transforms the ideas into things, my mimicry of sleep into effective sleep. *If the body can symbolize existence it is because it* realizes it and it is its actuality.[22]

There could hardly be a stronger declaration of the essentiality[23] of the body: it is the man. However, the questions referred to above, remain: for instance, why do I mimic one thing rather than another, so that my body accomplishes the metamorphosis one way rather than another? In the sick, the movements towards the future, towards life are blocked, so to speak, by the bodily symptoms, for the body has become the concealment of life, thus existence becomes tied up. Even the normal person engaged in intersubjectivity, insofar as he has a body, knows that he can withdraw from its activities, he may retire in that anonymous life which underlies his personal one, always through the body. And through the body, also, he can open himself to the world and place himself in situation. The movement of existence towards the other, can be resumed by the patient not "by an effort of the intellect nor by an abstract decree of the will, but by a conversion of the whole body wherein the whole body re-assembles itself, so to speak, by a true gesture."[24] Memories and voice are found again when the body reopens itself to others or to the past, in active coexistence beyond itself.[25] But the "return" of the body to its active engagement

---

[22] *P. P.*, pp. 191-92.
[23] Just what does Merleau-Ponty mean by "essentiality" of the body? The term for him has no classical connotation—that is, essential as opposed to accidental; for him it simply means that without the body there is no relation of any kind possible: his dialectic notion of being-in-the-world, of intersubjectivity, of temporality, of spatiality all involve the body; even the possibility of spirit is dependent on body—and therefore also thought and language. It is in this sense only that one can point to the body and say that it is essential.
[24] *P. P.*, p. 192.
[25] *P. P.*, p. 192.

Man: A Sexed Being

cannot be mere accident: just what triggers this re-activation?

The body, no matter how far cut off from the circuit of existence, is never completely shut within itself. I can never completely suppress all reference of my life to the world, even if I am absorbed within myself and in solitude. Again and again, some intention springs up within me towards the world. I never become completely a thing in the world, for I do not have the solidity of existence of a thing. As long as I have sense organs, my corporeal existence is never closed within itself; however, the senses alone do not assure my presence to the world, rather it is my existence which assures me of such presence. My corporeal existence, is the actual sketch of a true presence to the world; it founds at the least the possibility of such presence, it establishes my first pact with the world itself. No matter how I try to withdraw from the human world, I still find within my body the same power—nameless perhaps—which "condemns me to being." One could say that the body is the form of being itself or rather that personal existence is the resumption and the manifestation of a being in situation.[26]

Merleau-Ponty compares the way the body expresses existence to the way the word expresses thought. Besides the conventional means of expression, by which I manifest myself to others, there is also as a primordial operation, a kind of signification which does not exist apart from the signified. In the same way, the body expresses total existence, not as an exterior accompaniment to itself, but as an existence realized in it. "This incarnate consciousness is the central phenomenon of which body and spirit, sign and signification are the abstract moments."[27]

This is again a reference, and a more explicit one, to the body-soul relation as discussed by Merleau-Ponty in *La*

---
[26] *P. P.*, p. 193.
[27] *P. P.*, p. 193.

structure du comportement. Now he points out that the relation here is not that of expression to the expressed, as it would be in the case of the original and the translation. It does not have a univocal meaning.

> Neither the body, nor existence could pass for the original of the human being, since each presupposes the other; the body is existence congealed or generalized, and existence [is] a perpetual incarnation.[28]

The relation here is between the body and existence; how this existence becomes the body, or how the body incarnates this existence Merleau-Ponty does not say. His whole point of interest seems to be the observation of that which is presented to consciousness as a phenomenon, not the how or why of the phenomenon itself. This is understandable enough in a phenomenological context; Merleau-Ponty did not live to work out an ontology.[29]

4. *Existential Signification of Sexuality*

Returning to the express topic of sexuality, within the discussion of signification, he reconsiders the question proposed before: has sexuality an existential signification or does it express existence? He maintains that one must not think that the sexual drama is in the last analysis nothing but a manifestation or a symptom of an existential one. One

---

[28] *P. P.*, p. 194.
[29] Again we are confronted with Merleau-Ponty's abiguity: he describes the phenomena, but he never points out any line of demarcation or at least an indication of the possible superiority of one element over the other in any given problem: the contours are always blurred; there is mutual interdependence and mutual influence of one moment of the dialectic over the other, but all that we know is the process as it is taking place: we cannot look at the forces which go into its actualization. This may well be the only possible way to look at the phenomena—that is from an existential phenomenological point of view—for to dissect it by analysis might well result in its destruction as *that* given phenomenon.

Man: A Sexed Being

can neither reduce sexuality to existence nor existence to sexuality. There is rather a dialectic of existence and sexuality, there is a point in which they meet, an equivocal or an ambiguous point of contact, which is their common web, wherein the limits of the one are blended with those of the other

There is no doubt that desire, modesty, and love in general are incomprehensible if we treat man merely as a machine governed by natural laws or as a bundle of instincts. Love, desire, modesty have a metaphysical significance and concern man as a consciousness and as a liberty. This may explain why man does not—usually—expose his body to profane gaze; if he does he experiences shame as if the other's look might strip him of himself. Yet man is willing to expose his body as a means of conquest—he can make a slave of the other by fascinating him—"the exhibition of his body will deliver to him the other without defense."[30] This two-fold possibility of relation with the other, Merleau-Ponty maintains, is a dialectic wherein the ego and the other are in a relation of master and slave: modesty and immodesty are the thesis and antithesis—rather, for Merleau-Ponty, they are the two poles of the tension which characterizes his dialectic; as long as I have a body, I have the power to make a slave of another or to be made a slave by him. However, he points out clearly, either condition is illusory because from the moment I make a slave of another I no longer consider him a person: at that moment then I cease to be a master; he is a being without liberty from the moment that he has been fascinated by me, and therefore he does not count for me any longer.

To say that I have a body is therefore a way of saying that I can be made an object and that I seek to be seen as a subject, that another can be my master or my

---

[30] *P. P.*, p. 194. Sartre describes this in his *L'être et et le néant*.

slave; so that modesty and immodesty express the dialectic of the plurality of consciousnesses; they have a metaphysical significance.[31]

This passage harks back to the Sartrean thought so insistently expressed in *Being and Nothingness,* namely, that love is illusory because in love one wants to capture the freedom of the other, and this mutual attempt results in a mutual destruction as persons. Merleau-Ponty, however, expressed his thought in a clearer way than Sartre did; further, he does not consider this relation as love yet, but only a desire to fascinate the other. Love, for Merleau-Ponty will be something quite different: a reciprocity, a mutual engagement.[32] He does describe however, somewhat in the line of Sartre, the incongruity of having a witness to an expression of love or desire. It is a sort of impropriety, a third is felt as a menace because he prevents me from fascinating the other. Yet fascination also fails if the other is either too detached or too free. Perhaps this attitude of freedom suggests the virtual presence of another, or denotes a spirit too strong to succumb to fascination. So there is at least a possibility that my power of fascination be sometimes wanting. Merleau-Ponty gives the reason for this: that which I seek to possess is not just a body as physical organism but a body animated by a consciousness. This last remark suggests that in the sexual exchange the dialectic is not only between body-subjects, but also ego-consciousnesses. That is to say, the sexual relation is not at the pre-personal level—at that level in which a consciousness is at work which is not yet

---

[31] *P. P.*, p. 195.
[32] *P. P.*, Chapter IV, Part II. It is difficult, however, to see in Merleau-Ponty's relation of love a truly personal dimension. The fact that he assigns so much importance and so great a role to the body-subject in all intersubjective activities makes one wonder if and at what point, the intersubjectivity becomes "interpersonal relation." But this question will be discussed further.

Man: A Sexed Being

fully human—but it implies the full human awareness of the ego-consciousness.

> The importance attached to the body, the contradictions of love are therefore linked to a drama more general, depend on the metaphysical structure of my body, at once object for others and subject for myself. The violence of sexual pleasure is not sufficient to explain the place which sexuality holds in human life and the phenomenon of erotism, unless we understand the experience of sex as a possibility, given to all and always accessible, of experiencing the human condition in its most general moments of autonomy and of dependence.[33]

This then means that sexuality is part and parcel of man's very structure. Merleau-Ponty has said that sexuality is a dialectic; this does not make it a knowing process, nor does it make the history of man identical with the history of his consciousness. "The dialectic is not the relation between contradictory but inseparable thoughts; it is the tension of an existence towards another existence which denies it and without which, however, it cannot sustain itself."[34] Metaphysics—which Merleau-Ponty calls "emergence beyond nature"—has its point of departure in the act of opening of the ego to the "other" and is first realized in the development of sexuality itself. This notion, however, runs counter to Freud's generalization of sexuality. If it is all pervading, how can we speak of development? Further, can we even attempt to characterize as sexual a content of consciousness? In fact, we cannot. Sexuality is usually concealed under a mask of generality. The tension and the drama which it itself has stirred up do not reveal themselves as sexual, yet we cannot say that sexuality is subject to our life. Rather, should we say that it is transcended and submerged within

---
[33] *P. P.*, p. 195.
[34] *P. P.*, p. 95.

the more general drama of life. In this respect Merleau-Ponty introduces two possibilities, both erroneous: the first is a refusal to recognize in existence any content not specifically and distinctly manifest; the second, is to duplicate this manifest content by adding to it another hidden or latent content. For Merleau-Ponty, sexuality is neither transcended by human life, nor symbolized within it by unconscious representations. Rather, it is constantly present as an atmosphere, which is, however, ambiguous.[35] This means that the general movements of sexuality, the general functions of tactile experience, often take place without the expressed awareness of the consciousness involved. Likewise, sexuality, without being the object of an expressed act of consciousness, may motivate certain privileged forms of experience.[36] Merleau-Ponty insists that the equivocal is essential in human existence; all that which we live or think always has several meanings. Even a kind of life seemingly in contrast with that expressing affectivity, for instance, a tendency to solitude, may be a generalized expression of sexuality. On the other hand, the underlying signification of sexuality which has become existence, may express itself in such rational ways that it is impossible to find in them the form of sexuality as an explicitation of the form of existence. There is a sort of osmosis—Merleau-Ponty maintains—between sexuality and existence; that is, sexuality is diffused into existence and existence into sexuality in such a way that it is impossible to decide, with regard to a given action or decision, whether the motivation be of a sexual or non-sexual origin. This accounts for the element of indetermination in human existence—Merleau-Ponty calls it a

---

[35] *P. P.*, p. 197. "Prise ainsi, c'est-à-dire comme atmosphère ambiguë, la sexualité est coextensive à la vie. Autrement dit, l'équivoque est essentielle à l'existence humaine et tout ce que nous vivons ou pensons a toujours plusieurs sens."
[36] *P. P.*, p. 196: "Il y a là des formes confuses, des relations privilégiées, nullement 'inconscientes' et dont nous savons très bien qu'elles sont louches, qu'elles ont rapport à la sexualité, sans qu'elles l'évoquent expressément."

Man: A Sexed Being

"principle" of indetermination. Such indetermination is not just the human lot and the result of an imperfection. Not even a god could probe the heart so as to fix the boundaries of that which is from nature and that which is the fruit of liberty.

Merleau-Ponty gives reasons for this indeterminacy of existence.

> Existence is indetermined in itself by reason of its fundamental structure insofar as it is the same operation by which that which did not have meaning takes on a signification, that which had only a sexual signification takes on a more general meaning.[37]

Merleau-Ponty describes existence as transcendence, and transcedence as that movement by which existence reassumes and transforms a factual situation. It is therefore clear that existence is always indetermined and never goes beyond anything definitively—if it did, the tension which defines it would disappear, thus making a dialectic impossible. Existence, then, remains what it is, neither exterior nor accidental to itself. In the same way, Merleau-Ponty argues, sexuality, even more than the body itself, has to be taken into account as an indispensable content of our experience.

Opposing to the above the notion of contingency Merleau-Ponty asks whether it would be possible to "conceive" a man deprived of any one of his essential organs or integral parts: for instance, without hands or deprived of sex. In the first place, this "conceiving" could be done only on condition that man be considered merely abstractly—in which case the various organs would be viewed as mere fragments of matter. But if man were, in actuality, lacking any one of his systems of relation, he would no longer be a man, but something else. One could even conceive a man reproducing

---
[37] *P. P.*, p. 197.

Merleau-Ponty

by an a-sexual method, or even lacking hands or head for instance—but this would always remain pure thought, abstraction.[38] But, if we define man by his own experiential being-in-the-world, (and Merleau-Ponty maintains this is the only way we can define him meaningfully) then a man could not be described except as endowed with those organs which make him a man—specifically, with those organs which put him in contact with the world and with other men. Thus one could not think of man as lacking sexual organs any more than of one lacking the power of thought or without hands. His sexuality, his power of thought and speech, his tool making power (directly related to the structure of his hands), his manner of being in the world and of relating to the world through perception are not separate and independent functions of man. They are unified and integrated to such a degree that the impairment of one will affect the functioning of the others.[39]

All this seems to lead to a purely empirical definition of man. Merleau-Ponty states that in all this we do not interject any notion of necessity: that is to say, we do not posit any "a priori" such as a necessity of nature; rather, we simply point to existence. In the existential being of man it is not possible to distinguish that which is essential[40] from

---

[38] *P. P.*, p. 198. "On répondra [to a previous question on contingence] peut-être que l'organisation de notre corps est contingente, que l'on peut 'concevoir un homme sans mains, pieds, tête' et à plus forte raison un homme sans sexe et qui se reproduirait par bouture ou par marcottage. Mais cela n'est vrai que si l'on considère les mains, les pieds, la tête ou l'appareil sexuel abstraitement, c'est-à-dire comme des fragments de matière, non pas dans leur fonction vivante, —et que si l'on forme de l'homme une notion abstraite elle aussi, dans laquelle on ne fait entrer que la Cogitatio."
Compare the above with Merleau-Ponty's discussion, on same page, on the fact of man's opposable thumb—in relation to necessity.
[39] *P. P.*, p. 198. Cf. *S. C.*, pp. 161-62.
[40] Therefore it is nonsense to speak of the "essential"—considered in the classical meaning of the term. The notion of dialectic tension makes everything necessary because in such a relation every "moment" is required for the synthesis to take place. In Merleau-Ponty's tension dialectic, the poles are necessary.

that which is contingent as it is impossible to distinguish in man's expressions that which arises from the sexual from that which is otherwise motivated. Hence Merleau-Ponty concludes that all is necessary in man. And yet, all is contingent in the sense that this manner of human existence is not guaranteed to every infant which is born; he is not endowed with a certain essence which will develop itself constantly throughout his life and within the hazards of the objective body. "Man is a historical idea and not a natural species."[41] That means simply, that nothing in man is a brute necessity of nature and yet nothing is purely fortuitous. This certainly makes it difficult to assign man to any specified category of being; Merleau-Ponty admits that in this case we must revise our notions of contingency and necessity, for human existence *is* "the change" of contingency into necessity by the act of renewal and liberation.[42]

In other words, Merleau-Ponty holds that starting from a condition which we have not chosen, we are de facto transforming our situation continuously by a kind of escape which is never an unconditional liberty, but which nevertheless makes our condition human, that is, a choice. "There is no explanation possible which would make of sexuality something other than itself, because it already is something else; if one so chooses, even his whole being. Sexuality is dramatic *because* we engage in it our whole personal life."[43]

---

[41] *P. P., p.* 199. "Man is an historical idea" seems to lend itself to an interpretation quite different from the existentialist notion Merleau-Ponty has specifically embraced. Man is not "just" an idea for Merleau-Ponty, but his expression wants to convey the notion of a being which cannot be classified according to any closed and stable category, because man is in process.

[42] *P. P.*, p. 199. Not only must we revise our notions in this case, but to follow Merleau-Ponty we must revise most of our notions; he uses familiar terms with the most unfamiliar connotation. It is quite true, as he said in the *Preface,* that phenomenology is accessible only to a phenomenologist.

[43] *P. P.*, p. 199.

The reason for this is very significant: since our body is a natural self it reflects our very being. Because it [the body] is a current of given existence we never even know whether the forces which sustain and carry us are its or ours—rather, such forces are never either its or ours entirely.

> There is no going beyond sexuality as there is no sexuality closed within itself. No one is ever saved or lost completely.[44]

5. Some Implications of the Doctrine

Merleau-Ponty's investigation of the role of the body as sexual brings out very definitely the fact of man's position in the natural world; he does not belong to it and yet is in a sense part of it. Man is master of his own situation and yet he is made what he is by that very situation. The phenomena Merleau-Ponty investigates reveal that man's relations are not only tied in with his body but they are his body. Man could never be man without his bodily condition, and yet his body could not be body without the spirit of which it is the incarnation. The spirit however, is not a "being" residing *in* the body, for there is no spirit apart from the body. There is a sense in which we can even say that the spirit is, in fact, the body. What this means for the sexual life of man is that sexual expression is never a purely biological fact, but rather, it is a human act. Its characteristics cannot be detached from the spiritual current which makes of man a living human being. There is therefore a definite ambiguity in all of man's relations to himself and to others as well as to the world, for no act is ever attributable

---

[44] *P. P.*, p. 199. This expression is quite strong. If this is true, then it would seem that once one has discovered the sexual drama of a person everything is discovered. But then, if sexuality is not closed within itself, we are again in an open situation: does not Merleau-Ponty contradict himself? There is plenty of room for questions here, which may be answered in his later writings, particularly in his article "Le roman et la métaphysique," *S. N. S.*, pp. 45-84.

Man: A Sexed Being

to just one or the other living impluse which can be—abstractly—recognized in him. Thus, to know man in any of his manifestations is to know man in his totality, but not to know exactly the motivation of any one act in particular.[45] This may at first sight seem to be a poorer way of knowing or describing man, since there is an underlying ambiguity in whatever explanation one may seek to give, but it may well be a better and a richer way. Insofar as one does thereby recognize man—at least abstractly—as a certain essence one has a generalization of man; insofar, however, as one knows man in his undefinable and existential condition one knows his essence in its existing situation; therefore one knows not abstractly, but concretely human nature in its manifestation and in its signification. True, for Merleau-Ponty, as body and soul are but significations so also are the moments of sexual life. This view does not imply a denial of the objective body or of the soul, or of the fact of sexuality. It merely expresses the recognition of the integral nature of man which refuses to be compartmentalized in any form and still remain what it is.[46]

It is undeniable that Merleau-Ponty's study of man as a sexed being is not only true to fact, but also very profound. This is not to say that it is a result of a pure phenomenological investigation. In fact, probably it is not. A simple investigation of phenomena could not have disclosed the insights which we find therein. To take just an example, the dialectic of body and soul could hardly be revealed by a non-reflective phenomenological study; it must have been arrived at by a deeper phenomenological reflection. If we want to call it "second reflection" and consider it a "phenomenology

---

[45]Here we find a parallel to the assertion that he makes with regard to the certitude of perception; that is, there is no certitude of anything in particular, though there is a certitude of the world in general.

[46]Cf. *P. P.*, pp. 200-201. Merleau-Ponty refers again to ambiguity in history as well as in the existential situation.

of phenomenology"—as Merleau-Ponty intends to do with the Cogito—then, perhaps, we may accept the insight as phenomenological; but Merleau-Ponty himself does not make such a claim. His whole effort has been, presumably, to proceed by that phenomenological method which he describes in his "Preface," but there seems to be much more than an examination of the phenomena in his whole work. The very theories which he intends to refute or disprove often enough furnish him the insight for his own reflections; therefore, we could say that he incorporates some of them. It is ultimately to the benefit of his own philosophy, even if it is not his intention to incorporate them but rather to go beyond them and do away with the inconsistencies which he sees in them.

It also seems difficult to think that his discussion of intersubjectivity in relation to history and economics be obtained purely from a phenomenological investigation.[47] Economics, he maintains, is not a cycle of closed objective phenomena, but rather a confrontation of productive forces and of forms of production—again we have hint of a dialectic—and economics finds itself integrated into history, rather than history into economics. "Taking cognizance" of the relation, or of the dialectic, is itself a cultural phenomenon, and the whole relation rests on the manner of existing or of co-existing, that is, on interhuman relations. As he has done for the sexual relation with respect to human life in general, he asks whether the drama of coexistence has a purely economic significance or whether the economic drama dissolves itself into a drama more general and existential. His reflection brings him to affirm here also the essential ambiguity of an existential theory of history—understandable because arising from "things." But at the root of all this is always the fundamental thesis which Merleau-Ponty has sustained throughout, namely, that no one singular motivation is re-

---

[47]Cf. *P. P.*, p. 199, Note 1.

Man: A Sexed Being

sponsible for the conditions or the struggles of life—in this case the economic one—and that the human condition is of necessity caught up with the complexity of life at every level. Since economy is not a closed world and all motivations are integrated into history, the exterior becomes interior and vice-versa, and no component of our existence can ever be surpassed. As all our life breathes an atmosphere of sexuality without our being able to assign to any single act a purely sexual content,[48] so the economic and social drama is at the root of the life of each consciousness, without being identifiable with it—it is coextensive with history. Thus the act of the artist or of the philosopher is free, but not without motive; freedom merely consists of assuming a situation of fact by giving it a meaning beyond its own proper signification. "Thought is interhuman life such as it understands and interprets itself."[49]

As there is no unique signification of the life of man so there is no unique signification of history; it is in this recognition of many meanings that an existential conception of history distinguishes itself from both a materialistic and a spiritualistic one. However, (and here may be hidden a hint of Merleau-Ponty's Marxism) the whole cultural phenomena has, among others, an economic significance; although history cannot be reduced to it, nevertheless, it cannot transcend it.

Merleau-Ponty then compares the whole social structural unity to the unity of the body; in the one as in the other, it is impossible to reduce the whole to any one of its relations, even though in each case, one or the other component may be considered dominant. Thus one gesture may be classed as

---

[48]This last assertion might be contested: that many of our acts be ambiguous may be very true, especially if we are looking for the sexual meaning in them; but that no act may be so definitely sexual as to be able to be so classified seems untenable; much more so since he declares that "there is no going beyond sexuality."

[49]*P. P.*, p. 202.

sexual, another as belligerent; in the coexistence of men an historical period may be described chiefly cultural, another economic and another principally political. But philosophy can never predict the future; it can only indicate what might be expected from a consideration of the human condition—philosophy, that is—but does Merleau-Ponty mean by this "phenomenology?" If he does, it is hardly possible to admit as much. An examination of the content of consciousness could hardly be sufficient for such a development of reflexive thought, particularly when it is a question of history.[50]

---

[50]This theme will be taken up again later.

CHAPTER SIX

THE ROLE OF THE BODY IN MAN'S POWER OF COMMUNICATION

"Phenomenology is not considered as the function of the mind but the power to translate and enlighten, to make transparent and to express in language the darkness of prereflexive reality."[1] If this is the function of phenomenology, then the investigation of language has a very important place in Merleau-Ponty's philosophy. However, it is not so certain that Merleau-Ponty intended to assign the intentionality of language to some power in man divorced from the spirit. As a matter of fact, man's body *is* the incarnation of the spirit and therefore whatever communication is achieved by means of the bodily functions is necessarily also a function of the mind.

In turning his attention to the phenomenon of language, and in attempting to show its significance as bodily expression of a particular kind, he aims at overcoming the classical dichotomy between subject and object, between idealism and empiricism which has been the concern of philosophy for ages past.[2] This he will attempt to show by his phenomenological investigation of language, not as a tool of a preformed thought, but as an incarnation of thought itself through the verbal expression, and further, as a means of

---

[1] M. Virasoro, "Merleau-Ponty and the World of Perception," *Philosophy Today*, Vol. III, No. 1 (Spring, 1959, pp. 66-72), p. 71. [From *Ciencia y Fé*, Ano XIII, No. 2, abril-junio, 1957, pp. 147-57.]

[2] "Nous avons reconnu au corps une unité distincte de celle de l'objet scientifique. Nous venons de découvrir jusque dans sa 'fonction sexuelle' une intentionnalité et un pouvoir de signification. En cherchant à décrire le phénomène de la parole et l'acte exprès de signification, nous aurons chance de dépasser définitivement la dichotomie classique du sujet et de l'objet. *P. P.*, p. 203. Of course from the very declaration of his intention the phenomenological character of the investigation becomes doubtful; how could he anticipate the results if he were truly instituting a phenomenological inquiry?

intersubjective exchange. If, as was shown previously, intersubjective "object" is an object which is known by me and others, it is clearly seen how important the subject of language is for this exchange: it is necessary to name things in order to know them and to participate in one another's knowledge of such things."

Merleau-Ponty never departs from the notion that man's bodily condition is the milieu of his manifestation—of whatever kind it be: perceptive, sexual, intersubjective, mental. Further, he looks at man always from the existential point of view; thus, as sexuality is an existential movement, so is language existential; each of man's existential expressions, however, is in the dialectical relation of a polarity—a tension—so that not any one of man's expressions has a preeminence over another.

In his investigation of this facet of man's corporeity, Merleau-Ponty follows the same familiar procedure: to *prove* his points (if one can speak of "proof" in an existential phenomenology) he has recourse to the phenomena of the abnormal, and refers frequently to the data of psychology and psychoanalysis.

The fundamental data of his discussion of language are found in *Phénoménologie de la perception,* and in the articles "Sur la phénoménologie du langage,"[3] and "Le langage indirect et les voix du silence."[4] These are by no means the only sources of his thought on expression and language; they are simply the works wherein he discusses the problem explicitly. He makes very frequent mention of the role of language and bodily expression whenever the discussion centers upon man's experience of intersubjective

---

[3] This article was presented at the Colloque International de Phénoménologie, Bruxelles, 1951. It was printed in *Problèmes actuels de la phénoménologie,* Ed. Van Breda, 1952, pp. 81-109. It is also printed in *Signes,* pp. 105-22. References in this paper will be to *Problèmes* . . . .

[4] *S.,* pp. 4-104.

relations in one way or another; thus he also enters the discussion of language in his *Les relations avec autrui chez l'enfant*, in *Les sciences de l'homme et la phénoménologie*, and in general when he deals with man as a cultural being.

It is Merleau-Ponty's merit to have shown how the social character of language is revealed through the body, and to have made quite clear the intimate relation of thought to word. His study of the psychological behavior of the abnormal has convinced him that the word and language are far from being purely the result of a nervous mechanism in operation, even though one could study the operation from the purely mechanical point of view. This, of course, is not Merleau-Ponty's specific "discovery"—it takes little reflection to understand that the expression of words and language in general is much more than a stimulus-response process. Man has the capacity to speak, Merleau-Ponty says, just as the electric lamp has the capacity to light up; this is true from a purely physiological point of view. Since so many factors go to make up language—physiological, nervous, anatomical, psychological, etc., one can look upon it from any one of the above viewpoints and thus fragment language itself into so many parts: there can be spoken language to the exclusion of the written; the written to the exclusion of the spoken language. Thus one seems justified in concluding that the word is a "being of reason" in the most general meaning of the term.[5]

But for Merleau-Ponty language is much more than that. His psychological observations show that there is a connection between the power of language and the lived situation; it is clear that behind the word there is an attitude, a function of the word which conditions it.

---

[5]"Puisqu'il y à des troubles électifs, qui atteignent le langage parlé à l'exclusion du langage écrit, ou l'écriture à l'exclusion de la parole, et que le langage peut se désagréger par fragments, c'est qu'il se constitue par une série d'apports indépendants et que la parole au sens général est un être de raison. *P. P.*, p. 204.

Merleau-Ponty

Just what is the word for Merleau-Ponty? To put it in its most significant characterization, the word is the incarnation of the thought, or that wherein thought seeks its completion. As such then it immediately reveals its social character: for to what purpose would a thought seek an expression if not in order to be communicated to others? Indeed, Merleau-Ponty has stressed the social character of man's various forms of expression, but he has given primacy to language as the most explicit and significant social relation.

In fact, very significantly, Merleau-Ponty adds that the thought which is satisfied with existing for itself, that is, outside the word and communication, as soon as it has appeared will fall back into unconsciousness—it will not exist even for itself. He will deal at length with this aspect of language in his article "Sur la phénoménologie du langage." Making the point very clear: there is genuine thought only insofar as there is expression. Answering Kant's objection, he explicitly says:

> There is such an experience as thought in this sense, that we present ourselves our thoughts by the interior or exterior word. Such thought progresses instantaneously in flashes, but it is up to us to appropriate it, and it is by expressing it that we make it ours.[6]

Our thoughts are not real unless and until they are expressed. Language is therefore, then, the condition for thought; and because language is ultimately a bodily expression, we can in truth say that the body is the condition for thought. Hence Merleau-Ponty in attempting to describe the phenomenon of language, as well as that of bodily expression through gesture, will actually attempt to describe the genesis of thought.

Merleau-Ponty further points out that the naming of objects or things is not consequent to recognition of the same: it is precisely in the act of naming them that we recognize

---
[6] *P. P.*, p. 207.

them; the naming *is* the recognition. "God creates beings by naming them."[7]

In "Les relations avec autrui chez l'enfant" Merleau-Ponty clarifies this point by some very important observations: language must be conceived as an *operation for two*. There is a sort of indistinction between the act of speaking and the act of understanding. The word is understood only insofar as the hearer is ready to pronounce it; conversely, the subject who speaks is in a way transported in the one who listens. In a dialogue the participants "hold the two ends of the same cord, and it is this which explains how the phenomenon of speaking can pass into the phenomenon of understanding."[8]

At first sight one might think that the word understood brings nothing new to the listener and that the listener himself gives meaning to the speech heard—for there would be no understanding of words and expressions if the listener had not the power to grasp their meaning spontaneously. Therefore, consciousness would find in its own experience only that which it has put into it: with the result that there could be no communication at all. Does it simply mean that a certain consciousness has constructed a mechanical linguistic device by which it gives another consciousness the occasion to effectuate the same thoughts, but there is really nothing communicated from the one to the other? But how is it then that the consciousness in question really apprehends something? It cannot be that it has known it in advance. "The fact is that we have the power to understand beyond that which we spontaneously think."[9]

1. *The Word: Authentic or Empirical*

Of Merleau-Ponty's insights into the significance of the word and of language, that of the "authentic" word is worth

---
[7] *P. P.*, pp. 206-207.
[8] *R. A. E.*, p. 40.
[9] *P. P.*, p. 208.

considering in particular. He refers to the word which is uttered for the first time —not necessarily a new word (as to symbol or sound)—as the incarnation of a new thought; thus the child who has *named* a new thing, the lover who has discovered his love, the philosophers who have experienced a new "vision," or even "the first man who spoke," all express an authentic word—a word which is identical with the thought, in fact it is the thought which has thus found its incarnate expression. He contrasts this "authentic word" with the words used in everyday language: the latter he calls empirical language and maintains it is not creative, because it is made up of words and expressions which have become stereotyped by usage. Empirical language however, is derived from the creative.

> That which is "word" in the sense of empirical language—that is to say the recall, at an opportune moment, of the pre-established sign—is not word in regard to authentic language . . . [but] the true word, that which signifies . . . and delivers the captive meaning in the thing, is nothing but silence in relation to empirical usage, because it does not pass under a common name.[10]

Merleau-Ponty further asks: is the word an empty shell used to convey the significance of the thought? Or does the word itself have a meaning? Is human intercourse communion of intellects or an intersubjective exchange of man with man? He maintains that the thought *seeks* the word as its completion or its incarnation; the word is then not merely an accompaniment to thought. Since the thought is thought only in being expressed, even interiorly, in a creative or authentic word, then the word itself has a meaning—the very meaning of the thought it actualizes. Thus

---

[10] *S.*, p. 56. Cf. Kwant's criticism of this notion of silence: *Encounter*, pp. 36-37.

The Role of the Body in Man's Power of Communication

Merleau-Ponty concludes that one can overcome both empiricism and intellectualism by the simple admission that the word has a meaning. He further comments:

> If the word presupposed thought, if to speak were first of all to meet the object by an intellectual intention or by a representation, we could not understand why thought tends towards expression as towards an achievement, why the most familiar object seems indeterminate as long as we cannot recall its name, why the thinking subject himself is in a kind of ignorance of his own thoughts until he has formulated them to himself, or spoken them or written them, as is shown by the writer who does not know, when he first begins to write, just what he will produce.[11]

Thus a thought, an idea reaches its own fulfillment only when incarnate in the word—and not in any word whatsoever, but in just that word which is the idea's adequate expression (we admit this adequacy may not always be all that could be desired). It is this intimate relation of word to thought which accounts for Merleau-Ponty's conviction that the word *has* a meaning.

Kwant has this interesting comment on the subject:

> The idea that thought becomes itself in speech is concordant with the deeper essence of man. Man is embodied consciousness. The body is not a kind of living quarters for a spirit living a life all of its own. The spirit exists, realizes itself in the body. . . . Just as the person comes into full existence through embodiment, so does the thought, the idea exist in the word. . . . The "word" does not point to a reality already existing for us before it was named, but on the contrary it makes this reality exist for us. The "word" is not an acciden-

---
[11] *P. P.*, p. 206.

tal indication of a pre-existing vision, but it makes this vision exist.[12]

No one would dispute Merleau-Ponty's contention that we become familiar with a previously unknown thought by means of the "word"; however, how this takes place is a little less obvious. It is not sufficient to listen to another's word or to become acquainted with the printed page—the whole of which already implies a familiarity with the language used by the speaker or writer. We must further be familiar with the author's empirical language (Merleau-Ponty has specified this empirical language as the available wealth of words in common use: in any given case, different disciplines would differ in the empirical language used). Moreover, we must observe that the artist or the philosopher never uses the empirical language as given; the use they make of it transforms the words, so that they become creative or authentic words.

It is difficult, Merleau-Ponty observes, to understand the meanings of a language expressing a new thought—for instance that of a philosopher. It is then that we must explore first its possibilities existentially, by approaching the philosopher himself by a kind of sympathy. Then, if we do not grasp the thought at first, we at least become acquainted with the philosopher's own style, and this will facilitate our understanding of his language and thought. This grasp will come only after we have discovered the new meaning which his words embody in the context; hence, we must say that, no matter how painfully and slowly, we have become acquainted with the new philosophy by means of the *word*. "Ultimately, a language 'teaches' itself [s'enseigne] and signifies its own meaning in the mind of the hearer."[13]

The same thing happens in the artistic forms of expression we have in music and painting. Both music and paint-

---
[12]Kwant, *Encounter*, p. 37.
[13]*P. P.*, p. 209.

ing, if not at first understood, end up by "creating" their own public—if they truly "say" something they "secrete their own meaning." What about poetry and prose? Literature is less made up of common words than of that which it does to them: it modifies them, it transforms them into a new signification; the author himself does not have recourse to a ready-made language. He uses words which please him because they are in themselves (that is without relation to other models) just that which he creatively expresses; their perfection is not patterned after anything else except the words themselves. Hence, poetry and literary prose are perhaps the best examples of language expressing "authentic and creative words." This explains the distinctive uniqueness of each work of art in literature even though we don't always realize the power of words with which we are already familiar, but which the writer has transformed. Just as in painting or in music each stroke of the brush and each sound create a unique artistic expression, so in literature each word embodying a new meaning creates the inimitable expression which it is in its own unique language.[14]

There are really no merely exterior relations between thought and word; on the contrary one cannot be extricated from the other. "The speaker does not think before speaking, nor while he speaks: his word is his thought."[15] This can be seen in the case of a discourse; if the reader of a text is successfully expressing himself, then we are fully occupied with the words which give us at the same time the full meaning of the thought which they embody. This complete domination of our attention and understanding by the meaningful words proves to be such an enjoyment and a fulfilled expectation that the end of the reading (or of the discourse) "will be the end of an enchanting experience."[16]

---

[14]Cf. *P. P.*, pp. 210-11; also *Signes*, pp. 53-56.
[15]*P. P.*, p. 209: "L'orateur ne pense pas avant de parler, ni même pendant qu'il parle; sa parole est sa pensée."
[16]*P. P.*, p. 209.

Another experience resulting from the meaning of the spoken or written words will be this: we may come to a clear understanding of the whole discourse or text, for the whole meaning had already been present as a general thought.

The word is present to the speaker and to the hearer: there is no need to represent to oneself the word (in terms of physiological configuration or as a sound). It is sufficient to know its articulation and tonal mode as a possible usage of my body—as it suffices for a spatial movement that I actually make it without representing it to myself beforehand. Thus my body is involved in the word, for the word is a modality of the global consciousness of my body.[17]

What is the role of the body in my memory of words and language in general? The role of the body in memory, for Merleau-Ponty, can be understood only if memory is considered not as a continuing stream of consciousness, but as an effort to re-open time regressing from the present and considering our body as the medium of our relations with the past as well as of our lived "behavior." This, it must be admitted, is a rather different way of accounting for memory. Merleau-Ponty says that "the body displays in a panorama of the past the former attitude which it recaptures, then it projects in effective movement an intention of movement, because it is a power of natural expression."[18]

From the above discussion Merleau-Ponty comes to some conclusions about the nature of the word: it is not the "sign" of the thought—if one intends by "sign" that which announces something else—but it is thought itself. The re-

---

[17] *P. P.*, pp. 210-11.
[18] *P. P.*, p. 211: "La fonction du corps dans la mémoire est cette même fonction de projection que nous avons déjà rencontrée dans l'initiation cinétique: le corps convertit en vocifération une certaine essence motrice, déploie en phénomènes sonores le style articulaire d'un mot, déploie en panorama du passé l'attitude ancienne qu'il reprend, projette en mouvement effectif, une intention de mouvement parce qu'il est un pouvoir d'expression naturelle."

lation which obtains between thought and word is not exterior; on the contrary they are mutually enveloped in each other; meaning is caught up in the word which is not just the means of fixing or establishing the meaning, but exteriorized meaning itself.

> It must be that, in one way or another, the sentence and the word cease to be a manner of designating the object, or the thought, in order to become the presence of this thought in the sensible world; not its garb, but its emblem or its body.[19]

And words could not be the stronghold of thought nor could thought seek expression unless words themselves were already a comprehensible text possessed of a power of signification of their own.

The passage just quoted represents the central point of Merleau-Ponty's theory of language and expression; actually, it is nothing new, for the whole of his philosophy is constructed around the dialectical synthesis of moments, be they significations of body and soul, corporeity and existence, or the various syntheses of sexuality, spatiality, perception and intersubjectivity. The body comes up at every level to mediate our contact with the world, with our experiences and with the significations and meanings of other incarnate spirits. It is always the body which carries on the mediating function in the relational world of nature as well as of culture.

2. Relation of Word to Concept

Merleau-Ponty is aware of the fact that, as psychologists maintain, there must be a "linguistic concept" or a verbal concept upon which the language itself may be founded as upon a central experience; this central experience must of necessity be specifically verbal so that, in virtue of it, the

---

[19] *P. P.*, p. 212.

sound of the word, understood, pronounced—or even read—may reveal the language, or rather make up the language (formally that is). This permits the patients to read a text, even to pronounce the words correctly without however understanding the meaning of the words or of the sentences. There is therefore a first layer of signification in words and sentences which is their very own and which reveals thought itself as a style, as affective value and existential, before becoming a conceptual enunciation. In this existential signification found in the world-expressing-thought, Merleau-Ponty discovers a meaning which is not construed by the conceptual significations, yet it embodies them and is inseparable from them. The great merit of expression, when it is successful, is "to make signification exist as a thing in the very heart of the text itself, to make it live by an organism of expression, to instill in the writer or in the reader a kind of new organ of sense, and to open a new field or a new dimension to our experience."[20]

"This power of expression is well known in the arts, for example in music."[21] Here Merleau-Ponty shows in detail the relation of the sign to the signification—an indication of the closely knit relation of thought to word. The illustration of music will be valid for language. The signification of the "sonata" is inseparable from the sounds which carry it: before we hear it, it is quite impossible, by dint of analysis, to guess or predict what it would be; and once the execution of the sonata is over, we can only re-live the experience in its existential moment not recapture it by intellectual analysis; during the execution of the music itself, the "sounds"

---

[20] *P. P.*, pp. 212-13. The fact that expression can preserve the thought in writing is not so important for Merleau-Ponty; he maintains that the great works give us at the first reading all that which they will ever reveal to us; this might be disputed, at least for certain books and for certain readers.

[21] *P. P.*, p. 213.

are not "signs" of the sonata, but "the sonata is there, through and by them, it 'resides' in them"—the sounds *are* the music. The same thing is true of acting: the actor disappears and the character takes over—it appears as that which is signified. Thus, "the signification devours the 'sign.'" The aesthetic expression either confers on that which it expresses an existence in-itself, or it takes away the signs themselves (the person of the comedian, the color and the canvas of the painter) from their empirical existence and raises them to another world.[22]

In aesthetics, it is clear, expression is signification. But Merleau-Ponty holds that the same may be said of the expression of thought by word, for thought does not exist outside the word and outside of the expression. True, we refer to thoughts already formed before our expressions: we mean by them the ideas already constituted and already expressed which give us the illusion of an interior life. But actually that silence is filled with words (already available) and this interior life is an interior language; "pure" thought is nothing but a void of consciousness. By accepting a new signification in terms of a signification already disponible, that is, resulting from previous acts of expression (we are not speaking here of a creative or authentic word) we construct a net of significations and a new cultural being results.

> There is at this moment a new simultaneous constitution of thought and expression . . . similar to the movement of the body lending itself to a new gesture in the acquisition of a habit. The word is, in fact, a veritable gesture with its own meaning, much as the physical gesture has its. It is this immanent meaning which renders communication possible.[23]

---

[22] *P. P.*, p. 213. Cf. *S.*, pp. 56ff.
[23] *P. P.*, pp. 213-14.

As was pointed out previously, there is no more "pure" thought than there is "pure" human spirit—that is, not incarnate. However, it is interesting to note that Merleau-Ponty, in another context, speaking of the dialectic of thought and word affirms that all language is allusive and indirect, "or, if one wants to say so, silence."[24] It is not a contradiction, even though, being from a later work, it might represent a change in position. He simply means that there is ambiguity in language just as there is ambiguity in every man's existential expressions—an ambiguity which comes from the materiality or corporeity of language, dependent as the latter is on bodily expression.[25]

But there is another and more profound meaning in maintaining that language may be simply "silence": there are things which are not said because to say them would be to efface them; it is not necessary to "say" something explicitly in order to communicate: in certain cases our language speaks the loudest, the strongest, when it refuses to say a thing. When emotions are deeply involved, then language often becomes silent; but this silence is not less expressive than the word. To refuse to take a position is already a position. Merleau-Ponty will return often on this point when-

---

[24] *S.*, *p.* 54: "Or, si nous chassons de notre esprit l'idée d'un *texte original* dont notre langage serait la traduction ou la version chiffrée, nous verrons que l'idée d'une expression *complète* fait non-sens, que tout langage est indirect ou allusif, est, si l'on veut, silence."

[25] *S.*, pp. 55ff. Cf. *P.P.*, pp. 462-63: "Le *Cogito* tacite, la présence de soi à soi, étant l'existence même, est antérieur à toute philosophie, mais il ne se connait que dans les situations limites où il et menacé: par exemple dans l'angoisse de la mort ou dans celle du regard d'autrui sur moi. Ce qu'on croit être la pensée de la pensée, comme pur sentiment de soi ne se pense pas encore et a besoin d'être révélé. La conscience qui conditionne le langage n'est qu'une saisie globale et inarticule du monde, comme celle de l'enfant à son première souffle ou de l'homme qui va se noyer et se rue vers la vie, et s'il est vrai que tout savoir particulier est fondé sur cette premier vue, il est vrai aussi qu'elle attend d'être reconquise, fixée et explicite par l'exploration perceptive et par la parole. . . . Le *Cogito* tacite n'est *Cogito* que lorsqu'il s'est exprimé lui-même."

ever dealing with the existential position of man-in-the-world.[26]

3. Language. An Encounter

The possibility of communication, Merleau-Ponty has said, results from the meaning which is already contained in the word as a true gesture. But this is not sufficient; nor is it sufficient to know the language and vocabulary of the others. When I communicate, I actually come to an encounter with another whose personal being endorses a certain view of the world, just as much as I endorse the view of my world. Hence in this communication there is much ambiguity: our mutual relation is not clearly defined in expressed significations, it is rather a mutual expectation for an intention, the one from the other; hence, not yet at the intellectual level, a kind of meeting of existences takes place wherein each seeks to synchronize his existence to that of the other. The language used for the meeting may be simply that of words and phrases already "disponible" for which a signification is already at hand. There seems to be no special effort needed for communication of thoughts already formed and previously expressed. Understanding seems to take care of itself with the expressions of common language. This is the reason why we somewhat take the linguistic intersubjective exchange for granted; our reflections are carried out in the interior of a world already speaking and already spoken to. We actually lose sight of the contingent in our communication: this happens not only to the child who is learning to speak, but even to the creative writer who has suddenly seen a new light or to the man who witnesses an event which evokes a response: then silence is transformed into words. Then we come to the moment of realization: "everyday language" pre-supposes expressions already accomplished by a personal decision.

---

[26] *P. P.*, pp. 214-15. Cf. *S.*, pp. 55ff.

But our view of man will remain superficial, Merleau-Ponty asserts, unless we discover beyond the constituted word the primordial silence, and describe the gesture which has broken that silence—in other words, unless we discover the genesis of the signification in its nakedness and novelty, for, "the word is a gesture and its signification a world."[27] What that silence is for Merleau-Ponty can be gathered from his comparison of language to the work of art—main concern of his article on "Le langage indirect et les voix du silence."

> It is necessary to consider the word before it is pronounced, the foundation [root] of silence which never ceases to encompass it, without which the word would say nothing—or better, to bare the threads of silence of which it [the word] is intermingled.[28]

The truly expressive word, like the truly great work of art, is the authentic, creative word in its very moment of creation. It is not one already fossilized, so to speak, in the store of significations already defined; rather it is one which, of all the possibilities of expression, is the only one capable of expressing the insight or the vision of "this" particular moment.

4. Communication Without Words—Through the Body

Expression without word is another and more primitive form of communication—as well as a more direct way of reaching the other or of manifesting ourselves. Psychologically, it is proven that the witness to an expressive gesture is not first concerned with what the gesture would mean in his

---

[27] *P. P.*, p. 214. In the second part of "Sur la phénoménologie du langage" in *Problèmes* . . ., pp. 92-102, Merleau-Ponty studies in some detail the origin of language. Cf. Kwant, *Encounter*, p. 37 for interesting observation of topic of silence. He calls "silence" a "vision" and maintains that Merleau-Ponty has not been faithful to experience here.
[28] *S.*, p. 58.

own case. Gesture reveals meaning directly. I read anger directly, and not as a psychological meaning behind the gesture. That is, when I see an angry gesture I do not "think" of anger, I *see* it.[29] But the meaning of a gesture is not perceived as the color of an object is perceived. If it were, then I would grasp the meaning of mimic in beings other than human—as a matter of fact, I do not (except insofar as the science of psychology reveals it to me). This shows that to understand gesture I must in some way belong to the milieu wherein the person in question acts. It would be very difficult for a twentieth century man to understand the gestures of the cave man. I could not understand gesture or expression of persons whose milieu is too different from mine. Also, I would not understand the meaning of a certain expression if there were nothing in my experience to make me capable of giving it meaning. Even though, often, the knowledge of another is a help to self-knowledge, the gesture is not understood of itself: it is "understood," not simply given, that is to say, it is recaptured by an act of the spectator himself.

> The whole difficulty consists in rightly conceiving such an act without confusing it with an operation of knowledge. The communication or comprehension of gesture is obtained by the reciprocity of my intentions and the gestures of others, or of my gestures and the readable intention in the conduct of others. Everything happens as if the intention of others resides in my own body and mine in theirs.[30]

Merleau-Ponty maintains that the gesture of which I am witness designates and points out an intentional object which becomes actual and is fully understood when the

---

[29] *P. P.*, p. 215: ". . . Je ne perçois pas la colère ou la menace comme un fait psychique caché derrière le geste, je lis la colère dans le geste, le geste ne me *fait pas penser* à la colère, il est la colère elle-même."
[30] *P. P.*, p. 215.

powers of my body recover it and adapt to it. A gesture is at first a question put to me, an indication of a certain sensible direction of the world, and an invitation to follow it. If I do, communication occurs. At such a moment there is a confirmation of the other by me and of me by the other. Therefore, the closer to experience our understanding of a thing is, the nearer we are to a genuine grasp of the phenomenon in question. This holds true for perception in general as well as for the understanding of expression in interpersonal relations. Therefore, in perception as well as in language, not intellectual construction, but experience plays the decisive role. My engagement in things, by my body, is a coexistence with them of my incarnate self; this community of subject and things has nothing to do with a scientific objective construction.

In the same way, I understand the gesture of others, not by a common intellectual interpretation of the same, but by a sort of blind judgment or acknowledgment (my body's) previous to any elaboration of meaning. How is it that generation after generation understands naturally certain gestures without having been taught their meanings? For instance, the gestures of love, the expressions of grief are quite spontaneous and are easily understood; they are not taught. It is always by my body that I understand the others, as it is through my body that I perceive things. The meaning of the gesture is therefore one with the very structure of the world—that very world which my gesture outlines and signifies. And the meanings and significations of both are open to me in the same ambiguous and existential way in which all other intersubjective dimensions are at my disposal.[31]

---

[31] *P. P.*, pp. 216-17. Cf. *Problèmes* . . . , pp. 94-95. In relation to understanding others, Kwant observes: "Merleau-Ponty realizes that our life, no matter how much it is a participation in the common movement of life, is, nonetheless, à synthesis of this common movement and that, therefore, interpersonal contact is a real problem." (*Phenomenological Philosophy,* p. 59).

The Role of the Body in Man's Power of Communication

5. Gestures: Natural or Conventional Signs?

Merleau-Ponty admits that there is a difference between gesture and word, even though both are direct means of communication; gesture, of the two, is the least conventional—although some gestures develop in the context of a culture only. However, both expressions have their own inner meaning. This must be admitted specially in the case of a developed language or one would not even understand the possibility of language itself. Further, while gesture is limited to indicate a certain relation of man to the world and to other men, language has a more enlarged purpose: its communicative aim is cultural in addition to being a spontaneous exchange between men. The question of the "natural" and "conventional" sign is relevant here: is the gesture a "natural" sign and language a "conventional" one? Merleau-Ponty observes that to develop a system of "conventional" signs a sort of communication must already be in use. Therefore, it is quite difficult to say that language is conventional and gesture natural. Of course, we might say that the gesture is itself a sort of language, in which case we might say that a natural sign has developed into a conventional system—which is probably as close to what happened historically as any other supposition. Merleau-Ponty, unwilling as he always is to make any hard and fast distinctions, is of the opinion that nothing in the construction of a language is completely arbitrary and that even a "natural" sign is modified by a cultural influence one way or another. What is of more importance for him is this: in any event, both natural and conventional modes of expression are bodily expressions and living ones, not artificial constructions. Not even the sounds of a language are purely arbitrary, but they are the way a certain people "celebrate the world and live it."[32] Although Merleau-Ponty does not at-

---

[32] *P. P.*, p. 218. That is why no language can be translated perfectly, and fully, into another.

tempt to give any reasons for the differences in language—and there is no need for, perhaps no possibility of, any reason—he can in a way account for the differences since he maintains language is an expression of a lived world, not of an "objective" one. To assimilate a language completely one must assume the world which the language expresses. This is quite true, but it does not give us a clue as to the why of the different worlds of our experience; they are so different that they are expressed in languages which, at times, have practically nothing in common.

Obviously, then, a universal language would at present at least be impossible—presumably it would have to express a universal thought. Such a language would be "pure" convention and would serve, not to express man or the world, but only the store of words which are available to men in every more or less developed language. Such a language would never express Nature without man. Merleau-Ponty concludes:

> There are then, strictly speaking, no conventional signs, notations of pure thought and clear by themselves; there are only words within which is contracted the whole history of a language and which accomplish their communication without any guaranty, in the midst of incredible risks in the linguistic field.[33]

Even if universality of language were attained, says Merleau-Ponty, it would not be a language which furnishes us with a foundation to all possible languages, but rather an aid to pass from the language which I speak—and which I live, since it has initiated me to the phenomena of expression—to other languages for which expression is of an altogether different style. Yet no comparison could effectually be made among given languages except perhaps insofar as

---

[33] *P. P.*, p. 219.

they are human expressions—but no common element could be found to designate a unique structure.

Merleau-Ponty thinks it is an illusion to believe that language is a mode of communication more transparent than other forms—such as music or art perhaps—in spite of the fact that we have at our disposal, in most languages, a system of well coordinated expressions and means of expressions which can be put to use in what he calls empirical or common language (i.e., dictionaries, definitions, etc.).

Although it does have some advantages—for instance it is susceptible of more exact employment—Merleau-Ponty insists that it cannot be placed above music for instance, simply because the latter is tied to the very sounds which compose it for its meanings. For, language, in spite of its supposed clarity, rests on an obscure foundation;

> if we were to search far enough we would find that language, like music, does not express anything else than itself, and it is also inseparable from its expression. We would discover its genesis in the emotional gestures by which man has changed the given world into a world according to man.[34]

It is probably by basing his observations of language on this notion of an obscure beginning that Merleau-Ponty develops his theme of figure-background also in relation to language. He is true to his schemata of experience. Thus language, detaching itself from an obscure background, can never be clearly defined or detached from the ambiguity in which the world is shrouded.

For the same reason Merleau-Ponty maintains that it is plain nonsense to speak about natural and conventional signs; to him no sign is purely natural and no signification purely conventional. Man as a purely natural being does not exist; he is always influenced by interaction with the world

---

[34] *P. P.*, p. 219.

and with other men, so that no purely natural sign can come from him;[35] "one could speak of 'natural signs' only if to given 'states of consciousness' the anatomical organization of our body were to cause corresponding definite gestures."[36] But this is far from being the case: human beings act and react differently in different parts of the world. It is not only the gesture which is contingent with regard to corporeal organization, but also the manner of accepting and living a situation. The difference of mimics reveals a difference of emotions. "It is not sufficient for two subjects to have the same organs and the same kind of nervous system in order to express the same emotions by the same signs on a given situation."[37] Each makes a different usage of his body—as was observed in connection with sexuality—and that usage will reflect both his emotions and his world. There is no natural universal sign, because there is not either an instinct or a human nature given once and for all.

> The use which a man makes of his body as human is transcendental with respect to the body as purely biological. It is neither more natural nor less conventional to cry in anger or to embrace in love than to call a table a table.[38]

---

[35] And yet, some signs are more nearly natural and less conventional than others. Plato discusses this in the *Cratylus*. From a first position, that there is no correctness in names other than convention (*Cratylus*, 384), to the contention that a name is the instrument which distinguishes natures (389b), to the supposition that the gods must certainly call things by their right names (391b), and finally to the admission that convention also has a part in the naming of things (435a), Plato admits both natural and conventional signs. And to know names is to know things (435b).

[36] *P. P.*, p. 220. "Or en fait la mimique de la colère ou celle de l'amour n'est pas la même chez un Japonais et chez un occidental. Plus précisément, la différence des mimiques recouvre une différence des émotions elles-mêmes."

[37] Cf. *P. P.*, pp. 182 ff. "Il faut qu'il y ait un Eros ou une Libido qui animent un monde original, donnent valeur ou signification sexuelle aux stimuli extérieurs et dessinent pour chaque sujet l'usage qu'il fera de son corps objectif," p. 182. Cf. *supra*, Ch. V.

[38] *P. P.*, p. 220.

The Role of the Body in Man's Power of Communication

The above seems to be a bit startling; yet, it may well be true. Anthropological studies have discovered so many and so varied modes of expression that Merleau-Ponty's contention may well have a good foundation in experience. Yet, it seems too strong to assert that sentiments and passionate behavior are as much an invention as words are. However, as would be natural with Merleau-Ponty, these affirmations only lead to another sort of ambiguity—or, rather, they only end up by disclosing that in man nothing is possibly all one way or all another: thus nothing in man is purely natural and nothing is completely artificial, as if, upon man's natural being a cultural and spiritual superstructure were to be superimposed. The fact is that "all is natural and all is fabricated" in man; that is to say, there is not a type of behavior which does not in some way have a foundation in the biological; yet, at the same time, the same behavior surpasses the purely animal level of life; and there is no behavior which does not also surpass the vital level and attain to the human and thus to the spiritual. (We may recall here the three levels of structuration which Merleau-Ponty described in *La structure du comportement*.)

Then Merleau-Ponty observes how changed is the physical world even by one level of life, the animal; how much more does the presence of man give meaning to the world, for the manifestation of such behavior transforms in signification the irrational power of the world, and makes communication possible. The word is, for him, one case of this world-power of communication, but a special one because it alone not only achieves an intersubjectivity, but it has consciousness of sharing the world with others; other forms of expression, for instance music, do not have such consciousness. Merleau-Ponty does not explain the difference, but observes that in the case of language, the word can be indefinitely repeated, one can also speak about the word—whereas one cannot paint on the painting. The philosopher has dreamed about a word which would bound them all, (has sought for a thought of all thought—which would have to *be* word) but neither the musician, nor the painter could hope to exhaust all music or all painting.[39] Hence, Merleau-Ponty concludes that language has a privileged place— "there is therefore a privilege of Reason, but precisely in order to understand it properly, we must begin by replacing thought among the phenomena of expression."[40]

Thus the real point at issue is existential. That is why the pre-eminence of the word as a phenomenon of expression rather than as an intellectual signification is important for the study of the abnormal. Merleau-Ponty observes that recent studies of pathological conditions such as that of aphasia, reveal a clear movement towards an existential approach. A theory is being developed which considers man in his relation to the world precisely in that activity by which, through his body, "man projects himself towards a world."[41]

---

[39] Not that the perspective of finding a word which could embrace all words and exhaust all expression would be a very happy one. But language can try to accomplish it, whereas the other means of communication cannot even try it. That is, if we distinguish between spoken language and the system of notations by which the verbal expression is transcribed and preserved, we can conceive of a notational system universally valid, and capable not only of expressing in symbols universal thought, but also of making this thought available in any and every language. A system of this kind would certainly approximate the philosophers' dream of "a thought of all thoughts." But perhaps, the reason why the word encompassing all words has not yet been found is that language also is an art and as such it cannot be bound and completed, it is rather always open to wider horizons of expression.

[40] *P. P.*, p. 222. Cf. De Waelhens, *Une Philosophie* . . ., pp. 160-61. ". . . Le langage est . . . le seul capable d'édifier un acquis auquel il renvoie au cours de son propre progrès."

[41] *P. P.*, p. 223. Merleau-Ponty studies this problem in detail; he shows that the patient who fails to recognize colors, for instance, is not just forgetting the verbal expression, does not just lose the "thought of" or the knowledge of the color; it is the experience of the color itself which is behind the failure; that is to say, he does not have the thought because he does not know the "name" of the color, he does not recognize it. Cf. *P. P.*, pp. 222-25.

The Role of the Body in Man's Power of Communication

As he has constantly showed by concrete cases both from the normal and the abnormal, Merleau-Ponty holds that the attitude of man before the world is not pure thought, but existential relatedness. The "interior" of language, if we wish to call it that, is not thought closed within itself, but thought expressed; the word expresses, through the phonetic sound, a certain structuration of experience of the speaking subject, who is taking a position in the world by every act of exterior signification through both language and gesture.

> From the moment in which man makes use of language to establish a living relation with himself or with his likes, language is no longer an instrument, *it is no longer a means, it is a manifestation, a revelation of the intimate being and of the psychic link which unites us to the world and to our fellowmen.*[42]

But whether it be question of my body or of that of another, I have no way of knowing the human body except by living it,[43] that is to say, by recapturing the drama which goes through me and making myself one with it. "I am therefore my body to the extent, at least, that I have an experience; reciprocally, my body is as a natural subject, a provisional sketch of my total being."[44] For this reason Merleau-Ponty thinks that the experience of the body is opposed to the intellectual reflection which disengages the object from the subject, thus giving us merely the thought of the body or the body in idea rather than the experience of the body in reality.

---

[42] *P. P.*, p. 229.
[43] How I can "live" another's body Merleau-Ponty does not say expressly—however, from his former remarks we may infer that it could only be through intersubjective relations. Cf. *S. C.*, Ch. IV.
[44] *P. P.*, p. 231.

Merleau-Ponty is so convinced of the ambiguous reciprocity of body and spirit that he reiterates his position thus:

> If our union with the body is substantial, how could we experience in ourselves a pure soul and from thence accede to an Absolute Spirit? Before posing this question, let us consider well all that which is implied in the rediscovery of our own body. It is not only an object among all others which resists reflection and is so to speak glued to a subject. Obscurity gets the better of the whole perceived world.[45]

The above passage leaves us in no doubt with regard to Merleau-Ponty's belief about the spirituality of the soul, or rather, the substantiality and independence—ontological—of man's spirit. The spirit, as form of the body, would naturally *be* only insofar as the body it informs *is*. Admitting, however, as he does, that obscurity is here overwhelming, he reserves judgment on the matter. Yet, we may well foresee that further elucidations will not lead in any other direction: Merleau-Ponty is, so to speak, bound by his own conception of the relation of spirit to matter, and further studies will only emphasize the mystery, not help to solve it.

6. *The Phenomenology of Language*

Merleau-Ponty's investigation of language is taken up again in the article "Sur la phénoménologie du langage"[46]; though not the taking of a new position, his discussion reveals more directly the concern with phenomenological assessment of the same problem—from Husserl's viewpoint also.

---
[45] *P. P.*, p. 232.
[46] Reference has already been made to the above article in *Problèmes*. . . . Since it is quite representative of the author's investigation of the problem of language, we will have a closer look at it.

The Role of the Body in Man's Power of Communication

Admitting that Husserl had treated this problem more freely than others and that he had placed it in a central position, he thinks there is need for a more profound questioning of phenomenology, not only to follow in Husserl's footsteps, but to continue his own study by taking up the movement of his (Husserl's) reflection, rather than his thesis. Of the two positions which Merleau-Ponty attributes to Husserl, he would accept the one more consonant with his own notion of phenomenology—and this is the position taken by the late Husserl. Of the early position Merleau-Ponty had this to say: such a system of language as Husserl advocated would be a constituted language; an object before thought, language would not play any part except that of an accompaniment, a substitute, a memory aid—it would be a secondary means of communication in relation to thought. Such language would have the advantage of being one with consciousness, fully constituted, and capable of total explicitation.

Nothing could be further from the notion of Merleau-Ponty of what language discloses itself to be experientially. But the notion of the late Husserl, as Merleau-Ponty sees it, comes closer to experience: now language appears as an original way of seeing certain objects, as the body of thought, or even as the operation by which thought will acquire inter-subjective value and finally ideal existence. Philosophic thought reflecting on language will then be enveloped and situated in language itself.[47] It is easy to see why Merleau-Ponty would accept the late Husserl: for him (Merleau-Ponty) the phenomenological attitude to be adopted is not an effort at universalization, but a return to the speaking subject.

Merleau-Ponty's intention in the article is to reexamine the phenomenology of language and then the notions of intersubjectivity, rationality, and the philosophy implied by

---
[47] *Problèmes* . . ., p. 92.

phenomenology. Much of his discussion is a return to the topics already taken up in the *Phénoménologie de la perception*. He then examines the possibility of an history of language and the likelihood of a development of new forms of expression chiefly as a result of usage[48]; the theme of his philosophy is clearly seen in his contention that in language, as in all of the dialectical relations of man with the world and with others, there is much ambiguity. Language is always full of latent possibilities, hence never composed of absolutely univocal significations completely transparent to consciousness. Hence language is never

> a system of manners of significations clearly articulated one over the other, nor an edifice of ideas linguistically constructed according to a rigorous plan, but an ensemble of linguistic convergent gestures of which each will be defined less by a signification than by its use-value.[49]

Thus, particular languages will never be founded on some previous universalized forms; on the contrary it will not even be possible to achieve a universalization of signification if attempted as a universal language—for the simple reason that there is no such a thing as a universal human nature in the strict sense.[50] Even if I achieve a sort of generalization of expression by learning many languages, this is also quite limited: I only learn an equivalence of one expression for another; I do not really find in them a common categorical unique structure.[51]

---

[48] Merleau-Ponty thinks that the becoming of language is a sort of equilibrium in movement: when certain forms of language have lost their expressiveness through too much use, new forms are created by the subjects who really want to communicate—and this is done on the very emptiness created by the loss of meanings, and herein a dialectic is in progress. *Problèmes* . . . , pp. 94-95.
[49] *Problèmes* . . . , p. 95.
[50] *P. P.*, pp. 218ff.
[51] This topic has also been treated in *Phénoménologie de la perception*, pp. 218ff. Cf. *Problèmes* . . . , p. 95.

The Role of the Body in Man's Power of Communication

Discussing the quasi-corporeity of the "signifying," Merleau-Ponty points out that the word is not a product of intellectualization, but a corporeal one. There is a signification of language which is really a mediation between my intention and the expression still unspoken—the surprising thing is that sometimes the very word I express "surprises me and teaches me my own thought."[52] I am vividly aware of the scope of my gestures and of the spatiality of my body by which I communicate with the world, and if I do not reflect on it, the consciousness of my body is immediately significative of a whole environment. In the same way my word as well as my gesture is pregnant with signification to the point that a hesitation, an alteration of the voice, a choice of a certain syntax suffice to modify it. Yet all expressions appear to me impalpable, ideas are present to me in a sort of transparence, and all effort to take possession of the thought which resides in the word is futile—that is, it is futile to attempt to grasp the thought apart from the word.[53]

Further, "signification animates the word as the world animates my body." The significations of the word are always poles of a certain number of acts of signification which animate the discourse, but are not given directly of themselves and our expression is never total even if it seems to be so. "It is not because it expresses totally that it is ours, but it is because it is ours that we think it expresses totally."[54] There is always something hinted at in an expression. However, that does not imply imperfection. Rather, all expression is perfect if it admits the fundamental fact that the signified exceed the signifying; further, the transcendent expression of signification is an operation to which we have recourse not only to communicate, but also to take possession of the meaning of our thoughts, ourselves.[55] Again the

---
[52] *Problèmes* . . ., p. 97.
[53] *Problèmes* . . ., p. 97.
[54] *Problèmes* . . ., p. 98.
[55] Cf. *S.*, pp. 53-59.

notion of the body is used to express the incarnation of the word:

> The intentional signification gives itself a body and knows itself in seeking for an equivalent in the system of disponible significations which represent the language I speak and the ensemble of the writings and of the culture of which I am heir.[56]

7. *Philosophical Implications of the Phenomenology of Language*

Merleau-Ponty admits that the relation of the phenomenological analyses to philosophy proper is not clear. Often such investigations are considered merely preparatory and Husserl himself distinguished between phenomenological research in a large sense and philosophy. Hence, Merleau-Ponty admits contrarily to his assertion in the Preface to *Phénoménologie de la perception* it is difficult to maintain that phenomenology coincides with philosophy.[57] If the philosophic subject were a completely transparent consciousness there would be no problem to pass from phenomenology to philosophy. If there is a problem it is because man is steeped in ambiguity; reflection then, must focus on the mode of presence of the object and of the subject as they would appear phenomenologically and not as presented by intellectualized concepts derived from total reflection. But since—Merleau-Ponty insists—"phenomenology is all en-

---

[56] *Problèmes* . . ., p. 99.

[57] *Problèmes* . . ., p. 102. Since, according to Merleau-Ponty and Husserl's own admission the phenomenological investigation is never completely transcended—there is never a complete reduction—phenomenology is already a philosophy. That is to say, for Merleau-Ponty at least, the phenomenological investigation does not result in pure essences, but it retains existence—hence an ontological dimension perhaps?—and in this sense one is engaged in a metaphysics already, not merely in a phenomenological study. But this is pure interpretation: Merleau-Ponty has not spelled this out.

compassing with regard to philosophy, it cannot be simply joined to it."[58]

To Merleau-Ponty this is clear with regard to the phenomenology of language. If the word is as we have described it, he asks, how will the phenomenology of the word be other than a philosophy of the word? What further elucidation could we possibly make? "We must absolutely stress the philosophical meaning of the return to the word."[59]

However, Merleau-Ponty warns us that the relations of body and world, of word and thought cannot be considered merely psychological, for then all relations would be but appearances. Most certainly, I cannot say that the phenomenon of incarnation is merely an appearance, or a result of constitution. Rather, it is thanks to the perception of others, and through it, that I know, inevitably, my own body as a spontaneity. He points out that the position of others as other "myself" is not possible if I have to constitute them; for it would mean that I should constitute the other as constituting, that is, as constituting me in the act of my constituting him. Husserl saw and bypassed this difficulty; Merleau-Ponty criticizes him for not seeking a solution; since I do have the idea of the other I must in some way have surmounted the difficulty—this seems to be the implied contention for Husserl. But for Merleau-Ponty there is no need to live the contradiction which would ensue from this position. He states that "this subject, which experiences himself constituted at the moment he functions as constituent is my body."[60]

Merleau-Ponty describes in detail how this perception of the other's body occurs. Since when I perceive another I am at the same time perceived by the other (that is, in the case

---
[58] *Problèmes* . . ., p. 102.
[59] *Problèmes* . . ., p. 103.
[60] Herein we have Merleau-Ponty's clear enunciatoin of his term "body-subject, by which he refers to the body as animated. *Problèmes* . . ., p. 104.

of mutual perception). I am caught up by a second "myself" outside of myself. I am invested by the other at the same time I am investing the other by my glance. It seems here that object and subject exchange places. The same happens—Merleau-Ponty holds—with regard to language. As in certain ordinary cases of behavior I give the value of subject to certain objects (a body can also be viewed as an object) and thus reverse the ordinary way of relation (as a subject I have "objects"), so in the case of the word I reverse the usual procedure: that is to say, as I cannot consider the living body as a mere object—because it is a "body-subject" (mine or other's) so I cannot objectivize the word, because it is as much an incarnation as the body is; the word is the incarnation of the thought, hence it must be held as ultimate phenomenon and constitutive of others.[61]

The above seems a rather strong assertion; yet it is not surprising if we admit that the thought *is* only if incarnate: our constitution of the other does involve thought. Merleau-Ponty however goes a step further: unwilling as he is to give phenomenology only a second place, he affirms that if phenomenology does not truly involve our conception of being and our philosophy "we will find ourselves, when confronted by a philosophical problem, before the same problems already raised by phenomenology. In a sense, phenomenology is either all or nothing."[62]

However, I must recognize that I also have a relation to a world which is already constituted. Hence my references to this world and to the other subjects always imply more than I express, so that there is not just an equivalence between the signifying and the signified, strictly speaking. My word, my expression of truth always fall short of their signification, precisely because in the very utterance of one truth a whole new field of knowledge is opened to me. My

---
[61]*Problèmes* . . ., p. 105.
[62]*Problèmes* . . ., p. 105.

relation to others and my view of the world always enlarge my horizon at the very moment in which I express my present experience. At the very moment of my relation to others in time, there occurs a condensation, so to speak, of all other known truths in my present.

In the "density of personal and interpersonal time" a communication is established which concentrates in the present the truths of our knowledge. This is one of the few clear references to the personal in Merleau-Ponty's description of subjectivity. Unfortunately he does not develop the theme at any great length, except to affirm that it is thus that we have truth—"another name for sedimentation, which is itself the presence of all presents in our own."[63]

Merleau-Ponty further insists on the specifically philosophical implications of phenomenology by a declaration of his notion of the genesis of phenomenology:

> The characteristic of a phenomenological philosophy seems therefore to be its establishment by definite right in the order of the direct spontaneity which is inaccessible to psychologism and historicism, no less than to metaphysical dogmatism. The phenomenology of perception is, among all others, qualified to reveal to us this order.[64]

Enlarging on the above description of phenomenological philosophy, Merleau-Ponty comes to some very enlightening statements with regard to intersubjectivity:

> Whenever I speak or I understand another's word, I experience the presence of others in me and of myself in others—which is the touchstone of the theory of intersubjectivity; [further] I experience the presence of the represented,—which is the touchstone of the theory of time, and finally I understand the enigmatic state-

---
[63] *Problèmes* . . ., p. 107.
[64] *Problèmes* . . ., p. 108.

ment of Husserl, 'transcendental subjectivity is intersubjectivity.'[65]

It is Merleau-Ponty's contention that as long as what I say has meaning and in the measure in which I understand, I do not really distinguish between [myself] the speaker and [myself or another] the listener; the parties to a dialogue are one.

8. *Aesthetic Expression*

A further study of human expression—is found in the article "Le langage indirect et les voix du silence."[66] The stress here is on aesthetic expression. However, Merleau-Ponty's basic theme is the same: the gesture, the expression, of whatever kind, is the expressed and not merely a sign or symbol behind which I find or through which I infer a meaning. One basic difference between language and art— chiefly painting—is this: language expresses by word; painting, art, is a silent voice. Both ways of expression are corporeal, in situation, immersed in the world, have a meaning in themselves, not conferred on them exteriorly by anything else. Merleau-Ponty admits that the genesis of language is very obscure, historically; equally obscure is the process by which one language gives rise to another. However, it is Merleau-Ponty's contention that the word, like the work of art, gives itself its own meaning, and that the developments of new languages are a matter of internal rather than external influence.

> Language does not presuppose its table of correspondence, it divulges his own secrets, it reveals itself to each infant which comes into this world, it is entirely 'demonstration.' Its opacity, its obstinate reference to

[65] *Problèmes* . . ., p. 108.
[66] *S.*, p. 49.

itself, its turning and coiling upon itself are precisely that which makes of it a spiritual power: for it becomes in its turn something like a universe, capable of containing in itself the things themselves—after having changed their meaning.[67]

As in painting, the work of a master, the special movement by which he achieves a certain result, could have been made only by him,[68] so in language, a certain expression could have come to be only by a certain word—always speaking of authentic language.[69] Further, the choice of a word rather than another, is made in each case precisely because the speaking individual is this subject and not another: the choice is itself meaningful. Perhaps one should say that even in the use of secondary language[70] the choice reveals a personal signification if the words are of themselves not originally significant.

If we want to understand language in its original operation we ought to act as if we had never spoken before, submit it to a reduction without which it would escape us and bring us back to that which it means to us; we ought to regard it as the deaf regard those who speak, we ought to compare the art of language to other arts of expression, and at least attempt to see it as one of the mute arts. It is possible that the meaning of language be decisively privileged, but in attempting the parallel, we may begin to see

---

[67] *S.*, p. 54.
[68] The notion that only a certain artist could have accomplished a certain work will be discussed more fully by Merleau-Ponty in relation to modern art. He will look into the subjectivity of the expression and question the possibility of communication. Cf. *S.*, pp. 59ff. He also discusses painting in an article contained in *Sens et Non-sens*, "Le doute de Cézanne," pp. 15-44.
[69] This was discussed amply in *Phénoménologie de la perception:* he introduces it as "le mot comme instrument d'action et comme moyen de dénomination désintéressée" and further as *langage concret* and *langage gratuit. P. P.*, p. 204.
[70] This term is used by Merleau-Ponty to indicate empirical language or the language which is not creative or authentic, but the so-called "disponible" language.

that it may not be so after all. We will at least understand that there is a silent language and that painting speaks in its own fashion.[71]

Merleau-Ponty gives art a very wide compass: the perception of the classics was grounded in their culture; our culture likewise can modify our perception of the visible world; it is not necessary to abandon the visible world for the classical "recette" (formula), nor to enclose modern painting within the boundaries of the "individual." We cannot choose between the world and art, between "our meaning" and absolute painting; they pass from one to the other.[72]

He disagrees with the criticism of art which seems to claim that the contents of sensation have never changed throughout the centuries and that therefore the inspiration as well as the techniques of the classics are mandatory. Perspective for instance, is something that man has invented in order to project his own world, and not to copy it. It is an interpretation of our spontaneous vision and not the submission to a law which the perceived world demands—simply there is no such law; the world is not in the order of laws. Perspective is much more than a secret technique for the imitation of reality; it is the invention of a dominated world, one already possessed in an instantaneous synthesis.

He admits that the work of art needs not necessarily to be finished in order to be made; on the contrary it is the peculiarity of this kind of communication to invite the spectator to take over and complete the gesture which art has left incomplete. Thus other forms of art—poetry for instance—may lead us to carry on the theme just sketched, so that we may give free rein to our own power of expression.

---

[71] S., pp. 58-59.
[72] Here we find again Merleau-Ponty's notion of ambiguity and polarity at work. Just what he means by "absolute painting" is difficult to imagine; his whole philosophy is a study in the avoidance of this very notion at all costs. S., p. 61.

The Role of the Body in Man's Power of Communication

Merleau-Ponty does not see the problem of modern painting as an exaggerated expression of individualism in an attempt at creation. It is an altogether different problem from that of a return to the individual: it is rather to know how one can communicate without the help of a pre-established nature through which our meaning about everything can be disclosed, and how we are grafted on the universal by that which we have of most properly ours. This is certainly a philosophical problem on which much thought could be spent. Could it be that the artistic expression which more closely derives from and expresses the particular individual is also the most universal signification—a thing which is hardly ascribed to it by most critics at present. However, Merleau-Ponty is puzzled by the lack of a ground for communication in modern painting, and wonders whether such art can be truly a language.

A relation to others is necessary for the meaning to be disclosed. Painting's silent voice should be in relation to the other in the world just as much as language is.

Merleau-Ponty points out that modern painting, like modern thought, obliges us to admit a truth which is not mirrored in things, which is without an exterior model, and which nevertheless wants to be truth. This is not to condemn art, but to point out the characteristics of modern expression.[73] It is interesting to note that he brings into the discussion of art his notion of the perceptual field, which he now calls "field of pictorial significations": this field is open only after a man has appeared in the world.

> The quasi-eternity of art is confused with the quasi-eternity of incarnate existence, and we have in the exercise of our body and of our senses, insofar as they insert us into the world, that which understands our cultural gestures insofar as they insert us into history.[74]

---
[73] S., pp. 63-68.
[74] S., p. 87.

One would doubtless find the true concept of history if one were able to form it according to the example of art and of language. In fact the mutual intimacy of all expressions, their belonging to a unique order, obtain de facto the union of the individual and of the universal. The central fact to which the dialectic of Hegel reverts in countless fashions, says Merleau-Ponty, is that we do not have to choose between the *"pour-soi"* and the *"pour-autrui,"* between thought according to us and thought according to others, but rather, that in the moment of the expression the other to whom I address myself, and I, expressing myself, are already united.

Our mutual relations bring about this condition: the influences of man on man are so constant that each movement of our will and of our thought takes its impetus from the other, and in this sense, it is impossible to determine, except in general, that which is attributable to each.[75] I really make myself responsible for all, I provoke a universal life, as I install myself all at once in space by my living presence and by the density of my body. And like the operations of my body, those of the word and of painting remain obscure to me, because they are a spontaneous signification which does not allow itself to be confined or constrained.[76]

9. Silent Expression

Another kind of communication which for Merleau-Ponty expresses silently is the novel. He compares it to the painting. One can tell the subject of a novel as one can tell the subject of a picture. However, there are ways and ways of telling a "story." A language which does nothing but reproduce the "things," no matter how important they may

---

[75] Again we see Merleau-Ponty's notion of generality first encountered in his treatment of perceptive experience, but with more stress on the tension ensuing in the mutual exchange and influence.
[76] *S.*, pp. 91-95.

be, empoverishes its power of communicating. But a language which gives the reader perspectives on the things and brings them into relief, actually initiates a lively discussion which will continue indefinitely, and stimulate thought. This is precisely that which is priceless in the work of art, and which makes it much more than an object of pleasure: the artistic creation contains master ideas, which are never fully developed and which teach us to think in a way in which no analytic work would ever teach us. But this is precisely that which makes a literary work of art a "hazard," for its power of communication engages us in a continuing struggle: it introduces us into a new world far different from that of our experience—and this influence is not passing, it remains with us.[77]

"The meaning of the novel itself is not perceptible, except as a *coherent deformation* imposed on the visible."[78] Critics may judge the style and the techniques in the composition of the work; however, it is not legitimate to do so, unless it is done after one has had a global perception of the novel as a whole, wherein techniques and meaning are seen as a unity. Language ought not be analyzed as one would dissect a specimen. "Expression is not a curiosity which the spirit proposes to examine, it is its existence in act."[79]

The writer is not satisfied with continuing language; nor does he aim at replacing it by an idiom which may express only his intimate signification, as the painting expresses and immortalizes that of the painter. He destroys, in a sense, common language, but he does so in realizing it, in making it significant.

Merleau-Ponty returns to a theme which he has taken up before with regard to painting and language:

---

[77] *S.*, pp. 96-97.
[78] *S.*, p. 97.
[79] *S.*, p. 98. Cf. *P.P.*, pp. 457-59.

> It is essential for the truth to be integral, whereas no painting has ever pretended to be so. The Spirit of painting does appear only as a Muse, which is a Spirit outside of itself. Language, on the contrary, seeks to possess itself, to conquer the secret of its own inventions; man does not paint about painting, but he speaks about the word, and the spirit of language would wish to keep nothing that is not of itself.[80]

However, language is not a guide to the blind. Language does not only evoke other signs, but it leads us to produce, with the new significations, a new panorama of action; it is not just a replacement of signs, but a new signification, equivalent to the old, yes, but at the same time, a new structure.

Merleau-Ponty maintains that the word is the presumption of a total accumulation; hence the word presents to the philosopher the problem of the contingent and temporal possession of self, a possession which, though provisional, is not *nothing*. The problem of language is always this: it cannot give up the thing itself without ceasing to be in time and in situation. Hegel, Merleau-Ponty says, is the only one who thought that his system contained the truth of all other truths and that whoever did not know the truths through the synthesis did not know them at all. But, he continues,

> It is sufficient to see how a truth dwindles when it is integrated with the others . . . in order to agree that the synthesis does not contain effectively all the thoughts of thought, that is not all that which they [the thoughts] have been, and finally, that it is never synthesis and

---

[80] *S.*, p. 100. Yet, Merleau-Ponty says that the word and its meaning are not constituted by consciousness. In *Phénoménologie de la perception* he explains his thought in detail when he treats of the Cogito; Cf. especially p. 461.

The Role of the Body in Man's Power of Communication

pour-soi at the same time, that is to say, a synthesis which in the same movement is and knows, is that which it knows and knows that which it is, preserves and suppresses, realizes and destroys.[81]

If Hegel meant, comments Merleau-Ponty, that the past, as it becomes distant from us, changes in its meaning, and that therefore afterwards we may retrace an intelligible history of thought, he is right. But it is so only on condition that in this synthesis each term may remain the whole which it is to the world at the time considered, and that the chain of philosophies may keep such terms in their own place, as far as the open movement of anticipation and of metamorphosis allows. The meaning of the philosophies is the meaning of a beginning, it cannot then be totalized outside of time, and it is still "expression." Likewise, outside of philosophy, the writer cannot have the feeling of attending to things except by using language, and not beyond it. No one has ever made of the body a simple instrument; neither has anyone pretended to love just by principle—though it is equally true that the body does not love alone. Merleau-Ponty concludes that we may say, with equal rights, that the body does everything and that it does nothing, that the body is ourselves and that it is not ourselves. The body is neither end nor means, rather a mixture of both; it is always involved in everything and yet goes beyond all our doings; it acts autonomously and yet it is dependent; until the moment in which we ask of it for something, it has nothing to give. It would be interesting to know just "what" Merleau-Ponty means by the "we" he has been us-

---

[81]*S.*, pp. 102-103: "Il suffit de voir comment une vérité dépérit quand elle est intégrée à d'autres . . . pour convenir que la synthèse ne contient pas effectivement toutes les pensées révolues, qu'elle n'est jamais synthèse en et pour soi à la fois, c'est-à-dire une synthèse qui du même mouvement soit et connaisse, soit ce qu'elle connait, connaisse ce qu'elle est, conserve et supprime, réalise et détruise."

ing in describing the relations of the body-subject and the ego-consciousness. The following is even more puzzling:

> Sometimes, and it is then that we have the feeling of being ourselves, it [the body] becomes animated, it takes up a life which is not absolutely its own. It is then happy and spontaneous, and we [?] with it.[82]

It is the same with language, he adds. It neither governs nor is governed by meaning. Neither is subordinated to the other. Ambiguity always prevails, in everyday language as well as in fields of particular concern such as history or politics.

> Personal life, expression, knowledge and history advance obliquely, and not towards an end or towards a concept. One never finds that which he seeks too deliberately; on the contrary, ideas and values will not be lacking to him who, in his contemplative life has known how to set free the source of spontaneity.[83]

---

[82] S., p. 104.
[83] S., p. 104.

CHAPTER SEVEN

INTERSUBJECTIVITY AND PERSONAL RELATIONS

Communication—be it by language or by signs—involves us in the study of subjectivity and intersubjectivity. The terms have become very popular in modern philosophy. There is a sense in which it is correct to say that "subjectivity" was discovered. In what sense? Subjectivity is new in the sense that modern philosophers maintain that the "subject"—the conscious self, the "ego-consciousness," Merleau-Ponty would say—far from being a "lesser being" or an inferior kind of being is really the absolute form of being. This affirmation, which Merleau-Ponty does not explain, may be taken to mean that the subject is really the being which, alone, makes possible all other beings: without a consciousness it would make no sense to speak of any object. Kwant puts the matter thus:

> What is first and foremost accessible to us is the "being" of persons. Through the encounter with human person we become familiar with the infra-human. . . . The being which is first and foremost manifest to us is already personal. The question is ... what is the meaning of the impersonal being of the things? Is it not true that the infra-human world is accessible to us only insofar as it is humanized, in other words, when it is drawn within the human, the personal sphere? In the light of this view the non-human appears as an inferior form of being.[1]

Merleau-Ponty calls this being "the being of the soul or the subject-being"[2] thus making the point a little more am-

---
[1] Kwant, *Encounter*, p. 61.
[2] The soul has a singular power to ignore that which it knows and pretend to know that which it ignores; it has an incomprehensible capacity for error bound to its capacity for truth, a relation to non-being as essential in it as its relation to being. *S.*, p. 193. But Merleau-Ponty does not thereby define "soul."

biguous in the light of his previous discussion on the soul and its relation to the body,[3] for now we cannot know—merely from his discussion—the identity of this "subject" which is the significant core of modern subjectivity. Accepting the explanation of Kwant is certainly a way out of the difficulty, because he defines the subject as person, but for Merleau-Ponty the question is less definitely characterized: subject, for him, is not synonymous with person; intersubjective relations cannot be translated into "inter-personal relations." In fact, he reduces subjectivity to either of these meanings: the empty and strict meaning of subjectivity which is both intellectualistic and universal; the concrete, full, existential subjectivity which is engulfed in the world, and which therefore remains ambiguous.

This reference to the subject is necessary even for the attainment of the universal, Merleau-Ponty maintains. We do not attain the universal by renouncing our particularity, but on the contrary by using it to communicate with others. Likewise, he says, we have a metaphysics when we really perceive the radical subjectivity of all our experiences and its truth value. Metaphysics is founded on this double sense of the Cogito: I am certain that there is being; I cannot find this being outside of the being-for-me. It is precisely in the singularity of my experience that I can reach others, and communicate with them.[4]

For him, communication with others is possible at the very moment in which I realize that my experience, precisely because it is mine, puts me in contact with others; how this realization comes about Merleau-Ponty does not say—he seems to take for granted that it is a fact: it is for this reason that I am sensitive to the world and to others, and thus able to appropriate their thoughts. Insofar as I can understand others, respond to them, recognize an affinity

[3] Cf. *S. C.*, Ch. IV.
[4] *S. N. S.*, pp. 163-64.

with them, I realize that I am engaged in a life which is to me "absolutely individual and absolutely universal."[5]

It is easy to see, from modern philosophic works, how subjectivity may have achieved such an eminent place in modern philosophy and how Merleau-Ponty can maintain therefore that in a real sense subjectivity—as previously described—is something new in philosophical speculation.

The meeting of subjectivities in communication becomes an intersubjective relation which chiefly means that I have basically the same experience another has of a certain object or event. An intersubjective object is, for him, simply an object which is possessed by a plurality of subjects even though, strictly speaking, the experience cannot be common to all: there is a sort of solipsism which prevents me from ever sharing my own experience of an object with that of any other subject.

The understanding of intersubjective relations involves certain difficulties, more or less, depending on the presuppositions one has at the beginning of his investigation. For Merleau-Ponty, who makes at least an attempt to explore the intersubjective relations phenomenologically, the difficulty does not seem too great because he finds the relation already a fact (as will be shown shortly). However, as the investigation proceeds, difficulties emerge.

The problem of intersubjectivity takes up much of Merleau-Ponty's discussion in his major works as well as in his various articles. Recalling the meaning he gives to the terms "intersubjective" it is clear that intersubjective relations are for him fundamental to all human problems—in fact intersubjectivity is involved in perception and in man's relations to the world. He explains this when he affirms that whenever I perceive—without any notion of the organization of my perceptive faculties—I am vaguely conscious of integrating in my grasp consciousnesses which are outside of

---

[5] *S. N. S.*, p. 165.

my personal life, yet come under the sensible mode of perception. Every object is at first given to me as a natural object, made up of colors, tactile qualities and sounds; but besides these, there appears to be in and with my perceptions an added facet: I am not only aware of a physical world, but of a cultural dimension which is so to speak attached to the natural object. "Each of these objects bears the stamp of the human action for which it is made. Each spreads an atmosphere of humanity."[6] It is because of this human atmosphere that even perception of things implies an intersubjectivity—that is, it implies that I am not the only one to perceive such and such an object; there is no possibility of an unqualified solipsism: a community of subjects is always implied.[7]

The problem of intersubjectivity for the author is ultimately centered on the existence of the other for me and on my existence for the other. This for him does not present at first a really serious problem. According to Professor Lauer, Merleau-Ponty sees the fact that the world is the world; hence he "needs no explanation of intersubjectivity; he simply takes it for granted and then watches it work."[8] It is indeed Merleau-Ponty's method to present the fruit of his investigation and reflections without attempting to prove anything. He sees the "de facto" intersubjective relations which exist among men—at the cultural level—and describe these relations as they occur before him. However, he does not claim that his description is already philosophy. Answering an objection in "Le primat de la perception," he admits "a life" is not a philosophy and description is not the return to the "immediate." The problem is to see whether one seeks to understand that "immediate" which one sets out to describe. "It seems to me that to seek the expression

---
[6] *P. P.*, pp. 399-400.
[7] Cf. Kwant, *Encounter*, Ch. III, especially pp. 125 ff.
[8] Lauer, *Triumph* . . . , p. 180.

of the immediate is not to betray or abandon reason; it is, on the contrary, to labor for its advancement."[9] Thus, we may assume with good reasons that Merleau-Ponty, in describing the intersubjective relations at any and every level, is not merely "describing," but is aiming at a philosophical reflection on the immediate data of experience.

1. Being-in-the-World

The basis of intersubjective relations is the being-in-the-world of the subject. This "subject" is revealed by the body, whose spatiality and temporality is the very condition of its being perceived. This, however, would not by itself reveal each to the other as subject. Ultimately, it is true, it will be because of the body that the other is perceived as subject. But how? Merleau-Ponty says rather bluntly, "If my consciousness has a body, why would not the other bodies have a consciousness?"[10] He starts from the experience which my consciousness has of the vast field of perception—the phenomenal field—against which, as against a background, my particular sensory and perceptual experiences stand out. Obviously, by perception I do not constitute things. Further, I experience a past which is impenetrable to me—hence not of my making. I am, instead, "inserted" into this world which I perceive. Now, Merleau-Ponty seems to think that the perception of others is no problem (or does he refuse to see it as a problem?). If my perception of the other reveals him to me as endowed with a certain configuration and with a body like mine, I can logically suppose that he is endowed with consciousness also.

---

[9]"Le primat . . . ," p. 138: "Assurément une vie n'est pas une philosophie. Je croyais avoir indiqué en passant cette idée que la description n'est pas le retour à l'immédiat: on n'y revient pas. Il s'agit simplement de savoir si l'on se propose de le comprendre. Il me semble que chercher l'expression de l'immédiat ce n'est pas trahir la raison, c'est travailler au contraire à son agrandissement."

[10]*P. P.*, p. 403.

To affirm this requires a radical change in the notions of both body and consciousness. First, it is necessary to distinguish the body as described by physiology from the body as a human behavior manifesting itself to me: it is the latter and not the former which is here considered. Secondly, consciousness must no longer be conceived "as a constituting consciousness, and as a pure being-for-itself, but as a perceiving consciousness, as the subject of a behavior, as being-to-the-world or existence."[11]

Obviously, Merleau-Ponty is thinking of consciousness as it has been defined by certain types of idealism, and his aim is to consider instead the conscious subject in his existential milieu. For it is only on the condition of treating the ego-consciousness as existential that the other may appear to me as a phenomenal body and receive a certain "localization"— for I will then invest it with the same powers with which I see myself endowed. This new interpretation of the body and of consciousness immediately suggests to Merleau-Ponty a way out of the antimonies of objective thought. He thus finds in phenomenological reflection, an existential experience of the world as perceived. Moreover, it is precisely because I can see the other, and can be seen by others that "this instrument of expression which is called physiognomy can be bearer of existence."[12] Likewise my conscious encounter with others is a kind of reaffirmation of their existence. This is quite different from Sartre's notion of intersubjective relations among men. For him it is precisely the "look" of the other which far from discovering or affirming my existence as subject tends to effectuate my destruction. The "look," far from being a link binding one man to another, or providing a certitude of the perceived, is that which disrupts relations and tends to deprive the subject of

---

[11] *P. P.*, p. 404.
[12] *P.P.*, p. 404.

his world (the world he perceives, and to an extent, even of his own being).[13]

In Merleau-Ponty's notion of the perception of the other there is nothing resembling reasoning by analogy, for analogy presupposes that which it wants to explain. But the other-consciousness which I encounter cannot be deduced: it could be only if after comparing the emotions of the others and mine I were to find them identical. But this obviously cannot be the case, for in order to do that I should already presuppose the "perception" of the other—the very thing in question. It is therefore clear that there is no constitution of the other here. The correlations observed between my mimics and those of others, my intentions and my acts, can well furnish a lead to the methodic knowledge of the other, but they cannot reveal to me his existence.

> Between my consciousness and my body—as lived—there is an internal relation, as there is an internal relation between this phenomenal body and the body of others—as it appears to me from the outside—; this internal relation makes the other appear as the completion of the system.[14]

The meaning of the above is rather obscure: it may be interpreted to mean that the other's phenomenal body is so

---

[13] "It is a whole space which groups itself about other people, and that space is made 'with my space'; it is a regrouping in which I participate and which eludes me, of all the objects that people my universe. This regrouping does not stop here; the turf has a qualification: it is that green turf that exists for others; in this respect, the very quality of the object, its deep, original green, is in direct relationship with that man; that green turns towards another a face that eludes me. I perceive the relatedness of the green with another person, as an objective relationship, but I cannot perceive the green as it appears to another being. So, all at once, an object has appeared that has stolen the world from me." Sartre, *Being and Nothingness*, tr. w. introd. by Hazel E. Barnes (New York: Philosophical Library [1946]), p. 313.

[14] *P. P.*, p. 405.

interrelated with my behavior that I experience it as part of my own existential being-in-the-world; it is part of a whole system of perceived and perceiving: the body of the other is part of my perceived world. Now the evidence of the other is possible precisely because I am not transparent to myself—I am a body, not pure consciousness. But this means that, insofar as the other is in the world and visible and therefore part of my phenomenal field, he is not an Ego in the sense in which I am an ego for myself. To think the other an "Ego," I should be able to think myself a simple object for him; but this is impossible because of the knowledge I have of myself as subject. However, when, in the mutual relation of myself with the other, each sees the other's body not as an object but as a behavior, then neither will be reduced to the status of object by the other.

True, if one sees himself as an absolute, then he cannot at the same time consider the other as a personal being, unless indeed, a different kind of reflection on himself makes this possible. This reflection, Merleau-Ponty maintains, would have to show me that my self as a perceiving subject is grounded in a prepersonal subject, from whom actually stem both perceptions and judgments; it would also be necessary that the world appear to this subject as something neutral (that general certainty of which Merleau-Ponty often speaks) wherein the behavior of the other may find a place.

Merleau-Ponty affirms that

> this world can reside undivided between my perception and that of the other; the self perceiving has no particular privilege which would make a perceived self impossible [each perceiver is at once perceiver and perceived] for both of them are, not thoughts closed in their own immanence, but beings which are transcended by their world, and therefore also transcending each other.[15]

---
[15] *P. P.*, p. 405.

Intersubjectivity and Personal Relations

The above seems to point out quite clearly the possibility of a plurality of subjects—while asserting once more the generality of perception of the world. However, when Merleau-Ponty comes to the affirmation of a consciousness other than mine, he maintains that this act makes of my experience something private, no longer coextensive with being. Why is this so? Perhaps because from the moment I affirm another consciousness—whom I do not constitute—I recognize the fact that this consciousness other than mine possesses a world which is not mine, or rather, that this consciousness as a subject has an experience which I am unable to share. Thus, although the general perception of the world is common to consciousnesses, the being of the other is not just a part of that general grasp—hence my experiences are by that fact reduced to my own consciousness no longer all embracing, or coextensive with being. In fact, the author goes farther and says that the other's "Cogito" deprives mine of all its value, and makes me lose my assurance of achieving independently the only being conceivable to me, that being which I see and constitute. However, since we know that our individual perspectives cannot be realized apart from each other, for they pass from one to the other and converge in the thing, we must learn to find communication with other consciousnesses in a common world. Actually, others are not enclosed in my perspective of the world because this perspective itself is open, undefined, always shifting from one to the other; all perspectives are "gathered into a unique world to which we participate as anonymous subjects of perception."[16] "Anonymity of perception" seems to be contradictory to the term "subject" which Merleau-Ponty uses: his meaning is but a reaffirmation of that generality and dialectical tension which he declares to be at work at all levels of life, physical, vital, human. This is perhaps one of the weak points in his philosophy, for it will be

---

[16] *P. P.*, p. 406.

quite difficult to build on this "anonymity" the personal dimension.

It appears then, that perception of behavior is the key to the perception of each other as subjects and not merely as objects. However, as was just pointed out, his disconcerting note on the participation in the world as anonymous subjects of perception seems to run directly counter to his notion of intersubjectivity and to the oft-repeated assertion that in communication I am not concerned with a "language," with "words" or with "gestures," but rather with a living subject. This anonymity no doubt stems from his fundamental notion of ambiguity underlying all of his philosophy. Has he not maintained, throughout, that in the last analysis ambiguity always prevents us from saying the last word on perception, on behavior, on language, on any and every expression of life, precisely because there is interaction hence a blurring of contours at every level?

I achieve the first level of communication with others by virtue of my power of sensation as a psychological subject. When I gaze upon a living subject all of my other perceptions of things receive a new signification, take on a different meaning; besides being as they appear to me, they are also whatever the behavior of the other makes them to be.

> Around the perceived body a sort of whirlpool is formed towards which my world is pulled and sucked in; in that same measure it is not any more just mine, it is no longer only present to me, it is also present to X, to such other behavior which begins to take shape in him. Already, the other body is no longer a simple fragment of the world, but the locus of a certain elaboration and as it were a certain "view" of the world.[17]

In Merleau-Ponty's expression there is no strong emphasis of the negative aspect of the other's consciousness in relation to mine; rather, his presence is a sort of confirma-

---

[17] *P. P.*, p. 406.

Intersubjectivity and Personal Relations

tion of my own. In the same way, I experience my body as a possibility of contact with the world through a specific behavior; in and through this experience I realize that the behavior of others brings me back to my own experiences, and as it were, reveals to me the "other" as a veritable extension of my body. Thus, my relation to the other through my body, far from detracting from my contact with the world, adds to it the assurance of a familiar situation.

Thus, "the body of others and mine form a unique whole, the two sides of the same phenomenon; an anonymous existence is implied and it entails the two bodies at once."[18] However, this relation to the other does not yet reveal him as another *man*. At this stage my life, as the alien one of the other with whom I communicate, is still open, unprotected; it is still somewhat dependent on biological and sensorial functions; only by degrees it bypasses the natural objects which it has at first grasped in their natural sense, constructs for itself instruments which later give way to cultural objects by which it (this "alien life") projects itself into a cultural milieu. One of the cultural objects which will play a great part in the perception of the other is language. "The experience of the dialogue will constitute between him and me a common ground; my thought and his thought make up a single tissue, my conversation and his are inserted, so to speak, in a common operation of which neither is the creator."[19] Thus, we can say that the dialogue plays a very special part in intersubjectivity. This is the real problem which man encounters; for the child this is no problem—as for that matter very few things are for him.[20] The

---

[18] Here we have again the notion of anonymity—it does not fit well in the context of his previous remarks on the perception of the other, although there is something valuable in that it implies relatedness to a high degree.

[19] *P. P.*, p. 406.

[20] Merleau-Ponty also discusses dialogue in relation to the child's development and gradual insertion into the relatedness of the social milieu. He treats of this in detail in "Les Relations avec autrui chez l'enfant."

struggle of the adult for the recognition of the "other" as "other" arises from my awareness of the other consciousness, our meeting on a common ground (the world) and the realization of the lost peaceable coexistence in the world of childhood.

But Merleau-Ponty seems to step back in his investigation: the intersubjective relation which at first had seemed no serious problem is now doubtful: Is it really the other which I attain by the relation described above?

> We level the "I" and the "Thou" in the experience of the "many," we introduce the impersonal at the heart of subjectivity, we efface the individuality of the perspectives; but in such general confusion have we not caused the Alter Ego to disappear with the Ego?[21]

He admits that he has made the two exclusive of each other. If we realize that the Ego and Alter-Ego have basically the same pretensions, we will also understand why the Ego cannot perceive another ego (because he would destroy it as ego?). And whenever the subject which perceives is anonymous, the other "himself" which he perceives is also anonymous; thus we cannot discover therein the plurality of consciousnesses. True, Merleau-Ponty admits, I may perceive in the other a certain passion as behavior, without experiencing the same myself—grief or anger, for instance. However, these passions are after all a modification of the other and not the other, even if they are one with the phenomenal body which we perceive.[22] Moreover, a passion is not, for the one who experiences it, what it is for the one who perceives it: for him who experiences it, it is a lived situation, for the perceiver it is a witnessed fact. If I suffer

---

[21] *P. P.*, p. 408.
[22] Here there seems to be a denial of the "structuration" of behavior, as Merleau-Ponty calls it. Discussing behavior Merleau-Ponty has insisted that a new structuration was almost equivalent to a "new" or different being. Cf. *S.C.*, Ch. III.

Intersubjectivity and Personal Relations

because my friend suffers, if I share his anger, I do not thereby have his lived experience; even where two subjects share a project, each one's experience is his.

> Our consciousnesses try in vain, through our own situation, to construct a common situation by which we may communicate. It is from the depth of his subjectivity that each projects his "unique" world.[23]

The above seems in contrast with Merleau-Ponty's previous statement on the possibility and actuality of dialogue—dialogue is a being-for-two.[24] In dialogue the other is no longer for me a simple behavior in my transcendental field, nor am I for him; rather, we co-exist through the same world. In the dialogue I am free from myself; the thoughts of the other are indeed his, I do not form them, even though I may know them in advance or negate them; the questions and objections of the other, however, discover to me thoughts which I did not know I possessed. Thus there is an intersubjective relation in dialogue which, however, can afterwards change into a relation of opposition: this occurs when, reflecting on the dialogue, I can recollect my thoughts and make of the whole exchange an episode of *my* life; then the other can fade from my consciousness, or, if I feel his presence, I can resent him as a menace.[25]

Why Merleau-Ponty thinks of the other as a menace is not clear. Perhaps an unconscious reverting to Sartre? Perhaps the taking up of intersubjective exchange in my private life has made any reference to the other an intrusion. However, the author has made it abundantly clear in other discussions that the subjects are interdependent for the very

---

[23] *P. P.,* p. 409.
[24] It is quite true that man is at the same time in relation with others and alone, because communication, even at its best is never complete. Experience testifies to this fully.
[25] *P. P.,* p. 407.

realization of their personal being—at least at the cultural level.

2. *Intersubjective Relations*

But interdependence of subjects and the discovery that through behavior we can meet each other does not make the difficulty of intersubjective relations vanish. Neither is objective thought the sole problem that has to be solved in relation to the other. The conflict of myself and the other does not begin when I attempt to "think" the other, and does not disappear when I return to the irreflexive. In "Le Primat de la perception" Merleau-Ponty asks whether it is truly objective to regard man as an object susceptible of explanations by causes and not rather to seek by describing man's conduct (behavior) to constitute a true science of man; or, he also goes on to say, is it objective to apply to man tests which concern only abstract aptitudes, or is it not more so—be it by means of tests also—to learn the reaction of man before the world and before the others?[26] He maintains that both objective thought and the unity of the Cogito are to be investigated, for they are well-founded phenomena. But in his insistence that the true beginning must be a return to the pre-reflexive, he does not intend to deny or minimize the value of reason. By stressing the primacy of perception he has never intended to imply

> that science, reflection, philosophy are [only] transformed sensation or values of pleasure both differentiated and calculated. We have expressed in these terms [the notion] that the experience of perception puts us back in the presence of the [experiential] moment wherein things became for us. . . . It is not a question of reducing human knowledge to sensation, but rather of witnessing the birth of human knowledge, of rendering

[26]"Le primat . . .," p. 132.

such knowledge as perceptible as the sensible, of reconquering the consciousness of rationality which we [*l'on*] lose in thinking that it [rationality] stands by itself.[27]

He has attempted to find a method of approach to the cultural relations of men capable of making such relations "present and living" as the object of perception is present and living. This method would apply to language, knowledge, social relations and religious experience.

Merleau-Ponty enters thus a discussion of the solipsism which at first sight seems to be in direct opposition to his theory of relations. Yet, it is not so. It touches on a fundamental notion of human life, that is, the irreducible unicity of the person. There is a lived solipsism which is insuperable. Doubtlessly, I do not feel myself constituting either the natural or the cultural world: in each of my perceptions and judgments there are elements which are not really mine, because I receive them from the given world; at the same time, my own acts are transcendent to me—though I am the one who "lives" them. To such a being as man is, nothing can be given simply because he has in himself projects—or at the least the capacity for projects—for all possible being, because he has been plunged in his field of experiences.

But how can the ego alienate himself from himself? My subjectivity is inalienable and the fact that my body's comprehensiveness is compensated by the other's body makes it impossible to explain the fact that the ego may alienate himself from himself in favor of another. This needs elucidation: Merleau-Ponty has maintained that the body is in a dialectical relation with the world and with the other bodies —that is, the body entails a multitude of relations: but because the "Other" also *is* a body, its multitude of relations, its comprehensiveness, will perfectly balance those of the Ego

[27]"Le Primat . . .," p. 133.

Merleau-Ponty

alienating himself, therefore there is really no explanation; in fact, is there any alienation at all? Apparently not.

Thus Merleau-Ponty discusses the relation of the Ego to the "alter Ego" as the foundation of morality. This relation comes about when I realize that my incommunicable solitude is broken by the "realization of the paradox of an *alter ego,* of a common situation."[28] And here, as in every other respect, the primacy of perception—"the recognition, at the very heart of our most individual experience, of a fruitful contradiction which submits this individual experience to the consideration of others—is the remedy to both scepticism and pessimism."[29]

However, the "how" of the recognition of the other as discussed in *Phéoménologie de la perception* is not so easily understood. Merleau-Ponty seems to rely somehow on "constitution"—the very thing he does not admit is possible when intersubjectivity is concerned. He seems to be somewhat influenced by Sartre on this point. I actually have no common ground with the other; my position with regard to the world and the other's position with regard to the world constitutes an alternative. If the other is posited, once he turns his gaze on me, thus inserting me in his field, he deprives me of part of my being; obviously, I cannot restore my being except by demanding to be freely recognized by him; yet my liberty implies for the other the same liberty. Just how am I able to posit the other? "Insofar as I have been born, I have a body and a natural world, I can find in such a world other behaviors with which mine is interlaced (as was discussed before)."[30]

Still, according to Merleau-Ponty the very self which is conscious of its own acts, the "ego consciousness" as he calls

---

[28]"Le Primat . . .," p. 134.
[29]"Le Primat . . .," p. 134.
[30]*P.P.,* p. 410.

it, seems to be the chief impediment to the recognition of the other.

3. The Other and Solipsism

Merleau-Ponty then asks how I can find in my own field of perception this presence of the self to self. If I maintain that the presence of the other is a simple fact (it is at any rate a fact confirmed by experience), still I cannot extricate it from the category of "fact for me"; it arises from my own possibilities, therefore I can hardly suppose it is independent of me. Doubtlessly, I can recognize but one Ego, but if I consider it as a universal Ego, then it ceases to be my finite self in order to become an impartial spectator of the empirical self which I am. In this case the other will be equal to me, because we both will be confronted by this universal Ego. However, the consciousness which I now call my self and which I discover by reflection will no longer be able to be called "my self"; it will be "constituted" before the universal Ego—the same may be said for the other.[31]

Rather unaccountably for one who does not admit an Absolute (as Merleau-Ponty repeatedly declares)[32] he makes a strong assertion: "In God I can have consciousness of others as of myself, love others as I love myself."[33] This is a rather unusual way to say that there is no real transcendence of the ego. He further declares that *if there is a transcendence* I am ignorant of it. If I were to know myself and the others in an absolutely transparent way I should be God. (Obviously, the subjectivities I encounter cannot be called God.)

---

[31] *P.P.*, p. 411.

[32] That is, we have to say, in the last analysis, that he does not admit an Absolute in the sense of a first cause or a Supreme Being. If he speaks about an absolute other than the subject, in the sense in which he speaks of the subject as absolute in the "Preface," that does not mean he believes in his existence: cf. "Le Primat . . .," p. 150; "Je pense que c'est le propre de l'homme de penser Dieu; ce qui ne veut pas dire que Dieu existe."

[33] *P.P.*, p. 411.

Hence, the knowledge of myself as well as of the other is of necessity opaque and limited.[34]

Even love becomes doubtful in this framework. Reiterating the notion that I cannot love others as myself except in God, he goes on to say that even the love I think I have for God is not mine, but God's. It is simply God loving Himself in me that gives me the illusion of loving. Hence, for Merleau-Ponty "there would be really no love of others or indeed, others"[35]—a strange statement after all the discussion on intersubjectivity. There is only love of self, a love all tied up within itself, beyond our lives, and beyond our reach. Thus, "the movement of reflection and love which would lead to God, makes impossible that very God to whom it would lead."[36]

The net result of all this—for Merleau-Ponty—is that I am condemned to solipsism, with a pretention to divinity. My transcendence of others derives from the fact that all situations and all others have to be perceived by me to *be* in my eyes (to be for me). And yet I find novelty in others. This pluralistic solipsism is ridiculous—but inevitable if consciousness implies the situation described. Since, however, we live this situation, there must be a way of explaining it. Merleau-Ponty now has recourse to his dialectical interpretation again: solitude and communication are not two alternatives, but two moments of a unique phenomenon, for, de facto, others exist for me. The experience of the other is

---

[34] This is how F. Sandrini puts it: ". . . total communication, identification of self with others, not only is never accomplished in experience, but it cannot even be accomplished in principle, because it would simply be destructive of the human condition: it would destroy that impenetrable interiority given "for me" which is an inseparable face of my behavior. There is therefore no total communication and no total solipsism." "La Fenomenologia", p. 96.

[35] "De sorte que pour finir il n'y aurait nulle part amour d'autrui, ni autrui, mais un seul amour de soi qui se nouerait sur lui-même par-delà nos vies, qui ne nous concernerait en rien et auquel nous ne pourrions pas accéder." *P.P.*, p. 412.

[36] *P.P.*, p. 412.

like reflection; its object—the other—cannot escape it absolutely. Somehow, reflection must give us the irreflexive. In some way, I must have the experience of the other, else, how could I even speak of solitude. The existence of the other is incontestable on the horizon of my life, even if my knowledge of the other is imperfect.

Hence, according to Merleau-Ponty, in pre-reflexive existence the ego and the other are mutually related as two poles always in contact, in a necessary and inevitable meeting. This meeting is a reciprocal implication, yet the distinction and the transcendence of the one over the other are preserved. It is therefore a two-way or a bi-lateral relation, and between these two poles there occurs a dialectical exchange.

This kind of encounter is not different basically from the dialectical relations which, according to Merleau-Ponty, take place at all levels, beginning with the perception of things and of the world—here also when we come to reflection we turn to the pre-reflexive as to the primary source of our investigation. There is a difference, however, in the manner of the dialectic: whereas things and the world present themselves immediately to the sensing subject, the "other-ego" in this meeting is mediated by the body and by the world, that is, by significative gesture, and by the word. However, the reciprocal relation "I-other" is less narrow and less inevitable than that existing between subjectivity and things (obviously, I can refuse the relation on occasion).

However, the "other" is not "inferred" by me from the observation of his gesture and the understanding of his language. Rather he *is* the total behavior which I perceive. As he is an object of perception for me, he is not seen as a subject, he does not yet enter my solitude. To admit another as a subject, I must accept the fact of his universality which at once limits me to the dimension of particularity: I am no longer the sole possessor of my experienced world. Yet this situation does not destroy me as a subject: the fact of my insertion into the world, my being in situation as a body and as a social being grounds both my subjectivity and my transcendence over the other, and assures my liberty.

> It is my destiny to be free and to be unable to renounce such freedom and reduce myself to anything I experience; this fate was sealed the moment my transcendental field was open to me and I was thrust into this world.[37]

Therefore, I can refuse the social world, estrange myself from others, even doubt individual perceptions.[38] "The truth of solipsism is here. All experience will always appear to me as a particularity which cannot exhaust the generality of my being."[39]

Solipsism then would be a philosophy implying other men; it would actually be a willed withdrawal from this community of men by a very definite act. To deny something in particular, is to affirm something in general: we affirm being even through the negation of some beings. Merleau-Ponty spells out a condition for solipsism which is usually passed over in silence: that is, a solipsist cannot really be what he calls himself; a community of men is required if a solipsist is to have an audience. Even to refuse something implies something from which I am able to keep a distance. In choosing either myself or the other I really set one against the other, hence I affirm the two. However, for Merleau-Ponty the negation of the other by me and his negation of me do not occur at the existential level; this negation is possible only at the intellectual level. Very much like Sartre, Merleau-Ponty compares our way of looking at

---

[37] *P.P.*, p. 413. Is not "destined to be free" a contradiction?
[38] Merleau-Ponty has repeatedly said I cannot doubt the perception of the world in general.
[39] *P.P.*, p. 413.

each other as that of an insect; i.e., we observe each other's actions instead of understanding them. I resent the scrutiny of a stranger because it is a substitute for communication. Still,

> the refusal of communication is itself already a type of communication. . . . Communication cannot be abrogated. It can, however, be suspended by that unqualified existence which in me and in the other marks the limits of sympathy, and springs from that inalienable root, which is liberty. Yet each existence does not transcend the other unless it remains idle and silent.[40]

The moment one expresses his thought, he ceases to be transcendent, and he gives the other access to him. Solipsism would only be possible if one could know his own existence without *being,* or *saying,* or *doing* anything—an impossible situation for "to exist is to *be to the world* [italics mine]." The philosopher inevitably involves others in his reflection, even if and when he retires into solitude to meditate. "Transcendental subjectivity is a revealed subjectivity, that is to say, revealed to the self and to others, and in this sense subjectivity is an intersubjectivity."[41]

4. Existence and the Social World

Insofar as existence is engaged in behavior, it is perceived. But the social world is not made up of objects, it is a permanent phenomenal field, a dimension of existence. Our relation to the social is more profound than all expressed perceptions and all judgments: we are immersed in the social by the mere fact of being in existence. If I know or love someone, I seek to penetrate that inexhaustible source which he is—as a subject—an experience which may prove

---
[40] *P.P.,* p. 414.
[41] *P. P.,* p. 415. Cf. "Le Primat . . .," pp. 144-45.

disastrous because I may deceive myself. To know and to love someone is a risk. Perception itself is a violent act and not merely an illusion.[42] But we are linked to others in society. Before its realization by consciousness the social exists indistinctly and as a solicitation; it is not actual until it has *become* our existence, and a co-existence as well.

> The problem of the modality of existence of the social is linked to the problem of transcendence. Whether it be question of my body, of the natural world, of birth and death, the problem is always to know how I can be open to phenomena which transcend me and which, nevertheless, *are* only insofar as I recapture them and live them; how the presence to myself which defines me and conditions all extraneous presence to me is, at the same time, "de-presentation" and throws me outside of myself.[43]

Both idealism and materialism—as Merleau-Ponty has often pointed out—falsify the motivation which exists between the interior and the exterior, the first by making the exterior immanent to me; the second by submitting me to causal action. In neither case our individual past could be given us because the past would be, properly speaking, present. If the past has to *be* for us, it cannot *be* except in an ambiguous present, as a field to which we have access, and which is always present as a ground for our thoughts and projects.

> If the past and the world exist, they must have an immanence of origin—they can only be that which I see behind me and around me, a transcendence of fact—they exist in my life before appearing as objects of my express acts.[44]

---
[42] *P. P.*, p. 415.
[43] *P. P.*, p. 417.
[44] *P. P.*, p. 418.

Intersubjectivity and Personal Relations

Here again, Merleau-Ponty goes back to the existential situation—always ambiguous, always general and somewhat blurred. It is not the objective approach which gives me the contact with either my past or the world; I am in the world as a whole before becoming aware of the single "things" in the world; in other words, he reiterates the assertion that I have certainty of the world in general, but not of anything in particular. The object of thought comes only later on and I cannot make anything whatever an object of thought—without a distortion.

What is then my condition? Merleau-Ponty finally gives an answer to the question he has discussed throughout the investigation.

> Installed in life, relying on my thinking nature, steeped in this transcendental field which has opened at my first perception and in which all absence is but the reverse of a presence, all silence but a modality of sound, I have a sort of ubiquity and eternity of origin, I feel myself destined to the flux of an inexhaustible life of which I cannot think either the beginning or the end, since it is still my living self which thinks them; and thus my life both forestalls and survives itself at all times.[45]

Yet, in spite of this thinking nature which opens to me the world, I experience the feeling of my contingence, the anguish of being transcended, so that "if I do not think of my death, I live in an atmosphere of death in general";[46] there is, as it were, an essence of death lingering in my thoughts. But because I share the same cultural world with others, my life has a social atmosphere just as it has a sense of contingency.

---

[45] *P. P.*, p. 418.
[46] Note here again Merleau-Ponty's constant return to the notion of generality at every level, and in every field. This notion of generality will permit him to deal with the objections raised to his phenomenological philosophy. Cf. "Le Primat . . .," (discussion), pp. 135-53.

Concluding, Merleau-Ponty points out that the truly transcendent (which is not an assemblage of constitutive functions, before an impartial spectator), is the ambiguous life within the natural and social world, the source of transcendences, which, by a fundamental contradiction puts me in communication with them and makes knowledge possible. Merleau-Ponty disposes of the objections which might be raised against placing a contradiction within philosophy and proposing "unthinkable" descriptions. The objections would be valid if by phenomenology we meant a sort of "prelogical" or "magic" experience. Then we should either believe in description and renounce thought, or know what we are saying and renounce description. But neither position alone is correct, yet both are true if taken together. Such descriptions demand an understanding and a reflection more radical than objective thought. And it is precisely here that Merleau-Ponty hints at a phenomenology of phenomenology[47]—which he attempts in his subsequent investigation: the Cogito.

Merleau-Ponty notes that Husserl has said as much in his later works: all reflection must begin with the description of the lived world. But, he adds, by a second reflection (phenomenology of phenomenology—perhaps moving away from existence) the lived world must be replaced by the transcendental flux of a universal constitution in which all the obscurity is clarified. Hence, one of these things will obtain: either the constitution renders the world transparent and then there is no reason why reflection should pass through the lived world; or, such a constitution, in spite of reduction, still retains some existential overtones, some facticity, and hence it never frees the world from its opacity—another way of saying that reduction can never be complete.

Merleau-Ponty maintained that Husserl's thought—the late Husserl that is—was shifting more and more toward

---

[47]Cf. *supra*, Chapter VI.

the existential approach, and away from the purely essential which Merleau-Ponty labeled idealistic.[48]

5. The Phenomenon of Love

At this point we may ask what is the relation of consciousness to the affective life. Merleau-Ponty affirms that in the awareness we have of our psychic states, we face no danger of illusion. The feeling I experience comes from within: as a feeling, it is real, even if the object which inspires it (e.g., love or hatred) is nothing but a product of my own consciousness. In this case, it is quite true that the appearing *is* the being. And since consciousness of an object implies, necessarily, consciousness of oneself,

> to will and to know that one wills, to love and to know that one loves is one and the same act; love is consciousness of loving; to will is consciousness of willing. A love which is not conscious of itself is a love which does not love, and unconscious willing is a will which does not will, just as an unconscious thought is a thought which does not think.[49]

Hence, must one say that error is not possible with regard to interior states? Is everything true in consciousness? Is not love the same whether its object be true or fictitious? Considered in itself will not a sentiment always be true?

At first sight, we might think that the answer is affirmative. But we must not overlook the fact that we can distinguish, within us, between "true" and "false" sentiments, and therefore we cannot place all our feelings—simply because experienced—on the same existential level, nor take them to have the same degree of reality within us. As there are in exterior perception levels of reality, that is, differences between reflections, shadows and "things," so there are within

---
[48]*P. P.*, p. 432.
[49]*P. P.*, p. 433.

us illusory and false sentiments. A further distinction must be made with regard to erroneous interpretation and bad faith, in which latter case one only pretends to experience a sentiment, but does not believe for an instant to be truly engaged in it—in love, for instance.

"On the contrary, in false and illusory love, I have united my will with that of the person loved, she has truly been for a time the *mediator of my relations with the world* [italics mine]."[50] This is very significant: in the light of Merleau-Ponty's doctrine, this relation would bring about a new type of behavior and therefore also a new structuration—hence a new being, not to be equated with the one who did not love, for the mediation implies a closeness and a reciprocity truly existential. Thus a false and illusory love, on the contrary, is believed to be true, one's life is actually engaged in it, and only after the disillusion does one come to the realization that the sentiment experienced was other than love. I did not love the manner of existing of the person, but only certain qualities of the latter, such as beauty, youth; but the manner of existing of the person is the person itself, whereas the qualities are not.[51]

Merleau-Ponty asks whether it is not the case of a true love which ceased, if I did not know the nature of my sentiment; or if I knew, then there was never love—not even false. He claims that neither supposition holds. (Note again the ambiguity prevalent in all of man's relations with his fellow men).

> One cannot say that this love has been, while it existed, undiscernible from true love, and that it has become "false love" when I disavowed it.[52]

---

[50] *P. P.*, p. 433.
[51] The implications of what Merleau-Ponty says here run counter to his theory of structuration; that is, according to a *behavior* I live I supposedly "become"—that is, the qualities I manifest in my behavior *are* myself because I become according to my structuration. Cf. *S. C.*, Chapter III.
[52] *P. P.*, p. 434.

Evidently, Merleau-Ponty holds that there is a real difference between true and false love, not just that there has occurred a misunderstanding somewhere in the relation. When Merleau-Ponty observes that as in the mystic attitude resulting from a true vocation and not merely from a fortuitous accident, the whole life of the mystic is involved, so in true love the whole life is engaged, and such love does not cease except if and when either of the lovers changes; but false love reveals itself when the Ego reflects upon itself. The difference between the two is intrinsic. There is a lack of authenticity in a false love as in a false sentiment; there is always a part of the self which is not touched—as it happens in hysteria as contrasted with true sorrow.[53] But is there a clear knowledge of myself and my thoughts in love? Am I certain of my sentiments within my consciousness? We do not possess ourselves at every instant in the fullness of our reality; we can admit an interior perception, as a certain witness which however is not a knowledge coextensive with our being. When love pursues its dialectic through me, I am not aware of it as knowledge, rather I experience a movement towards another which involves all my thoughts and influences my behavior.

In the article "Le Roman et la métaphysique," Merleau-Ponty answers some of his own questions on love. Commenting on Simone de Beauvoir's *L'Invitée,* he comes to some deep insights concerning the personal relations exemplified in the characters. Although the basic doctrines of Merleau-Ponty reappear in this article without substantial change, a marked development is evident: he now brings out the implications of that which he barely sketches in *Phénoménologie de la perception.* In particular, he makes clear the basic demand of love to be total, and, in a sense, exclusive:

---

[53] *P. P.,* p. 435.

Merleau-Ponty

> It is essential for love to be total, for he who loves loves someone, not some qualities, and the person loved wants to feel his very existence justified by such love. The presence of a third, even if also loved—and precisely if loved—introduces a reservation in the love of each for the other.[54]

In fact, Merleau-Ponty maintains that it is difficult enough to obtain a relation between two lovers, let alone a trio. In a sense, he questions the success of love even in the best of circumstances, without, however, looking at it from a totally negative viewpoint.

Merleau-Ponty shows it is an illusion to think that one can have at the same time mutual love and mutual independence as De Beauvoir describes it in two of the characters, Pierre and Françoise. They have built their life on utter sincerity and have a system of language which, they think, makes it possible for them, while leading each his own life, "to be free in their union." They are transparent to each other and their individual world is completely shared. But such love is a myth: it is impossible to love and to be free from commitment, to love one person and to be free to love and be loved by another without breaking faith with the first, even if, by mutual consent, each proclaims the other free. In the novel, Françoise discovers this truth in the metaphysical drama which results from the introduction of a third (Xaviére) whose love destroys the previous supposed unity of the two. At that moment the world Françoise had created for herself disintegrates; she feels herself alienated from Pierre, and no amount of "verbal communication" can take the place of "living a love," for this time Pierre lives his love for Xaviére. At this point, Merleau-Ponty shows that the dramatic realization also shatters the image Françoise had of herself as pure consciousness. A whole

---
[54] *S. N. S.*, p. 61.

new view of life emerges, she understands that each one must exist for himself, "each one must decide for himself, each is condemned to acts which are his own."[55] Thus the illusion of perfect communication, happiness and purity vanish from Françoise's life. Merleau-Ponty points out also that personal responsibility and yet personal innocence are made evident in the drama; and the notion of ambiguity and of a multiplicity of intentions in human actions is brought out.

There is no knowledge of self to a degree of transparence, wherein our thoughts are absolutely and unequivocally present to us. On the contrary, in every lived situation—be it love, sexuality, or any other personal expression—we have at best an equivocal contact with ourselves, for our being in situation prevents us from seeing ourselves as a mere spectator would see us. This poses the question of the possibility of certitude. If I can be victim of illusion, if I am not entirely engaged in certain sentiments, how can I determine an authentic experience? If I am deceived once how can I be assured that I am not always deceived? It seems that we are before an alternative of either an absolute consciousness or an invincible doubt. If I do not effectively will, love, act, I do fall prey to doubt with regard to the world and to my own conscious thoughts. There is a sort of gradual revelation of self to self by an "inner perception" by which—always in retrospect—I discover my true self. Thus, in illusory love, I may become aware of the emptiness of my first emotion which, however, was true as an emotion. Man is not wholly transparent, nor is he capable of projecting his consciousness with an all-embracing grasp of future life. But Merleau-Ponty, looking back, says we can reconstruct our progress as a "synthesis in the making."

The love which worked out its dialectic through me, and of which I have just become aware, was not from

---
[55] *S. N. S.*, p. 60.

the beginning, a thing hidden in my unconscious, nor an object before my consciousness, but an impulse carrying me towards someone, and a transformation of thoughts and behavior . . . it was a matter of experience rather than knowledge, from beginning to end.[56]

The thoughts of love, hate, will, are steeped in existence and that is why they are indubitable as thoughts. Interior perception does not suffice to give me certitude, because I am a subject which *becomes* what he is not, not an object to be observed.

6. *The Cogito: Merleau-Ponty's Interpretation*

Now a question presents itself: if intersubjective relations are rooted in the body and founded on the perceptive existential experience of the subject, what is the function of the Cogito? Merleau-Ponty's fundamental criticism of Descartes is this: if the object of my perception can be doubted, why not the subject also? Thus Merleau-Ponty questions the indubitability of consciousness. The "cogito" of Merleau-Ponty will be open to doubt just as much as the object of his thought. If it is indubitable that I think, am I always sure that the object of my thought is actually there? It seems easy to disassociate the "I think I see" from the evidence of *what* I think—that is, its existence. But, in fact, I cannot disassociate the two. Perception is a kind of act wherein it is impossible to separate the act itself from its term. Perception and the perceived have necessarily the same existential modality: it is impossible to disassociate from perception the consciousness which attains the thing perceived. Obviously, I cannot maintain the certitude of perception while rejecting that of the thing perceived. The whole problem is precisely this: *when* do I see in the true sense of the word? If I see, in the true sense of the word,

---

[56] *P. P.*, p. 436.

the thing I see is there: to see is to see something. It is essential to my vision to be referred to something actually seen, and not merely to a pretended vision of a thing—that is, the thought of seeing. We cannot disassociate the certitude of our existence from the certitude of the existence of the perceived object. This, however, does not yet tell me *whether* the thing is there, *when* I perceive—just how do I know that I truly perceive—that the object is truly there? If I have a doubt about the existence of the thing perceived, such doubt necessarily reverts to the perceiver, that is to say, "I have not *perceived* [seen] *truly,* I admit that in each moment there has not occurred this adequation between my intention and the visible which is vision in act."[57]

It follows then that there are two possibilities: a) either I am not certain of the things themselves—in which case I cannot be certain of my perception taken as a simple thought, because perception itself involves the affirmation of the thing; b) or I may know with certitude my own thought—but this pre-supposes at once the existence which it endorses.

Descartes' contention therefore, that the existence of visible things can be doubted but that our own vision, considered as simple thought, cannot be doubted is not tenable. Neither is it tenable if we understand by our vision a mere possibility of seeing or a probability of seeing; here "the thought of seeing" implies a resemblance to actual vision in which the certitude of the thing was assured. But Merleau-Ponty says quite strongly that after all "the certitude of a possibility is only the possibility of a certitude"[58] and the thought of seeing is only "vision in thought" and therefore not actual vision. However, no matter under which aspect you consider it, the thought of seeing has no more certitude than actual vision has; that is to say, I am only certain of my thought of seeing if it is derived from effective vision

---
[57] *P. P.,* p. 430.
[58] *P. P.,* p. 430.

and not in any other way. For an absolute idealism of course, the thought of seeing would stand on its own merit, because the thought *is* the real. Thus transcendental idealism becomes a realism in the absolute sense. Hence Merleau-Ponty denies that sensation *in itself* (whatever that may mean, for there is no possibility of sensation without an object or apart from a sensing subject) is always true and that, therefore, error is the result of the transcendental judgment. For, how is the judgment motivated? Is it not precisely the perceived phenomena which give rise to the judgment itself? The interpretation is therefore not independent of the actuality of the perception. Nor is the danger of error eliminated in the domain of consciousness for "consciousness is through and through [de part en part] transcendence, but not a passive transcendence [transcendance subie] . . . but an active transcendence."[59] The certitude of thought can only be based on the certitude of vision of this or that thing (not on the purely interior vision—which would be something immanent). The vision of this or that thing is an act and therefore it must have an actual, concrete object, and not merely the thought of an object; it must be a "contingent" operation and not an eternal one— "eternal operation" is contradictory, for something eternal is not in process and does not achieve at a point in time a definite status which it previously lacked. Hence, the notion of seeing or sensing "in itself" is simply nonsense: there is no perception without the perceived. We must then conclude that the Cogito reveals to me not the notion of an act in the abstract, but the movement of my own transcendence in the very act of being immersed in the world by actual perception. Only thus, Merleau-Ponty claims, the notion of the Cogito according to Descartes can be re-interpreted in an existential and therefore valid way.[60]

[59] *P. P.*, p. 431.
[60] *P. P.*, pp. 431-32. Descartes had attempted this already, without much success. (Cf. Sixth Meditation.)

Intersubjectivity and Personal Relations

Perception is then an operation which always surpasses itself; it does not come from the interior except insofar as the perceiving subject has had a first contact with a transcendent world. Yet perception does not dispel ambiguity, not the possibility of error—I must in fact, expose myself to the risk of falling into error if I want to find the truth. The truth of the "real" will not be an eternal, but a temporal truth—the only one Merleau-Ponty freely admits possible. Thus consciousness must be inserted into the temporal and the self must find a way to connect the "eternity" of ideas (in the sense that ideas are unchanging) with the moments of time.[61] Both my perception and my consequent thoughts are quite contingent.[62]

Further, not only my actual perception, but even my doubts must be steeped in actuality, for even in doubt the only way to achieve certitude of it is to doubt completely and effectively: one must doubt something, or even everything, in order to achieve certitude of the self-doubting, and, indirectly at least, of the things doubted—that is, to assume them as doubtful. It is only in relation to things that I know myself: interior perception comes later and only after I have *lived* my doubt. I cannot verify the reality of my doubt as I cannot verify the perception of the thing; if I were to attempt this I would become involved in an endless regression, having to doubt the thought of my doubt, then the thought of this thought, ad infinitum.

> The certitude comes from the doubt itself as an act [a doubt in the concrete] and not from these thoughts, as

---

[61] *P. P.*, p. 427.

[62] "If the Cogito reveals to me a new mode of existence which has nothing to do with time, if I discover myself as the universal constituent of all being which is accessible to me, and as a transcendental field without folds and without exteriority, I must not only say that my spirit . . . is the God of Spinoza . . . I must say without restrictions that my spirit is God." *P. P.*, pp. 426-27.

the certitude of the thing and of the world precedes the knowledge of their properties.[63]

It does not follow that Merleau-Ponty considers doubt not an act; he refers here to the "mere" thought of a thing as contrasted with a thought arising from a concrete situation. This is the crucial point of Merleau-Ponty's new Cogito: not the "thought of" an activity, but the act which gives rise to the thought is at the heart of my consciousness. In this consists the existential meaning of his Cogito. Thus, he will also say that it is not the "I think" which will contain the "I am," but rather the "I am," in its transcendence, takes up the "I think" and incorporates it in its existential movement, through which consciousness also becomes existential.[64]

The cogito is really the recognition of this fundamental fact: there are acts by which I can be conscious of myself and at the same time transcend myself—but this same condition makes possible both truth and illusion with regard to myself.[65]

Not even in pure thought is it possible for me to achieve absolute identity with myself, for even in considering abstract geometrical truths I am involved in the materiality of my imagination constructing the figures in question. Therefore, be it question of sentiment, of pure thought, or of expression—language or painting—my existential subjectivity is always involved and I am never a thought transparent to itself; in order to have absolute evidence of myself and of the world "it would be necessary for me to become a pure knower of myself, and for the world to cease to exist around me in order to become a pure object before me."[66]

Merleau-Ponty's interpretation of the Cogito consists in this: he gives it a temporal thickness. If I am not victim of an interminable doubt and if "I think" it is because I am

---
[63] P. P., p. 439.
[64] P. P., p. 439.
[65] P. P., pp. 436-38.
[66] P. P., p. 453.

engaged in existential experience. The ontological contingency of the world is the foundation of all my ideas of truth. "Both the unity of the world and the unity of the subject are invoked rather than proved each time I perceive"; it is through the universal subject that both perception and evidence are founded, as "it is through a present thought that I achieve the unity of my thoughts."[67]

7. Presence and the Subject

The most important thing is to know that the world and the view of the world are inseparable: if we understand this we can understand subjectivity as inherence in the world.

We do not affirm that the *notion* of the world cannot be separated from the notion of the subject, or that the subject "thinks" of himself as immersed in the world and therefore inseparable from it; if it were so the thinking would not affect the being—to think a relation does not establish it, the independence of the thinking subject would remain untouched, and the subject would not be situated in the world thereby. If he is in situation it is because he effectively has entered in situation with his body-in-the-world. That is why I find, if I reflect on subjectivity, that its essence is bound to that of the body and of the world; it is so because there is some sort of identity of thought and being (which, however, Merleau-Ponty has closed to himself by his approach). My existence as subjectivity and my existence as body are one with the existence of the world, because my being as subject is inseparable from this body and this world. The ontological body and the ontological world we find at the center of the subject are not merely "ideas of" the world or of the body; they are "the world itself compressed in a global view and the body itself as conscious."[68]

---

[67] *P. P.*, p. 465.
[68] *P. P.*, p. 467. In other words, existence, at all levels, is a meeting with things and with the world; the temporal synthesis functions as conditioning form and the lived reality of the world as conditioned content, the subject is at the center of this relation.

However, if the world and the subject are not the result of a constitution, how do we explain the concordance of appearances so that a truth or an idea emerges? Merleau-Ponty answers: this is the problem of rationality, which remains unsolved.[69] Absolute thought can only be as clear to me as my finite mind can conceive it. We *are* in the world, things appear, we understand our own and the other's existence.[70] All that is needed is to recognize the phenomena which form the foundation of all our certitudes. Belief in an absolute spirit and in a world in itself, detached from us, is nothing but a rationalization of that primitive faith.[71]

We can thus consider the world as the cradle of significations and the means by which we can overcome the idealism-realism dichotomy; hence it is the home of all rationality. The analysis of time clarifies that of the meaning of the world: the past is not past, nor the future future; time exists only when a subject breaks the fullness of being and, introducing the phenomenon of perspective, injects non-being into it.[72] The object and the subject, then, are but two moments of a unique structure, "presence." It is only through time that we can think being, and by the relation of time as both subject and object we come to understand the relation of the subject to the world: the subject is essentially temporal—a presence—and the world is "subjective" inasmuch as its texture and its articulations are designed by the transcendental movements of the subject.[73]

---

[69] One might ask whether it really is the problem of rationality. Why rationality and not the evidence of sensation?

[70] This is certainly a bold statement. Do we really *understand* each other? To a degree, yes; completely, no; as Merleau-Ponty has said so often. Yet here he says: "chaque existence se comprend et comprend les autres." P. P., p. 468.

[71] P. P., p. 468.

[72] P. P., p. 481.

[73] P. P., pp. 491-92. Merleau-Ponty deals with the problem of temporality in great detail (which we treat only briefly). Cf. pp. 467-95; also: pp. 484; 398-99; 516-17.

Intersubjectivity and Personal Relations

The analysis of the notion of presence, involving the presence to self and the presence to the world, and the identification of the Cogito with the engagement in the world, makes us understand how we can find the other in his visible behavior. Obviously, the other will never exist for me as I myself exist—we can never witness in him as we do in ourselves the power of temporalization. But since two temporalities do not exclude each other—as consciousnesses do—for each can relate to the other as they project themselves in the present, the presence of the other far from being a menace to me is a gain. This is a positive reaffirmation of intersubjectivity in direct contrast with Sartre's negative notion of the same. My world is enlarged in the measure in which my private existence assumes collective history.

> The solution of all the problems of transcendence is found in the thickness of the pre-objective present wherein we find our corporeity, our sociality, the pre-existence of the world, that is to say, the point of departure for all "explanations"—insofar as they are legitimate—and at the same time the foundation of our liberty.[74]

8. *Human Liberty*

There remains one more aspect of the human subject to explore: liberty. Merleau-Ponty seems to have neglected this aspect of man's experience if we are to judge from the few pages dedicated to it in *Phénoménologie de la perception*. He hasn't, however; the fact of man's freedom has been treated from the very beginning of his investigation when he undertook to study the relation of consciousness to nature. Throughout his works and particularly in his articles he emphasized the independence of the subject from

---
[74] *P. P.*, pp. 494-95.

physical, biological and psychophysical causes. Although for him freedom is rather ambiguous, and not without limitations, he maintains that the subject is an "absolute," not the result of antecedents or of physical and social environment. Man's choice of these things for his own development and use, and not blind forces makes him what he is. Thus, if man's freedom is conditioned, for world and subject reciprocally determine each other, even this determination is not deprived of choice; even though the choice is not radical, since man begins and remains in situation, still he can choose within the possibilities given. In fact, he is so free that he can also choose not to choose. The world chooses us—we have an "essence"[75]—and we choose the world. Our freedom arises against a background of existing meanings:

> There is, as Husserl says, a "field of liberty" and a "conditioned liberty," not that freedom is absolute within the limits of this field and non-existent outside of it, (as the perceptive field, also that of liberty is without confines) but inasmuch as I have both near and remote possibilities. Our commitment sustains our power and there is no liberty without some power.[76]

History forms the background for our freedom, a freedom within a given manner of life, which is determined by our corporeal situation as well as by our cultural milieu. For Merleau-Ponty there is certainly room for an existential

---

[75] As an existentialist Merleau-Ponty maintains that man is already in situation, has the choice of this or that project, but within a certain framework and not from nothing. Even if all of his projects come from his choice, what he is, and the possibilities of his choices are not pure liberty; they arise from a certain "essence" which man already is, arising from a developmental process, and not from pure creation. When he speaks of structuration (*S.C.*) he implies as much. We may contrast Merleau-Ponty with Sartre, who said that "choice and consciousness are . . . one and the same thing." *L'Être et le néant* (Paris: Gallimard, 1940), p. 539.

[76] *P.P.*, p. 518.

choice, but there is no unlimited freedom as we would find in Sartre, for instance, when he considers man "condemned to be free." In Merleau-Ponty's view

> I am the one who gives significance and future to my life; but this does not imply that this meaning and that future arise from conception; they spring from my present situation, and from my past, most of all, from my past and present coexistence.[77]

Of course, I could refuse to choose to be what I am, but this does not necessitate a constant choosing of myself; not to refuse is different from choosing, as not to interefere is different from doing. It is difficult to distinguish the part played by situation from that played by freedom. We are so involved in the world and with others that we are veritably in an inextricable relation. Yet this does not destroy the freedom of our acts—a condition quite compatible with our engagement in history.[78]

As noted, for Merleau-Ponty freedom starts from a limiting situation: I exist a certain situation; over this I have no control. Beyond this situation, my choice is not so much conscious as existential, that is to say, preconscious. This existential limitation illustrates once more Merleau-Ponty's notion of ambiguity and indeterminacy. I am not free absolutely; my freedom does not spring from nothing; I am only free to interrupt a certain project, in which I already find myself engaged, and start another—but always within a given situation. Thus my freedom is really a freedom to change or shift existing conditions, not to create radically new ones. Very aptly does Merleau-Ponty express this notion when he remarks, at different times, that not to act is

---

[77] *P.P.*, p. 510.
[78] *P.P.*, pp. 516-18.

Merleau-Ponty

already taking a position, not to speak is already expressing something. Here meaning is made very explicit:

> It is true that at each instant I can interrupt my projects. But what is this power? It is the power to begin other things, for we are never suspended in nothingness. We are always in the full, in being, as a face which, even at rest, even in death, is always condemned to express something.[79]

Concluding, Merleau-Ponty makes it very clear that my liberty is enmeshed with others through interpersonal relations. For, not only is my existential situation ambiguous and limited because of my relations to the world, but my liberty is molded, and, in a way, limited by other liberties, which like myself are condemned to "express" even in their silence. Thus, the "knot of relations" which constitutes man, is made up of the corporeal as well as of the spiritual ties which bind him to his fellow man. My liberty is assured if I but accept the human situation and live it:

> I cannot fail to have freedom, unless I seek to go beyond my natural and social situation by refusing to assume it at the beginning, instead of rejoining through it the natural and human world.[80]

---

[79] *P.P.*, p. 516.
[80] *P.P.*, p. 520.

CHAPTER EIGHT

CONCLUSION

Concluding such limited study of Merleau-Ponty's philosophy it is hardly justified to pause and ask some questions about the import of his phenomenological investigation and its value as a philosophy. Yet, one must,[1] not to compare him with other thinkers, but to bring to light whatever merit his thought may have, as well as to point out possible flaws.

First of all, the question arises: "Is Merleau-Ponty's phenomenology only a description of experience, or is it, as he claims it to be, already a philosophy? There are diverging opinions on the matter. Some of Merleau-Ponty's texts[2] would lead one to say that it is only a phenomenology; yet if all of his writings are considered one cannot doubt that his work is philosophical. The important thing is to see whether his investigation of the ultimate structure of reality reached a truly philosophical dimension.

The most outstanding structure of existence he describes is the dialectical relation of the reciprocal poles of exchange between any two aspects of experience. These occur at various levels and in different dimensions; we find them in the description of knowledge resulting in a synthesis: myself and the other, myself and the world; in the description of man: everything in him is intentional, and these intentionalities are structured among themselves—they condition,

---

[1] We refer the reader to the last chapter of Kwant's book, *The Phenomenological Philosophy of Merleau-Ponty*, p. 224ff., for a searching critique of Merleau-Ponty's philosophy. This chapter is particularly important because it considers the author's thought without comparing it with that of other philosophers. In general, we agree with Kwant's criticism except for some minor points to which reference will be made later.

[2] For instance where he asserts that existential experience *is the solution* of every philosophical problem. Cf. Preface to *Phénoménologie de la perception*.

imply, and "recall" each other;[3] in the categories of interiority, the "cogito," reflection, freedom: they are situated in a dialectic and are in relation with the historical and world situation.[4] The world has need of man to be "the world"; being is being when it is "being-for-me." In the historical context, phenomenology reveals intersubjectivity at the cultural level: individual and class are then the two poles of tension enacting the drama of history.[5]

Intentionality, temporality and incarnation are the key themes of Merleau-Ponty's existential phenomenology. Such approach to the world and to man-in-the-world is not yet a complete philosophical account.[6] However, insights gained by Merleau-Ponty's phenomenological investigation certainly provide us with a solid basis for a philosophical development. Even if phenomenology alone is thought to be insufficient as a philosophy,[7] it is certainly adequate, in fact necessary, as a point of departure for the philosopher intent on investigating reality, and not merely "constructing" an abstract "theory," of being.

De Waelhens admits that in some cases Merleau-Ponty gives us reasons to doubt his philosophical attitude. For instance, when Merleau-Ponty says that all knowledge is rooted in perception, this ambiguous statement can be taken in two senses: it may mean that all knowledge begins with the concrete and that it must be made explicit; or it may mean that we can never emerge from the immediate; and that to "live" our experience would be our "explicitation" of the same; in the latter case, obviously, the whole enter-

---
[3]Cf. the three levels of structuration, *S. C.*, Ch. III.
[4]Cf. *P. P.*, p. iii; p. 417; *Eloge*, p. 12, pp. 25-27.
[5]"L'homme est une idée historique et non pas une espèce naturelle. En d'autre termes, il n'y a dans l'existence humaine aucune possession inconditionnée et pourtant aucun attribut fortuit." *P. P.*, p. 199. Cf. also *Les Aventures de la dialectique*, wherein he re-examines the Marxist philosophy as well as the historicity of man.
[6]He did not live to complete his work.
[7]It remains to be seen, however, whether a radical phenomenological investigation can be made without a philosophical involvement.

Conclusion

prise of the philosopher would simply be contradictory.[8] The same thing appears in Merleau-Ponty's treatment of the historical dimension of man-in-the-world. If the spectator's attitude is not at all possible, how can he avoid a measure of subjectivism? This lack of distance would, of course, prejudice the philosophical attitude of the phenomenologist. Professor Kockelmans, while admitting that Merleau-Ponty is right in insisting that we are totally immersed in the world, comments:

> I am in the world with my whole being and the world penetrates to the heart of my subjectivity; but I am not entirely in the world, since the human mode of being by its very essence keeps its distance from the world. . . . We have to view this distance from the world as an essential characteristic of our being-in-the-world. Merleau-Ponty does not deny this, but he has not underlined this idea sufficiently.[9]

It is precisely this lack of stress on the possibility—indeed necessity—of a secondary reflection which makes it difficult to assess Merleau-Ponty's phenomenology as genuinely philosophical. His fault lies in having taken for granted certain ontological presuppositions and having overlooked the necessity of clearly defining the transcendental dimensions of man. For, as Kockelmans observes, if man is mundane, he is also "more than mundane. In this light the presence of man in the world becomes a real problem, indeed perhaps the most important problem for any philosophical system."[10] In this Merleau-Ponty has not reached the truly philosophical level which marks his other investigations.

---

[8] De Waelhens, *Une philosophie*, p. 386.
[9] Joseph A. Kockelmans, "Merleau-Ponty's Phenomenology of Language," *Review of Existential Psychology and Psychiatry*, Vol. III, no. 1 (Winter 1963), p. 81. However, Kockelmans is far from denying the greatness of Merleau-Ponty as a philosopher. Cited hereafter as *Phenomenology of language*.
[10] Kockelmans, *Phenomenology of language*, p. 81.

However, De Waehlens definitely holds that Merleau-Ponty's phenomenology is a philosophy. In the last two parts of his *Une philosophie de l'ambiguité,* in which he considers the ontological status of Merleau-Ponty's philosophy, he says it is possible to find in it an ontological character of both man and experience. He maintains that there is no need of elaborating a general ontology, but simply of disengaging the ontological implications already found in description; reflection may then be raised to the level of intelligibility required of a philosophical system. He thinks this possibility must be admitted in order to preserve the real import of the phenomenological insights gained into the self and the world.[11] No doubt, his contention is supported by Merleau-Ponty's references to that effect, although, in his study of essences, both phenomenologically and dialectically, the latter fails to work out the ontological implications of either the essences or the structures he describes.[12]

However, some criticism of Merleau-Ponty's method of philosophizing from his own viewpoint itself is mandatory. The development of his thought and the conclusions he reaches are often not warranted by his original data. If, as he claims, philosophical reflection must be based on the prereflexive and have no presuppositions of any kind, it must then proceed purely from the given in perceptive experience. This very laudable intention, as explained by Merleau-Ponty in his Preface to *Phénoménologie de la perception,* could be considered as a sort of blueprint for an adequate and fruitful investigation of reality in its most mysterious depth, in its fundamental, ontological ground, as well as in its various manifestations at existential and transcendental levels. According to this phenomenological method it should

---

[11] De Waelhens, *Une philosophie,* p. 259.
[12] In De Waelhens, "In memoriam Merleau-Ponty" (*Tijdschrift v. Philos.,* 23, 1961) mention is made of a book, *Le visible et l'invisible* which Merleau-Ponty was writing at the time of his death. In it he was attempting an ontological interpretation which he would borrow from Heidegger.

Conclusion

be quite possible to arrive at a valid philosophical appraisal of our existential experience. Since he understands philosophy as a profound reflection on experience such that the philosopher himself is not outside his investigation (not a mere spectator), but within it, the attitude of the philosopher becomes quite relevant to the character reality will disclose. Therefore, phenomenology should lead to the very heart of being through an authentic grasp of the originally given in perception as ontological ground and not merely as the psychological datum of a conscious being; it would involve man's becoming gradually aware of himself in the world and of the world itself in relation to—or rather, interrelation with—other men.

A further reflection on one's own experience, a phenomenology of phenomenology, should reveal the "cogito" as a deepening of the intentional and the rational interpretations of that experience which is the first genuine contact with the world and with others. As Merleau-Ponty's phenomenology is "already a philosophy," it should be expected to answer philosophical questions with a certain degree of completeness, or at least, to indicate the general lines of inquiry to be followed for a solution of proposed problems.

Now, looking exclusively at the development of Merleau-Ponty's thought through his various works—particularly his two major ones—it should be possible to see therein the realization of the theory put forth in the Preface, according to his own design. It should be possible to say that the phenomenological investigations of man as a body-subject, of perception as the basis of one's communion with others and with the world, have yielded the results Merleau-Ponty describes. It should appear that place and time as dimensions of man's being-in-the-world, and the "cogito" as a condition for choice and therefore for personal liberty, do indeed constitute the natural development of a primordial pre-conscious state of existence. But it is here that exception must be taken. Merleau-Ponty's investigation could not produce evidence that the above mentioned philosophical insights and conclusions were arrived at while remaining purely and constantly within the phenomenological investigation of man-in-the-world. This is not to say that there is any other being besides "being-for-man,"[13] but, rather, that the philosophical investigation he pursues is not purely phenomenological, but has its point of departure or support in a rational *a priori* which goes beyond the phenomenon, understood as manifestation of being at the perceptive, bodily level. It must always be remembered that *Phénoménologie de la perception* is concerned with the fact of perception, and that Merleau-Ponty did not develop any other theme in an exhaustive manner. If he had, then it might be possible to ascertain whether or not the phenomenological investigation could reveal the fundamental roots of being at every level. It is entirely possible that Merleau-Ponty may have done this kind of phenomenological investigation and then incorporated its results into his works without indicating the process by which he attained such results; in this case we would find no fault with his conclusions; but since we do not have evidence of phenomenological investigations other than those presented in his published works, we have to point out this deficiency as a flaw in his philosophical development.[14]

---

[13] We do not consider that Merleau-Ponty's entire synthesis is "suspended in mid-air . . ." *because* "all meaning exists thanks to the presence of man and this presence is a contingent fact." (Kwant, *Phenomenological Philosophy*, p. 233). We should like to point out that, without man there would indeed be no meaning possible—who or "what" could either give or find meaning? Even if one were to posit the Supreme Being as giver of meaning, in this our human world— the world we know—man alone could make such an assertion, also based on the way he knows and understands being.

[14] Kwant criticizes Merleau-Ponty on this point precisely for the reason mentioned. He claims that Merleau-Ponty is not entitled to draw the conclusions he draws in relation to truth, for instance, because he has not "analyzed the proper inner character of truth." (Cf. *Phenomenological Philosophy*, p. 227). But we may observe that since Merleau-Ponty maintains ambiguity prevails, we may hardly expect from him *clear* descriptions.

Conclusion

Yet, it is entirely possible that, while intending to follow the phenomenological revelations of being, he may have found in his experience precisely that which he had "thought" such experience should reveal. Thus his phenomenology would involve more a priori elements than he is willing to admit, hence less of that openness he claims characterizes his thought.

1. *Prevailing Ambiguity*

Another characteristic of Merleau-Ponty's philosophy is *ambiguity*. This term does not apply to his way of expressing himself (though he is also, at times, ambiguous), but to the way reality manifests itself and to the degree of understanding and "meaning" of this reality which he discloses. Whatever be the manner or mode of the relations he describes, or the elements of the dialectical exchange he presents or illustrates, the *results* of his reflection are always an intertwining and a relative confusion of the "related"—yet, a confusion which admits of a relative distinction of entities.

Just what are the reasons for this ambiguity, according to Merleau-Ponty? Primarily, (and ultimately), ambiguity results from the condition of being-in-the-world, or from the materiality of existents. Since man's spirit is not a disengaged and disinterested spectator, it naturally follows that all of man's accounts of reality can never have the clarity and lucidity which they might claim to have in an idealistic philosophy—that is, one maintaining absolute independence of the spirit from the material conditions of the body and of the world. The basic contention is that, even consciousness, as awareness of the world and of men in the world, is not a disengaged consciousness, but one immersed into the very situation it perceives, experiences, judges, or reflects upon. Naturally, this is so because of the involvement of the spirit and the physical body—for Merleau-Ponty, as was discussed, there is man, the Ego-subject, the body-subject,

Merleau-Ponty

the conscious being, but not any such entity as a "body" or a "soul," one apart from, or independent of the other. According to Merleau-Ponty, not only does not man ever judge a situation from a disinterested point of view, but his very viewing of the situation also modifies it. We must never lose sight of the fact that the whole of his phenomenology is an attempt at elucidating the fact of man's situation in the world. That ambiguity prevails is not the outcome of confused thinking on his part; the truth is that existence is itself ambiguous; beginning from the *Cogito* down to the last and most material level of being, that which is experienced is not clear. Thus, the cogito is really consciousness reintegrated in existence which grasps itself in an obscure manner. My presence to myself is possible because of my presence to the world, but this presence reveals to me my utterly ambiguous situation. Thévenaz says that this existence will not be for Merleau-Ponty either anxiety, restlessness, or damnation, but ambiguity, chance and risk.[15]

The transcendental, Merleau-Ponty says, is the world itself; it is the existential being-in-the-world, the *ambiguous* life, for we are involved in each other's existence and therefore the intentional threads of our consciousnesses mix and are inextricably confused with one another. It is therefore no wonder that, when Merleau-Ponty says that the world is the cradle of all meaning, he immediately qualifies this by admitting that meaning also is ambiguous.

> But "meaning" has a new sense for Merleau-Ponty: it is the ambiguous but fundamental Logos, already present in our original relation to the world. "There is meaning," not *a* meaning. Meaning is ambiguous, mixed up with non-meaning (Non-sens) because the reduction is never complete. One can no more say that everything has meaning then that everything is non-

[15] Thévenaz, *Phenomenology* . . ., p. 84. Obviously he refers to other existentialists, e.g., Sartre.

Conclusion

sense. But we take up this meaning, which is unreflected rationality, by reflection; we prolong it, and each of our thoughts expresses or gives a meaning to the world, without ever expressing it completely.[16]

Merleau-Ponty discovers the same ambiguity at the level of action and of social life; history also is ambiguous. There would be no human history if everything were either wholly meaningful or totally absurd. Meaning emerges from the mixed and ambiguous situation of our being in the world, from our language, from the intentions of our actions, which cannot be fully and clearly qualified at any one time as deriving purely from this or that motivation. There is ambiguity also, and particularly, in our psychophysical relations as there is ambiguity in our direct contact with the world by perception. It is very significant that Merleau-Ponty never tires of saying that we can have certitude of everything in general, but not of anything in particular, precisely because ambiguity always prevails. Merleau-Ponty is fully aware of this and accepts it as the only possible way of appearing of reality. Alquié doubts that anyone has ever pushed further the philosophic acceptance of ambiguity than Merleau-Ponty has done in his theory of the immanent-transcendent object—the theory which would overcome the idealistic-realistic problem. Intersubjective communication and social world relations previous to judgment are modes of coexistence. The world of immanence and that of transcendence coincide—immanence of principle and transcendence of fact, which, as existence, are ambiguous.[17]

We must note, however, that Merleau-Ponty's thought, if followed to its logical conclusion on the score of ambiguity alone could cause havoc to his whole philosophy. Ambiguity

---

[16]Thévenaz, *Phenomenology* . . ., p. 88.
[17]Alquié, "Une philosophie . . .," p. 57: "For Merleau-Ponty there is a être-à-deux of dialogue, and there is a social world previous to all judgment. Class and nation are 'modes of coexistence.'"

could become an excuse for retreat whenever a questioning of reality affords no answer; it could even impede man's intersubjective relations: if, for instance, we can never ascribe a decision or a choice to a specified motive then human communication may become doubtful. Further, if, as Merleau-Ponty claims, we can never be sure of anything in particular, we run a great risk of falling into doubts in the concrete—in spite of the fact that the general certitude he posits may save us from complete skepticism. Therefore, while it is quite true that the light of our knowledge is always accompanied by much darkness, a faithful adherence to Merleau-Ponty's thought, might result in a serious underestimation of man's intellectual potential. We must therefore admit that the things Merleau-Ponty has left unsaid and the problems he has neglected to study[18] leave some serious gaps in his philosophy.

Yet, in spite of lacunae, Merleau-Ponty's thought is rich and fruitful, as well as novel to a degree. Roland Caillois maintains that Merleau-Ponty's philosophy is no less revolutionary than others; more so in fact, for it assumes the task of

> understanding human existence as historical existence, as unique fact as well as actual destiny. It does not pretend to "eternity";[19] rather, it inserts itself in the becoming of history; it attempts to help man "of today" to take notice of his situation, of his ties with the world; and, finally, [it strives] to understand itself as a philosophy. It is for this reason that it puts itself on the philosophical level as well as on the level of facts in the daily battle for a more human future.[20]

---

[18] Cf. pp. 322 ff.
[19] This observation obviously absolves Merleau-Ponty from the accusation that he denies the absolute.
[20] R. Caillois, "De la perception . . .", p. 59.

Conclusion

According to Caillois, a thought which embraces both the philosophical level and the concreteness of facticity is not only a philosophy, but a richer one. This he claims to be Merleau-Ponty's merit. In fact, he goes so far as to say that, if Merleau-Ponty is not absolutely original he has certainly seen what no one else has.

> If Merleau-Ponty owes all to Husserl, it is equally true that no one before Merleau-Ponty read what he did in Husserl. Hence, Merleau-Ponty can be called an original philosopher.[21]

2. *Experience and the Absolute*

The question of the validity of his dialectic of experience, which could be better qualified as a tension between poles in relation, should not even be raised. It is quite true that description of lived experience of itself does not remove any of the philosophical problems. However, what basis would we have for philosophical reflection if we were to neglect experience—that is where would we find a point of departure if we were to refuse our *lived* experience? To begin with the "Cogito" or with "pure consciousness" would not free us from the necessity of seeking the origin of such "Cogito" or of the content of consciousness. Therefore we must say that, if the description of lived experience does not suffice to solve philosophical problems, it is nevertheless necessary for a philosophical reflection true to the nature of reality. A philosophy which does not come to terms with the historicity, contingency and finitude of man, or an idealistic or a rationalistic position which refuses to consider and cannot accord with the phenomena and character of human and intersubjective experience condemns itself. However, once these basic facts of human life and experience are accepted,

---

[21] R. Caillois, "De la perception...", p. 60. This very strong assertion of Merleau-Ponty's philosopical stature is much more valuable in that Caillois is not sparing in his criticism of Merleau-Ponty's weak points.

we must proceed to a deeper level of reflection—and it is here that Merleau-Ponty stops short of the mark. He does not ask, for instance, how knowledge is attained, or why being reveals itself; he does not "wonder" about the ultimate meaning of being; he does not ask whether man has a wider openness than that of being-to-the-world-through-the-body and of being-for-the-other-through-the-body. This is to say that Merleau-Ponty does not really come to grips with the question of the Absolute.[22] He definitely remains in the realm of the purely contingent, and human, and wordly. He does not really ask the ultimate questions. The contention that a reflection going beyond phenomenology is neither required nor possible is a flaw in Merleau-Ponty's philosophy. Wahl comments:

> Merleau-Ponty says that the signifying has an immanent meaning, that there is no place for a further elaboration, that phenomenology is everything or nothing: we belong to a pre-constituted world, truth is theoretically impossible, truth is a sedimentation, there is a phenomenological philosophy, phenomenology is a philosophy and it must establish itself there definitively.[23]

He does not agree with Merleau-Ponty's point of view. Merleau-Ponty has insisted that there is a logic which gathers into a totality all that which needs be understood and one wants to understand; and while there are risks with regard to reason, there is a spontaneity of the body in the word; my body shows the other, it reveals to me my presence to the world. But then, Wahl asks, is it not time to

---

[22] R. Jolivet discusses this aspect of Merleau-Ponty's philosophy in "Le problème de l'absolu dans la philosophie de M. Merleau-Ponty," *Tÿjdscrift voor Philosophie,* 19 (Mar.-June, 1957), pp. 53-100, an article which, in its critique of Merleau-Ponty's thought discloses perhaps the deepest signification of the phenomenological method and of the import of phenomenology as a philosophy. Cited hereafter as "Problème de l'absolu . . ."
[23] Wahl, "Conclusion," *Problèmes . . . ,* p. 149.

Conclusion

redefine phenomenology? (This is a task to which Husserl consecrated all his efforts).[24] Commentators are usually reluctant to accept Merleau-Ponty's contention of the supremacy of phenomenology—aside from the fact that, as is usually the case with phenomenologists, he has limited his description to certain facets of human existence: he has chosen to study perception. Other aspects of human dimension he has either neglected or treated rather summarily: we find references to the moral and the religious in some of his articles and a defense of his position in "Le primat de la perception."[25]

Phenomenology demands further reflection. Without further reflection it is not possible to reach an intersubjective and universal truth and even a degree of necessity.[26] What does it mean to say that "existences understand each other"[27] (in a mysterious way)? Merleau-Ponty affirms "that it is so," but he does not really solve the problem: he offers no explanation.

Moreover, further reflection is needed to complete phenomenology where it is lacking, in the phenomenological field itself: phenomenology must ask the questions which it has neglected, that is, questions about knowledge, the rela-

---

[24] We may recall the assertion that "La phénoménologie est enveloppante par rapport à la philosophie," *Problèmes*, pp. 102-103; cf. Wahl, "Conclusions," p. 150.

[25] In answering an objection, Merleau-Ponty has this to say: "Il n'a jamais été dans mes intentions de ne pas poser autrui comme sujet moral, et je suis même bien sûr de ne pas l'avoir exclu comme sujet moral. . . ." He further states: "Du seul fait que je fais de la moralité un problème, vous concluez que je la nie. Or le problème en question se pose pour nous tous. Comment savoir si nous avons quelqu 'un en face de nous, sinon en regardant devant nous? Que voyons nous d'abord, sinon des apparences corporelles? . . . Ce n'est pas la méthode phénoménologique qui fait surgir ce problème; quoiqu'elle permette mieux, à mon sens de le resoudre.

. . . La moralité n'est pas donnée mais à faire. Je ne vois pas comment personne pourrait poser autrui sans moi; c'est une impossibilité pour mon expérience," p. 139.

[26] On this point Bréhier also questions Merleau-Ponty and doubts that his doctrine is truly philosophical. "Le Primat . . . ," p. 138.

[27] *P. P.*, p. 468.

tion between experience and thought, corporeity and consciousness. Dialectic phenomenology cannot be definitive: it requires a superior reflection for its own justification, and for its own completion—in fact, for its own understanding of itself.

But this ulterior reflection always presents the danger of relapsing into the error of absolutizing experience—a thing which Merleau-Ponty wants to avoid at all costs. It is precisely to avoid this danger that he maintains in his philosophy a constant tension between the two positions he is trying to avoid,[28] and from whose opposition he is attempting a new synthesis, dialectical, but ambiguous.

All this seems to point inevitably to relativism. Fontan claims that Merleau-Ponty's phenomenology is precisely that. However, he maintains that such relativism does not "deny anything—neither God nor more proximate transcendental beings. Their affirmation subsists and the 'metaphysics' wherein man finds himself is reconstructed within phenomenology. A little index only has changed. It is question of human experience indefinitely provisional, temporal, ambiguous, each term reflecting the others without respite."[29]

Jolivet, however, strongly doubts that Merleau-Ponty has realized in fact, that which he has held all along—that is, that there is no absolute, and that truth can, at the most, be contingent and relative. All the problems which Merleau-Ponty investigates (reason, values, man within the world, the constitution of history which man himself effectuates, man's very relation to the world and to other men) are nothing but ways of orienting him towards the Absolute of being, of thought and of values. But this Absolute, far from blocking the elan of reason and the progress of morality makes him more and more aware of the impossibility in which men find themselves of stopping any attempt to reach

---
[28] I. e., idealism and realism.
[29] Pierre Fontan, "Le primat de l'acte sur l'énoncé: A propos de la 'Phénoménologie de la perception,'" *Revue Philosophique de Louvain*, 53, 1955, p. 46.

Conclusion

it—for the Absolute is precisely that which maintains man's questioning attitude always open,[30] and does not permit an answer that would end the search. Jolivet goes farther and says that "one should not plead for the Absolute, for no one ever renounces it except in words."[31] This may very well be the case for Merleau-Ponty. To affirm the relative is another way of invoking, at least virtually, the absolute. But Merleau-Ponty also affirms that the very absolute which we seek beyond our experience is already contained in the experience itself. "There is neither destruction of the absolute nor of rationality, except of the absolute or of rationality as separate."[32] Thus, it would seem, he does not really deny the absolute, except insofar as it is divorced from experience. He holds that Christianity has already replaced the abstract Absolute by the Absolute in man. God thus ceases to be an exterior God to become one with human life.[33] He thus reaffirms the dialectic nature of reality and the fact of man's intersubjective exchange also at the spiritual level. Once more we can see the ambiguity and interdependence of factors at play in human relations. This is, at bottom, the fundamental tenet of Merleau-Ponty's phenomenology and philosophy as well. This is equivalent to saying that reality is mysterious and that no amount of investigation can dispel the ambiguity of the mystery about anything: nature, the world, man, and God.

3. *The Personal*

Another interesting aspect of Merleau-Ponty's philosophy is his theory of intersubjectivity, and of personal relations. One expects to find in his philosophy a completely developed theory of persons in relation: the investigations of

---

[30] Does not Merleau-Ponty maintain that philosophy is a perennial beginning and that our philosophical endeavors are never definitive—that is, our search for truth must always go on?
[31] Jolivet, "Problème de l'absolu . . .," pp. 190-91.
[32] "Le primat . . .," p. 135.
[33] "Le primat . . .," p. 135.

structure, of the relations of body and soul, of the sexual exchange, and of the incarnation of thought in language seem to point to a final synthesis. Unfortunately, the ambiguity prevailing in all relations, at every level, precludes the possibility of a definitive plan of intersubjectivity at the personal level. Besides, the very basis on which his dialectic is built makes it difficult to have an authentic philosophy of personal relations: his notion of man as "incarnate spirit" (with all the implications involved—previously discussed) almost defines man as a dialectic between a body-subject and an ego-consciousness. All of man's relations, besides being ambiguous, are so expressed that the body, in the role of an indispensable "moment," seems to reduce the relation of intersubjectivity to a less than personal level. The overall view of relations between the Ego and the alter-Ego leaves us very much with the impression that human relations are not necessarily on a spiritual plane, but, rather, that the body is already gifted with intelligence, so that when one speaks of consciousness in man one needs not speak of the personal. It seems to us that for Merleau-Ponty even the act of encounter can take place at the pre-personal level. Of course, there is an encounter of man with the world, but it is precisely made possible by the human element. Kwant makes the point very clear when he affirms that we become familiar with "things" through human encounter: "We become familiar with things because of a previous familiarity with people. We become sensitive to the world because of our sensitivity to other people."[34]

Merleau-Ponty affirms that there are two levels of experience: the pre-personal and the personal. Now, even though he admits that the pre-personal is eventually absorbed by the personal existence, for Merleau-Ponty this prepersonal is very important; it is so basic that we cannot be free from it: it is the body understood as the relationship with the world, as subject. It is the body-subject which is the em-

---

[34] Kwant, *Encounter*, p. 31.

Conclusion

bodiment of the relationship with the world. This relationship gives meaning to the world: hence, there is a sphere of choice previous to conscious choice which we cannot avoid, about which there is nothing we can do. This he maintains to be fundamental: only if we understand this ego-body we can understand the world of our experience. No doubt this insight is very profound and very valuable, and according to Kwant, to a great extent, original.[35] Yet, it seems to us that once Merleau-Ponty has thus qualified the structure of intersubjective relations, he has not done enough. His emphasis on the pre-personal overshadows his study of the personal relation at a higher level; the investigation of the former seems to leave no further questions to be answered. Granted that the pre-conscious and the pre-personal are always present as a sort of substratum, does it not follow that a complete investigation of intersubjectivity should also concern itself with those phenomena which are, no doubt, built on the basic foundation of the personal—the pre-personal—but surpass it? Merleau-Ponty seems to neglect this to a great extent.[36]

A further cause of disappointment to us is Merleau-Ponty's treatment of the personal relation par excellence: love. In *Phénoménologie de la perception* he does not really develop the topic satisfactorily, nor does he seem to come to grips with the problem. His description is rather confused, too brief, at times almost incidental. It seems to us that there is a wealth of possibilities for a phenomenology of love which have been overlooked.[37] Love seems to be just an-

---

[35] Kwant, *Encounter*, p. 31.

[36] *P. P.*, pp. 502 ff. "Au-dessous de moi comme sujet pensant, qui peut à mon gré me situer dans Sirius ou à la surface de la terre, il y a donc comme un moi naturel qui ne quitte pas sa situation terrestre et qui esquisse sans cesse des valorisations absolues. Davantage: mes projets d'être pensant sont visiblement construits sur elles; si je décide de voir les choses du point de vue de Sirius, c'est encore à mon expérience terrestre que j'ai recours pour le faire . . ." p. 502.

[37] If one compares Merleau-Ponty's treatment of this subject with that of Kwant (*Encounter*) or of Luijpen (*Existential Phenomenology*, Ch. III) the difference is even more striking. But then,

other phase of the dialectic of the body—sometimes even at the pre-conscious level. However, in his articles—particularly in his criticism of Simone de Beauvoir's *L'invitée*,[38] he looks more profoundly into the truly personal relations, and reveals his strong disapproval of the a-moral atmosphere which pervades the novel. The most important characteristic of love which he notes is that it *makes one exist:* the lover makes the beloved *to be* for him. It is quite clear that he does not deny the possibility of love—as Sartre does—and that he considers love much greater and more enduring than a flair for certain qualities of the body or of the intellect. We can build on the few hints he gives us— there is much suggested that Merleau-Ponty does not develop, even in *L'invitée*.

In the article, "Le primat de la perception" he expresses what is perhaps his best evaluation of love when he says that love promises more than it can ever accomplish, it promises sincerely, for, at the moment of the promise one truly loves *beyond* the qualities, *beyond* the body, *beyond* the moments (of the dialectic), even though one cannot love without qualities, without body, without moments.[39]

If only Merleau-Ponty had further developed the insights contained in the above affirmations we would have something very valuable on which to build, perhaps, a philosophy of the person.

4. *Groundwork for Development*

Does Merleau-Ponty's investigation contribute in any way to the advancement of philosophy? Undoubtedly. In line

---

Merleau-Ponty did not undertake to write a phenomenology of love, but of perception, therefore his summary treatment is understandable.
[38]"Le roman et la métaphysique," *S. N. S.*, pp. 45-71.
[39]"On mesure la hardiesse de l'amour, qui promet au delà de ce qu'il sait, qui prétend être éternel alors que peut-être une maladie, un accident, le détruira . . . Mais il est *vrai*, dans le moment de cette promesse, que l'on aime au delà des *qualités*, au delà du corps, au delà des moments, même si l'on ne peut aimer sans qualités, sans le corps, sans moments, . . . L'absolu qu'il cherche au delà de notre expérience est impliqué en elle." "Le Primat . . .," p. 135.

Conclusion

with the direction of modern philosophy, he attempts to do away with the dichotomy of subject and object, body and soul, spirit and matter. For him, man is neither a thing among other things, nor an interiority completely turned upon itself, but an interiority which realizes itself only in relation with others,[40] a consciousness and a freedom, essentially open towards the world, in contact with others through sensible, living, and bodily means.[41] Man is a subject totally bound to the world and yet transcending it because he is also spirit—rather, his body is body only because of the vivifying spirit within. The existence of man is to contemporary philosophers a special kind of existence, one, namely, that is a sort of ground for the being of all that which is not man. It is in this role of consciousness-making-things-to-be that man plays such an important part in the existence of the world as a meaningful "world" for himself. Now, it is precisely in this that the contribution of Merleau-Ponty is outstanding: he emphasizes the point that the real merit of the *new philosophy* is specifically to seek in the new notion of existence (as discussed previously) a way of understanding the human condition. He has worked out a coherent doctrine of human embodiment quite close to that of Gabriel Marcel—to whom he often refers in his writings.

---

[40] De Waelhens puts it thus: ". . . la pluralité des sujets s'éprouve directement au sein de l'existence irréfléchie comme dialogue des comportements. Elle ne suppose ni déduction, ni inférence. A ce plan, nous sommes *avec* autrui. Mais l'immédiateté de l'existence à plusieurs n'éclaircit pas toutes les difficultés." *Une philosophie* . . ., p. 247.

[41] Sciacca expressed this notion of the world of man thus: "Le réel est le monde d'expérience, de l'acte humain de faire expérience; mais une telle activité d'expérience est celle d'un principe sentant intellectif et que ce principe vienne à cesser d'exister, toute expérience cesse aussi et avec elle le monde comme monde d'expérience. Si l'homme venait à cesser (ainsi que tout autre existant possible) le monde sombrerait dans le néant, il cesserait d'être monde d'expérience et il n'existerait que pour le Principe créateur." M. F. Sciacca, *Acte et être*, tr. F. Authier. ([Paris] Aubier Editions Montaigne [n.d.]), p. 128.

He has also provided us with a method for making clear and explicit the living experience of the body as *my own*.

Thus, even though taken as it is, Merleau-Ponty's philosophy is insufficient for the development of a philosophy of the person, we must admit that it is his merit to have done the ground-work for such a development. It should be entirely possible, beginning where he left off, to develop a phenomenology of the person in relation, and from there, by a new kind of reflection, study the ontological and metaphysical implications of this phenomenology and thus come to a meaningful synthesis. All this is to say that his work, such as it is, is a good and solid foundation for further development—even if, to be faithful to his thought, one might perhaps not be expected to seek anything beyond the phenomenological level. But it is not to say that if we were to realize a new philosophical synthesis, we would then have found the answer to all philosophical questions. Well has De Waelhens affirmed that philosophy, in its twenty-five hundred years of existence not only has never once been accepted implicitly—in fact its right to exist has always been questioned[42]—but also, as history shows, has never been able to answer its own questions; further even its right to pose the questions has been challenged. Thus, we may be somewhat reconciled to the fate of philosophy which, according to Merleau-Ponty, cannot be anything else except a perennial beginning—a thing which is however not as sad a fate as one might think, if, by a new beginning, we understand the dynamism of a true dialectic ever renewing itself in a constant ascent towards the Absolute Spirit.

---

[42]"La philosophie existe depuis vingt-cinq siècles sans que jamais son droit à l'existence ait cessé d'être en question. En un certain sens, on pourrait représenter son histoire tout entière comme une sorte de mouvement dialectique dans lequel on la voit affirmer inlassablement sa prétention à l'être, mais sous des formes toujours nouvelles, apparemment au moins, en riposte à des négations tout aussi diverses d'elle-même et commandées par sa propre évolution. *La Philosophie et les expériences naturelles,* Phaenomenologica—collection publiès sous le patronage des Centres d' Archives-Husserl (La Haye: Martinus Nijhoff, 1961), p. 1.

APPENDIX ONE

PHENOMENOLOGY

Husserl is usually acknowledged as the Father of Phenomenology as a philosophical approach to reality. But the term itself was already used before Husserl. It seems that it was first used by J. H. Lambert, in 1764, when he attempted to construct a theory of knowledge of his own.[1] Kant and Hegel used the term, giving it a signification consistent with their respective philosophies. But Husserl initiated that which was to be the phenomenological movement properly so called. His phenomenology differed from that of Hegel. In their turn, the disciples of Husserl differ from their master widely.

The phenomenology of Husserl comprises the following:

a) the plan to make of philosophy a strict science;

b) the adoption of a serious method, including: the avoidance of all prejudices and of uncritical acceptance of data which might vitiate the immediately given; the use of immediate intuition as the one means of grasping reality in its purity and in its varied complexity;

c) a new conception of consciousness: intentionality, which would overcome every form of empirical phenomenism and assure both the independence from and the relation of the datum to the constituting consciousness;

d) the epochè, by which the world is not denied or destroyed, but understood as a pure object of thought for a transcendental consciousness, and by

---

[1] Lambert, 1728-1777, German, noted mathematician, attracted the attention of Kant by his works in logic and epistemology.

which the totality of being appears as phenomenon for the "I" which contemplates it;

e) the arrival at a metaphysical position of transcendental idealism.[2]

Characteristic of the Husserlian idealism is a great preoccupation with absolute objectivity, so that the datum may be reconstituted in consciousness without any distortion or modification. Of all the insights of Husserl, his mode of investigation—pure, eidetic and intentional intuition of reality—is that which his disciples have found most valuable. It is also that which, especially in the case of Merleau-Ponty, has contributed to the sense of ambiguity prevalent in contemporary existential philosophy, an ambiguity which was already present in Husserl's own thought.

---

[2] *Enciclopedia filosofica*, III, col. 334-40. Cf. also Van Breda, "Note sur: Réduction et authenticité d'après Husserl," *Revue de Métaphysique et de Morale* (Jan.-March, 1951), 4-5, for a detailed outline of the Husserlian reduction, which he considers imperative to any serious minded philosopher.

APPENDIX TWO

EXISTENCE AND EXISTENTIAL

Existence can be defined as a manner of being common to every kind of being; or the state of being common to brute matter, living things, objects of thought, in fact, anything at all. Existence can be predicated of both phenomena and noumena. It can be applied to beings to delimit them in some way, or to specify certain aspects or modes of being; it can also be applied to our own experience as the act of experiencing being.

In Scholastic philosophy, existence means being in its actuality as opposed to being as essence (some would say that being is essence become actual, or an existing essence).

In Existentialism, existence is the condition of man in his facticity; the existential condition of man is characterized by consciousness of self, a sense of responsibility, derived from the realization of human contingency, and solidarity with others.

Reference to something as "existential" is the assertion of the actuality of the thing as opposed to its mere possibility, ideality or conceivability, or to some purely conceptual expression or definition of meaning independent of being. It also means that something is grounded in existence, it has a temporal kind of being (that is, is a being which is both in place and time); it is a being which is experienced—empirical, as opposed to theoretical or abstract.

Referring to the existence of an object of thought, the existence in the mind is considered, that is, *intentional* existence: this is therefore real existence as an act of an existing consciousness; however, this is a different kind of existence: not empirical in the sense of an experienced material being.

The terms "existence" and "existential" occur frequently in the language of Existentialism, which is precisely the philosophy which is concerned with the existent, man, and with his existential problems. Thus, Existentialism—one of the philosophic movements outstanding in the 20th Century—has set about to re-examine the chief philosophical problems, not in the abstract, but in their existential import of the *here* and *now*. In this philosophy, existence, that is the existence of man for whom *only* the problems exist, becomes the central theme. This concern for the concrete existence is in direct opposition to mere conceptualization and speculation on an intellectual abstract level. The philosopher can never be a disinterested spectator reflecting upon the world or upon problems concerning man in the world: he is always caught up in this existential condition, so that, even while reflecting on the data of his experience, he always modifies these same data by his very act of reflection. The act of the philosopher is part of the very reality he is considering, therefore included in the very world he investigates.

This explains why, to contemporary existential philosophers and phenomenologists, philosophy can never be a completed science, but must be a perennial beginning and a continual development: the dynamism of man modifies his world and therefore an ever new vision results from his philosophical reflection.

APPENDIX THREE

BIOGRAPHICAL NOTES

Maurice Merleau-Ponty was born at Rochefort-sur-Mer (Charente Maritime) on March 14, 1908. He studied at La Sorbonne, where he formed a friendship with Jean Paul Sartre.

He taught at St. Quentin, at Lions and at the University of Paris (1950). From 1952 on, he taught at the *Collége de France* where he succeeded Louis Lavelle in the Chair of Philosophy.

Besides his interest in psychology and philosophy, he was concerned with art and literature and took a lively interest in politics. In fact his writings in this field are particularly interesting and perhaps his best. He also belonged to the Resistance Movement.

His thought was influenced by the late Husserl, by Hegel, and less strongly perhaps, by Heidegger and Sartre. Moreover, he was open to all developments in both psychology and science, thus enriching his philosophical insights considerably.

Merleau-Ponty was editor of *Les Temps Modernes,* with J.-P. Sartre, until the time (about 1953) when their ideological differences caused them to drift apart from each other. Sartre gives an account of his relations with Merleau-Ponty in his article "Merleau-Ponty vivant,"[1] wherein he brings out Merleau-Ponty's political thought in particular.

Merleau-Ponty always considered man in his concrete, contingent reality, and within the historical framework—this became the foundation of his existential phenomenology.

---

[1] *Les Temps Modernes,* Numéro Spécial: Maurice Merleau-Ponty, XVII, No. 183-187 (July-Dec., 1961), 304-76.

Merleau-Ponty

He directed his philosophical investigation to the ontological significance of man when he undertook the writing of "Le Visible et l'invisible,"[2] but he was not able to complete his undertaking. He died on May 4, 1961, hailed by some as "the foremost academic French philosopher of the post-war period."

---

[2]This work is unpublished, but it is mentioned in several articles; e.g., Calude Lefort, "L'Idée d'*être brut* et d'*esprit sauvage*," *Les Temps Modernes*, Numéro Spécial: Maurice Merleau-Ponty, XVII, No. 184-185 [July-Aug., 1961], 225-86.

BIBLIOGRAPHY

PRIMARY SOURCES

Merleau-Ponty, Maurice. *Les aventures de la dialectique.* Paris: Gallimard [1955]

———. "Apprendre à lire," *Les Temps Modernes,* XXII, 3 (July, 1947), 1-27.

———. "Les cahiers de la pléiade, avril 1947. Gallimard, éditeur," *Les Temps Modernes,* XXVII, 3 (December, 1947), 1151-52.

———. "Communisme-anticommunisme," *Les Temps Modernes,* XXXIV, 4 (July, 1948), 175-88.

———. "Le doute de Cézanne," Fontaine, XLVII, 9 (December, 1945), 80-100. Trans. abridged "Cézanne's doubt," *Partisan Review,* XIII, 4 (September-October, 1946), 464-78.

———. *Éloge de la philosophie.* Leçon inaugurale faite au Collège de France, le jeudi 15 janvier 1953. 3ᵉ éd. Paris: Gallimard [ᶜ1953]

———. "L'homme et l'objet," (J.-L. Dumas "Les conférences"), *La Nef,* XLV, 5 (1948), 150-51.

———. *Humanisme et terreur, essai sur le problème communiste.* Les essais XXVII. Paris: Gallimard [ᶜ1947]

———. "Le 'Manifeste communiste' a cent ans," *Le Figaro Littéraire,* 3 avril 1948.

———. "Marxisme et philosophie," *Revue Internationale,* Trans., abridged "Marxism and philosophy," *Politics,* IV, 4 (July-August, 1947), 173-75.

———. "L'Oeil et l'esprit," *Les Temps Modernes,* Numéro Spécial: Maurice Merleau-Ponty, XXVII, No. 184-85 [July-Aug., 1960], 193-227.

———. *Phénoménologie de la perception.* (Bibliothèque des Idées) Paris: Librairie Gallimard, 1945.

———. *Les philosophes célèbres.* [Paris] L. Mazenod [1956]

———. "Pour les rencontres internationales," *Les Temps Modernes*, XIX, 2 (April, 1947), 1340-44.

———. "Préface de Merleau-Ponty," in *L'Ocuvre de Freud et son importance pour le monde moderne* by A. Hesnard. (Bibliothèque scientifique) Paris: Pagot, 1960.

———. "Le Primat de la perception et ses conséquences philosophiques," *Bulletin de la Société Française de Philosophie*, 41e année, 4 (October-December, 1947), 119-53.

———. *Les relations avec autrui chez l'enfant*. [1re partie] (Les Cours de Sorbonne) Autographié. Paris: Tournier et Constans [1953].

———. *Les sciences de l'homme et la phénoménologie*. Intr. 1re partie: Le problème des sciences de l'homme selon Husserl. (Les Cours de Sorbonne) Autographié. Paris: Tournier et Constans [1953].

———. *Sens et non-sens*. (Collection Pensées) 2e éd. Paris: Nagel [°1948].

———. *Signes*. Paris: Gallimard [°1960].

———. *La structure du comportement*. Précédé de "Une philosophie de l'ambiguïté" par Alphonse de Waelhens. 4e éd. Paris: Presses universitaires de France, 1960.

———. "Sur la phénoménologie du langage," in *Problèmes actuels de phénoménologie*, textes de P. Thévenaz, H. J. Pos, P. Ricoeur, E. Fink, M. Merleau-Ponty, J. Wahl; éd. H. L. Van Breda. (Actes du Colloque International de Phénoménologie, Bruxelles, avril 1951) Paris: Desclée De Brouwer, 1952.

———. "Le yogi et le prolétaire," *Les Temps Modernes*, XIII, 2 (October, 1946), 1-29; XIV, 2 (November, 1946), 253-87; XVI, 2 (January, 1947), 676-711.

———. As the book was going to press, the following posthumous works of Merleau-Ponty were released:

———. *L'oeil et L'esprit*. Paris, 1964.

———. *Le visible et L'invisible* suivi de *Notes du travail*. Ed. by C. Lefort, Paris, 1964.

WORKS BY MERLEAU-PONTY IN TRANSLATION

Phenomenology of Perception, tr. Colin Smith. New York: The Humanities Press [1962].

In Praise of Philosophy, tr. with a preface by J. Wild & J. M. Edie. [Evanston] Northwestern University Press, 1963.

The Structure of Behavior, tr. by Alden Fisher. Boston: Beacon Press, 1963.

The Primacy of Perception. Evanston, Ill.: Northwestern University Press, 1964.

Sense and Nonsense. Evanston, Ill.: Northwestern University Press, 1965.

Signs. Evanston, Ill.: Northwestern University Press, 1964.

For a complete and up-to-date bibliography of Merleau-Ponty we refer the reader to the following:

Kwant, R. C. *The Phenomenological Philosophy of Merleau-Ponty.* Pittsburgh: Duquesne University Press, 1963.

For Phenomenology and Existentialism:

Kaelin, F. E. *An Existentialist Aesthetic; The Theories of Sartre and Merleau-Ponty.* Madison: The University of Wisconsin Press, 1962.

Spiegelberg, H. *The Phenomenological Movement: A Historical Introduction.* 2 vols. The Hague: Hartinus Nijhoff, 1960.

SELECTIVE BIBLIOGRAPHY

BOOKS

Berl, Emmanuel. *De l'innocence* (Etudes et Essais). Paris: R. Julliard [1947].

It is a commentary on Merleau-Ponty's article, "Le Yogy et le Prolétaire." The author discusses the deterministic theory that violence is to be found in any type of government—the consciousness of guilt which is characteristic of the existential "responsibility" for everything and for everyone is the presupposition of the discussion.

Centineo, Ettore. *Una Fenomenologia della Storia. L'esistenzialismo di M. Merleau-Ponty*. [Palermo: (Palumbo ed.) Cappucci & Figli, 1959].

The author studies the phenomenology of Merleau-Ponty following the development of *La structure du comportement* and *Phénoménologie de la perception*, then relates the study of man-in-the-world to the historical dimension implied by the phenomenological approach to space and time. He takes into account the relation which Merleau-Ponty's thought has to other contemporary thinkers as well as the effort of the former to overcome the idealist-empiricist dichotomy.

Chiodi, Pietro. *Il Pensiero esistenzialista* (Kierkegaard, Jasper, Heidegger, Marcel, Sartre, Merleau-Ponty, Abbagnano, Paci). Milano: Garzanti [1959].

The author examines the various existential motifs in relation to each of the philosophers chosen so as to bring into relief the individual approach of each to the same problems. Some of the topics are the following: existence, being, reason, situation, time and history, world and science, and death.

Dondeyne, A. *Contemporary European Thought and Christian Faith*. (Duquesne Studies, Philosophical Series, 8) Pittsburgh: Duquesne University Press, 1963 (2nd impr.).

Selective Bibliography

It is a study of phenomenological and existential movements from the viewpoint of and in relation to traditional philosophy. The author points out the advantages as well as the dangers of existential philosophies, touching on those of Sartre and Merleau-Ponty. It is the author's conviction that a dialogue between contemporary thought and traditional Christian faith is both possible and necessary. From it ought to derive new and fruitful insights into the philosophy of man.

Kaelin, Eugene F. *An Existential Aesthetic. The Theories of Sartre and Merleau-Ponty*. Madison: The University of Wisconsin Press, 1962.

This work is an attempt to specify the nature of aesthetic, not in relation to some other aspect of philosophy, but as a theory of aesthetic creation properly so understood. It is a critical study of the existential aesthetics of J. P. Sartre and M. Merleau-Ponty in their treatment of human creativity. Kaelin brings out both the similarities and differences between these two philosophers, particularly their study of consciousness, in relation to imagination for Sartre, and in relation to perception for Merleau-Ponty. Kaelin also brings out the important fact that, ultimately, these two philosophers are very much concerned with the problems of man in his expression of freedom and moral values. Although both philosophers are considered followers of Husserl since they use the phenomenological method, of the two Merleau-Ponty is the most faithful to this intention, while Sartre is more critical and his method not truly phenomenological.

Kwant, R. C. *The Phenomenological Philosophy of Merleau-Ponty*. (Duquesne Studies, Philosophical Series, 15). Pittsburgh: Duquesne University Press, 1963.

This book is a survey of Merleau-Ponty's thought embracing all phases of his development, from the notion of the body-subject (which is the central theme of his phenomenology) to the political views which he for a time shared with J. P. Sartre. The author offers a critique of Merleau-Ponty's philosophy from the viewpoint of the philosopher himself, and points out both the insights and the deficiencies. Thus, while he admits that the phenomenological investigation of Merleau-Ponty is very significant in the field of perception, he deplores the fact that Merleau-Ponty did not so investigate other aspects of human existence, such as, for instance, thought; while he cannot criticize an author for the books which he did not write, he maintains that some of the conclusions Merleau-Ponty reaches are not warranted by his investigation. Kwant also discusses Merleau-Ponty in relation to Sartre, to Marxism, to the sciences and to phenomenology, showing in each case how he has developed his thought. Merleau-Ponty's rejection of the absolute, his atheism, his philosophy of history are also discussed in detail. Kwant shows very clearly that Merleau-Ponty is to a great extent an original thinker and that his philosophy, based as it is on the phenomenological investigation of man-in-the-world, has great potentialities.

Kwant, R. C. *Encounter.* (Duquesne Studies, Philosophical Series, 11) Pittsburgh: Duquesne University Press, 1960.

The author takes his point of departure from the fundamental notions found in Merleau-Ponty's philosophy of the body-subject and develops the implications of phenomenology and subjectivity to a greater degree than Merleau-Ponty himself has done. The main point of the work is this: it is only in relation to man, and because of man that the world is a world, that is, it has meaning. It is the encounter of persons in relation that makes possible the understanding of subjects in the world, as well as of objects—be they considered scientifically or humanistically.

"This book is written to show the extent to which our existence is involved in a state of being-together. . . . human involvement . . . gives full significance to all things, even to matter." (Introduction, p. 2).

The author is compelled to rethink the traditional themes of philosophy. Thus the book becomes a dialogue with and at the same time a critique of such views as Scholasticism, Marxism, Existentialism, and a new confrontation with scientific developments. From this dialogue derives a new light on the social nature of man.

Selective Bibliography

Moreau, Joseph. *L'horizon des esprits. Essai critique sur la phénoménologie de la perception.* (Bibliothèque de la Philosophie Contemporaine). Paris: Presses Universitaires de France, 1960.

It is a kind of dialogue between idealism and the perception theory of Merleau-Ponty; the author brings out the thought of Merleau-Ponty in opposition to idealism, admits that the phenomenological approach has rehabilitated the sensible, but holds fast to the notion of the absolute which he deplores finds no place in Merleau-Ponty, whose world is contingent through and through.

Luijpen, W. A. L. *Existential Phenomenology.* (Duquesne Studies, Philosophical Series, 12). Pittsburgh: Duquesne University Press, 3rd impr., 1963.

"It is *not* our intention to write *about* existentialism or phenomenology. It is not possible to philosophize in an authentic way if our thinking does not consist in a relatively independent rethinking of the eternal problems which have always occupied the thinking man. Authentic philosophy is the aim of this book. The rethinking, however, presented in this work, takes place in the 'climate' of thought proper to existentialists and phenomenologists, because we are convinced that nowadays existential phenomenology, enriched by the profound insights attained by medieval philosophy, offers the most promising perspectives for any endeavor to express the ultimate meaning of integral reality." (Introduction, p. 2).

The content of the book justifies the statement of aims above. The philosophy of Merleau-Ponty is very faithfully presented, along with that of many other modern thinkers whose development follows the lines of either phenomenology or existentialism. The content of this study is grouped under four headings: 1) the metaphysical question of man as being-in-the-world; 2) phenomenology of knowledge including the consideration of truth; 3) phenomenology of intersubjectivity with a stress on love, hatred, indifference, all based on the body as intermediary; 4) the phenomenology of freedom and its destiny in relation to the meaning of life and its implications within a processual world.

The whole book is a profound rethinking of the human problems in the light of history, never divorced from transcendence.

Tilliette, Xavière. *Philosophes contemporains: Gabriel Marcel, Maurice Merleau-Ponty, Karl Jaspers.* (Textes et Études Philosophiques). Paris: Desclée de Brouver [1962].

The author treats Marcel as the new Socrates—Christian—and develops the motifs of love and hope. Of Merleau-Ponty he discusses the thought embodied in his major works touching briefly on all problems connected with a philosophy of ambiguity, marxism, and the role of the body in man's relations to others and to the world. He discusses Jaspers as the philosopher of "unbelieving faith" —the thinker of philosophical faith.

Spiegelberg, Herbert. *The Phenomenological Movement. A Historical Introduction.* 2 vols. [Phaenomenological Collection "publiée sous le patronage des centres d'Archives-Husserl"] 6. The Hague: Martinus Nijhoff, 1960.

This is a developmental approach to the history of phenomenology; the author treats in detail the major exponents of the movement such as Husserl, Scheler, Heidegger, Sartre, Merleau-Ponty; he relates to the movement also lesser figures and philosophers who have prepared the way for phenomenology (e.g., A. Pfänder Brentano, Reinach, Geiger). The work is particularly helpful because the author treats the philosophers according to a geography grouping, and gives accounts of specific sections of phenomenological works. He further relates the phenomenological movement in Europe to parallel developments in America (e.g., W. James, J. Royce, Santayana).

Thévenaz, Pierre. *What Is Phenomenology? And Other Essays,* tr. J. Edie et al.—Intro. by J. Edie. Chicago: Quadrangle Books, Inc. [1962].

The volume contains three essays taken from *L'homme et sa raison* by Thévenaz. In these three essays the author treats in an original way of the problems of consciousness,

Selective Bibliography

anthropology and metaphysics in the light of phenomenology. The first essay treats of phenomenology and develops the thought of Husserl, Heidegger, Sartre and Merleau-Ponty with both accuracy and clarity. The work can be a very good introduction to phenomenology and existentialism.

De Waelhens, A. *Une Philosophie de l'ambiguïté: l'existentialisme de Maurice Merleau-Ponty.* (Bibliothèque philosophique de Louvain). Louvain: Publications Universitaires de Louvain, 1951.

This book can be considered a classic on Merleau-Ponty In it the author interprets Merleau-Ponty's philosophy with remarkable understanding. He terms Merleau-Ponty's philosophy "ambiguous" not because the expression of the former is not clear, but because Merleau-Ponty has disclosed the mysterious and ambiguous nature of reality. De Waelhens sees in the phenomenology of perception not a mere approach to philosophy or a method of philosophizing, but a truly ontological interpretation of reality. The book touches on all relevant problems raised by Merleau-Ponty in his major works and shows that the richness of Merleau-Ponty's philosophy needs only to be uncovered.

ARTICLES

Abbagnano, Nicola. "Outline of a Philosophy of Existence," *Philosophy and Phenomenological Research*, IX, 1948, 200-11.

Alquié, F. "Une philosophie de l'ambiguïté: l'existentialisme de M. Merleau-Ponty," *Fontaine*, no. 59 (April, 1947), 47-70.

Bannan, J. F. "Philosophical Reflection and the Phenomenology of Merleau-Ponty," *Review of Metaphysics*, VIII (March, 1955), 318-442.

Bayer, Raymond. "Merleau-Ponty's Existentialism," *Monographs in Philosophy*, XIX, 3 (September 1951), 99-107.

Berger, Gaston. "L'originalité de la phénoménologie," *Etudes Philosophiques*, N. S., IX, 3 (July-September, 1954), 249-259.

Callois, Roland. "Destin de l'humanisme marxiste (à propos d'Humanisme et Terreur)," *Critique*, IV (March, 1948), 243-251.

———. "Note sur l'analyse réflexive et la réflexion phénoménologique. A propos de la 'Phénoménologie de la perception' de M. Merleau-Ponty." *Deucalion*, I (Paris, 1946), 127-39.

———. "De la perception à l'histoire. La philosophie de M. Merleau-Ponty," *Deucalion*, II (Paris, 1947), 59-85.

Fontan, P. "Le primat de l'acte sur l'énoncé. A propos de la Phénoménologie de la perception," *Revue Philosophique de Louvain*, LIII, 1955, 40-53.

Jolivet, R. "Le problème de l'absolu dans la philosophie de M. Merleau-Ponty," *Tyjdscrift voor Philosophie*, XIX, (March-June, 1957), 53-100.

Kockelmans, J. A. "Merleau-Ponty's Phenomenology of Language," *Review of Existential Psychology and Psychiatry*, III, no. 1 (Winter 1963), pp. 39-82.

Articles

Kullman, M. and Taylor, C. "The Pre-Objective World," *The Review of Metaphysics,* XII, 1, issue 45 (September 1958), 108-32.

McCleary, Richard Calverton. *Ambiguity and Freedom in the Philosophy of M. Merleau-Ponty.* Film Reproduction. (M. A. Thesis). Chicago: University of Chicago Press, 1954.

Olafson, Frederick A. "Existentialism, Marxism, and Historical Justification," *Ethics,* LXV, 2 (January, 1955), 126-34.

Sandrini, F. *La fenomenologia di Merleau-Ponty e il rapporto dialettico.* (Dissertation pour le doctorat en Philosophie, Université Catholique de Louvain, Institut Supérieur de Philosophie). Louvain: 1957.

Scharfstein, Ben-Ami. "Bergson and Merleau-Ponty: A Preliminary Comparison," *The Journal of Philosophy,* LII, 14 (July 7, 1955), 380-86.

Spiegelberg, H. "French Existentialism: Its Social Philosophies," *Kenyon Review,* XVI, 3 (1954), 446-62.

Symposium: Existentialist Thought and Contemporary Philosophy in the West, *Journal of Philosophy,* LIII (November, 1956), 739-71.

Wells, Rulon. "World and Object," *The Review of Metaphysics,* XIV, 4, issue no. 56 (June, 1961), 695-703.

Wild, John. "Contemporary Phenomenology and the Problem of Existence," *Philosophy and Phenomenological Research,* XX, 2 (December 1959), 166-80.

Yale French Studies. "Critical Bibliography of Existentialism." Special Monograph (The Paris School), No. 1 Supplement (July, 1949).

―――. "Existentialism," I, 1 (Spring-Summer, 1948).

INDEX OF NAMES

Abbagnano, N. 26, 30, 31, 288
Adorno, T. 31
Alquié, F. 8, 71, 72, 261, 288
Baillie, J. 2
Baldwin, J. 4
Bannan, J. 44, 288
Barnes, H. 219
Bayer, R. 46, 47
de-Beauvoir, S. 239, 240, 270
Bergson, H. 56
Berl, E. 282
Binswanger, L. 21
Brentano, F. 11
Caillois, R. 72, 73, 262, 263, 288
Cairns, D. 17
Camus, A. 20
Centineo, E. 282
Chaix-Ruy, J. 44
Chiodi, P. 282
Conrad Martius, H. 21
Copleston, F. 19
Descartes, R. 11, 46, 58, 242, 243, 244
Dondeyne, A. 63, 65, 282
Duffrenne, M. 22
Edie, J. 7
Farber, M. 25
Ferrater Mora, J. 66
Fink, E. 15, 26
Fontan, P. 266, 288
Freud, S. 150, 161
Geiger, M. 21
Gibson, W. 6
Gurwitsch, A. 13, 15
Hartmann, N. 22
Hegel, F. 2, 3, 5, 10, 19, 36, 56, 68, 69, 208, 210, 211
Heidegger, M. 17, 19
Hering, E. 22
Husserl, E. 2, 3, 6, 11, 12, 13, 14, 15, 16, 17, 24, 25, 26, 27, 31, 32, 35, 36, 38, 42, 43, 44, 57, 60, 98, 100, 110, 126, 196, 197, 200, 201, 204, 236, 250, 273, 274, 277, 283, 286, 287
Hyppolite, J. 5, 22
Ingarden, R. 22
Jaspers, K. 20
Johann, R. 21
Jolivet, R. 264, 266, 267, 288
Kaelin, E. 52, 53, 281, 283
Kant, I. 4, 9, 55
Kierkegaard, S. 1, 19, 20

Kockelmans, J. 20, 93, 146, 255, 288
Kullman 26, 32, 289
Kwant, R. 47, 48, 49, 51, 54, 63, 84, 85, 135, 176, 177, 186, 188, 213, 214, 216, 258, 268, 269, 281, 283, 284
Lambert, J. 273
Lauer, Q. 21, 22, 25, 26, 27, 30, 35, 60, 100, 126, 216
Lefort, C. 278
Lipps, H. 22
Luijpen, W. 21, 50, 51, 269, 285
Marcel, G. 17, 20, 21, 47, 62, 65, 67, 271, 282
Malraux, A. 22
Mattew 116
Marx, K. 67, 68, 69
McCleary, R. 289
Moreau, J. 127, 128, 146, 283
Mounier, E. 21
Mueller, G. 5
Nédoncelle, M. 21
Nietzsche, F. 20
Olafson, F. 289
Otto, R. 22
Pfänder, A. 21
Plato 192
Ricoeur, P. 21
Sandrini, F. 78, 230, 289
Sartre, J. P. 17, 20, 47, 61, 62, 63, 64, 65, 66, 67, 68, 125, 160, 218, 225, 249, 250, 260
Sciacca, M. 271
Scharfstein, B. 289
Scheler, M. 21
Simmel, G. 22
Spiegelberg, H. 33, 35, 43, 44, 45, 123, 281, 286, 289
Spinoza, B. 58, 245
Taylor 26, 32, 100, 289
Thevenaz, P. 7, 12, 260, 261, 286
Van Breda, H. 12, 16, 172, 247
Van der Leeuw, G. 22
Virasoro, M. 171
Von Hildebrand, D. 20
DeWaehlens, A. 44, 194, 254, 256, 271, 272, 287
Wahl, J. 19, 29, 264
Watson, J. 79
Welch, E. 17
Wild, J. 49, 289
Wells, R. 289

INDEX OF SUBJECT MATTER

Abnormal 151, 152, 172, 173, 194; behavior 146, 148
Absolute 52, 66, 220, 250, 264; abstract 267; and experience 263; in man 267; and openness 267; and the relative 266; Spirit 196, 248, 272
Absolute Spirit 20, 40, 196, 272
Absolute subject 52, 250
Action, 140
Acts 152, 241, 245, 246
Aesthetic 183, 204, 283; and art 206 as expression 204; as language 204
Affective 144, 151; life 151; relation 152; states 148
Affectivity 134, 144, 147, 148, 151
Aphasia 152, 153, 194
Ambiguity 54, 57, 61, 72, 88, 109, 116, 193, 222, 259; and existence 260; language 191, 212; and man, 200; in man's relations 166, 167, 168. 268; of perception 109, 121, 245; and the present 234; and social life 261
Ambiguous 159, 169, 188, 235, 252, 266; situation 235, 252; language 198
Anonymous 156, 224
Appeal 14
Appearance, 4
A-priori, 138, 145, 164, 257, 258
Art 138, 139, 204, 205, 206, 207

Bad faith 238
Behavior 36, 79, 80, 82, 83, 84, 85, 86, 87, 92, 93, 193, 228; pattern of 135, 150, 224, 226; and perception 231; reflex 82; sexual 149; structures 153; superior 82
Being 4, 54, 60, 62, 65, 150, 238; in being 252; cultural 183; for man 257; -for-me 254; of persons 213
Being-to-the-world 86, 124, 218, 233, 264
Being-in-the-world 36, 51, 62, 73, 126, 164, 217, 220, 257, 159, 285, 261
Biological 192, 193
Biology 74, 80, 134
Body 47, 48, 53, 74, 82, 90, 91, 93, 94, 96, 97, 108, 128, 131, 137, 157, 159, 165, 169, 177, 220; autonomous 211; my body 101, 119, 138, 143, 145, 152, 188, 195, 201; and consciousness 77, 137, 140, 152, 154, 160, 219; as existence, 154, 155, 156, 158; ideality of 98; as involved 211; as object 132, 136, 165; ontological 247; as perceived 130, 131, 132, 138, 149; and perception 101, 102, 141; as phenomenal 219; and relation 122, 143, 166, 227; as sexual 119; and sexuality 148, 149, 160; and soul 84; as space 137; as spirit 195; as spontaneity 264; as subject 217
Body-subject 47, 48, 49, 50, 52, 73, 74, 122, 135, 140, 144, 202, 212, 257, 259, 268, 283
Body-soul 90, 91, 92, 96; dialectic 90, 92, 95, 97, 105, 115, 126; as distinct 95; problem 103, 104, 105, 106; relation 90, 95, 96, 97, 105; as significations 167

Choice 125, 152, 250; as choosing 232, 251; existential 251; pre-conscious 269
Cogito 46, 113, 122, 123, 168, 226, 242, 244; condition for choice 257; as existential 244, 246; and experience 257, 260; function of 242; as temporal 246; unity of 226; and the world 249
Commitment 111, 125, 250
Communication 122, 152, 153, 185; ambiguity 262; as bodily function 171; and consciousness 175, 186; inter-human 135, 145, 174, 184, 214; and meaning 183, 193, 207; with others 222; refusal of 233; and subjectivity 213, 214; total 230
Condemned to be free 251
Condemned to express 252
"Conscience engagée" 44, 61
Conscious subject 10, 18, 73
Consciousness 7, 8, 9, 31, 36, 48, 73, 76, 79, 80, 123, 193, 225, 273, 287; and being 57, 117, 135, 221; and body 199; as committed 44, 68, 111, 123, 259; and experience 114, 130, 175; and existence 111, 112, 113, 114, 271; image of 240; as intentional 12, 152; as perceiving 218; and perception 99, 104, 109; and relation 135, 154; as struc-

ture 79; and temporality 245; as transcendental 103, 104, 111, 141; and truth 237
Constitution 100, 228; of body 132, 201; of others 201, 219, 221; of subject 201; transcendental 12; universal 236
Contingency 115, 235, 245

Contingent 165
Corporeal 142, 147, 148, 150, 157, 192, 250
Creating 178
Creation 138
Creative 178
Cultural objects 223
Culture 200

Desire 144, 149, 150, 159
Development 270; existence 271; groundwork for 270
Dialectic 56, 57, 67, 88, 92, 95, 268; of being and nothingness 67, 68; of body and soul 126, 167; existential 55, 93, 159, 198; and freedom 124; of master and slave 159; and phenomenology 127, 266; and relation 121, 230, 231, 253; tension 221; and sexuality 147, 158, 159
Dialogue 223, 225
Disponible 98

Economics 168, 169
Ego 220, 227, 229; and alter-ego 224, 268; ego-body 84, 85, 269; ego-consciousness 160, 213, 218, 228; ego-poles 14, 18; ego-subject 74, 147, 220, 259; universal 229
Emotion 192
Empiricism 58, 75, 77, 78, 87, 148, 171
Encounter 135, 143; and language 185; and man 268; pre-personal 268
Engagement 156, 157, 251
En-soi 62, 63, 86, 114, 130
epochè 273
Equivocal 162
Eros 147
Erotic experience 149; perception of 150
Essence 5, 17, 20, 29, 30, 52, 98, 145, 250; and existence 137; knowledge of 100; and man 127, 165, 166, 167; and ontology 256
Essential 164

Essentialism 30, 58
Eternity 115
Existence 61, 98, 141, 147, 157, 233; anonymous 151; and body 158, 218; co-existence 112, 151, 152, 225; as consciousness 61; movement of 150, 169; as perceived 233; pure 20, 22, 29, 48, 51; and the social world 233; structure of 163, 185
Existence 242, 271, 275; as ambiguity 260; and the cogito 242; and the perceived 243
Ex-istence 5, 51
Experience 3, 4, 73, 104, 162; authentic 241, 253; as change 153; existential 38, 188, 193, 203; lived 57, 81, 100, 105, 114, 152, 225, 263; of the other 231; and philosophy 129; privileged 162; traumatic 152
Expression 157, 177, 182, 191, 193, 194, 199, 204; artistic 178, 182, 183; bodily 189; living 189; verbal 171
Existent 19, 20, 101
Existential 124, 153, 158, 172, 275; being of man 164, 167; experience 147, 153, 246, 257; milieu 218; phenomenology 44; relation 195
Existentialism 17, 18, 19, 20, 55, 59, 60, 67, 69, 275

Figure-background 138, 191
Finality 64, 80, 127
Form 82, 89, 112, 116, 117, 131, 145, 247; amovible (revocable) 82, 83; as behavior 87; as constituted 117; symbolic 83, 84, 85; syncretic 82, 83
Freedom 124, 125, 169, 232, 250, 285; as ambiguous 250; as conditioned 250, 251; and consciousness 249; and human world 252
Future 123, 139, 156, 248, 262

Genesis 38; of being-for us 144; of consciousness 110; of meaning 38; of signification 186
Gestalt 32, 98, 99, 138, 153
Gesture 156, 183, 185, 186, 187; and communication 187, 188; and culture 189, 192; as sign 189
God, 175, 229; denial of 266; one with human life 267; impossible 229; and mystery 267; others in God 230

Habit 140
Hallucination 120
History 37, 38, 39, 67, 68, 150, 168, 169, 208; as existence 262; and freedom 250; historical dimension 282; and intersubjectivity 254; of language 198
Human 80; act 166; condition 153, 161, 165, 170; conduct and behavior 80, 81, 217; embodiment 271; nature 167, 192, 198; person 213; relation 143
Humanism 64

Idea 101, 139, 183, 199
Idealism 146, 171, 234, 248; absolute 244; of Husserl 30, 31, 67; idealistic philosophy 259; transcendental 273
Identity 153
Impersonal 146, 224; and consciousness 268; and relations 187, 188; and subjectivity 224; and time 203
"Incarnate spirit" 63, 88, 89, 90, 106, 112, 151, 171, 268
Incarnate 139; consciousness 157; expression 176; existence 207; self 188; spirit 181; subject 143; of word 200
Incarnation 254
Indetermination 162
Individual 149, 207; life 215, 240
Immanence 261
Immanent 234
Intellectual 146, 188
Intellectualism 75, 76, 87, 117, 141, 148, 176
Intelligence 148
Intelligibility 141
Intention 35, 79, 80, 141, 256; and the body 157, 180; and communication 185; and conduct 187
Intentional 79, 141, 152, 253, 260; activity 140; analysis 15; existence 275
Intentionality 35, 36, 140, 147, 149, 150, 273
Intersubjective 23, 144, 145; communication 261; exchange 176, 197; object 172; and phenomenology 215; relations 146, 172, 195, 215, 216, 217, 226, 261; world 155
Intersubjectivity 13, 14, 92, 143, 145, 146, 213, 216, 233, 249; and culture 254; meeting of 215, 223; personal 147, 193; transcendental 14
Irriflexive 226

Knowledge 28, 135, 144, 145, 285; human 226, 253; objective 144; and perception 254; of self 241, 245
Knot of relations 252

Language 139, 155, 171, 172, 178, 179, 181, 189, 194, 195, 198, 208; as allusive 184; as art 194, 198, 209; as ambiguous 184, 198; as authentic 205; as bodily expression 174, 184, 204; as communication 209; condition for thought 174; as cultural 189, 209; differences in 190; as encounter 185; as existential 172, 173; as indirect 184; as intersubjective 173; and love 240; as "operation for two" 175; phenomenology of 196, 197; and physiology 173; as silence 184, 186; as spoken 173, 194; and things 211; universal 190, 198, 210; and word 182, 183, 185, 210; as written 173
Lebenswelt 13, 14, 15, 16
Liberty 45, 55, 61, 64, 65, 66; and commitment 125; and consciousness 112, 113; and contingency 165; field of 250; human 249; and relations 252; and world 232
Life 80, 116, 150, 156, 216, 235; as ambiguous 236; levels of 88, 223; living subject 222, 235; as value 116
Logos 40, 122, 260
"Look, the" (Sartre) 218, 219
Love 144, 159, 160, 161, 237, 269, 270, 286; and behavior 239; beyond moments 270; and commitment 240; and consciousness 237, 242; as dialectic 270; and existence 270; as false 238, 239; to love 233; phenomena of 237, 239; phenomenology of 269; possibility of 270; as total 239, 240

Man 28, 47, 127, 166, 167, 193, 241, 271; absolute source 28; and body 156, 177; center of intelligibility 57, 63; and contingency 163; condemned to exist 20; as historical 165; and space 139; and time 127, 139; as unity 108, 208; and the world 29, 51, 104, 257
Man-in-the-world 126
Marxism 66, 70, 169, 286
Materialism 234

Matter 89, 97, 138, 145; brute matter 50; materiality of body 136
Meaning 127, 137, 169, 175, 176, 177, 178, 181, 193; and ambiguity 259, 260; and being 264; and world 260
Mediation 238
Memory 151, 180; and body 180
Metamorphosis 156
Metaphysical 135, 153
Metaphysics 24, 161, 200, 214
Modesty 159; immodesty 159
Moment 5, 164, 181, 183, 230, 248, 268
Morality 114, 115, 228, 265
Motion 136, 140
Music 182, 194

Naming 174, 178
Nature 98, 143, 167, 190
Necessary 165
Negation 232
Non-sense 260

Object 127, 130, 131, 132, 146; body as 136, 138; mode of presence 200, 220; and relation 141, 145; and space-time 138, 140
Objectify 130
Objective 145; thought 225
Objectivity 121, 127, 146
Ontological chiffre 57, 58
Ontology 255, 256; ontological ground 257; ontological implications 272
Organs 150, 164, 192; organism 81, 88, 96, 151
Other 228; and body 264; and presence 249; and solipsism 229

Painting 204, 205, 209; as absolute 206; modern 206, 207; as silence 207
Past 123, 180, 234, 248
Passion 224
Perception 25, 32, 34, 82, 92, 145, 233, 245, 258; and ambiguity 261; and anonymity 221, 222; of behavior 222; and the body 118, 137, 140, 152, 217; the cogito 243; and consciousness 218; evidence of 34; and experience 99, 108, 110, 120, 201; field of 229; as a field 138; as inner 241; and knowledge 29, 116, 136; as lived 109; and the object 243; and the other 219; as phenomenon 203; as primary 131, 206; theories of 103, 119; and things 141
Perceptual field 100
Person 121, 213, 240; philosophy of 272; pre-personal 143, 160, 220; in relation 284
Personal 1, 19, 37, 121, 143, 144, 152, 185, 203, 212; and consciousness 268; level of 268; life 267
Personalism 20
Perspective 109, 110, 121, 141, 248
Phenomenal body 224; field 7, 109, 118, 129, 220, 232, 265
Phenomenological 10; existentialism 21; investigation 171, 258; method 25, 167, 168; movement 285; reflection 218
Phenomenology 2, 42, 72, 122, 260, 284; and being 257, 259; existential 18, 24, 50, 52, 254; according to Husserl 12, 13, 14, 15, 16; and language 171, 197; limitations of 116; as a movement 2, 8; of phenomenology 122, 236, 257; as a philosophy 39, 47, 72, 202, 253, 254, 257, 264, 265; as strict science 273; task of 40, 42, 171, 236; transcendental 6, 7, 42, 43, 126
Phenomenon 3, 5, 9, 98, 128, 258; body as 128, 158; according to Brentano 11; as cultural 168; according to Hegel 10; according to Husserl 11; as intentional object 11; according to Kant 10
Philosophy 27, 40, 97, 170, 221, 285; contemporary 1, 2; and experience 257, 263; existential 283; of man 147; and meaning 210; and phenomenology 197, 200, 203, 254; perennial beginning 272, 275; task of 36, 59; as transcendental 117
Physics 74, 134, 237; physical 151, 193, 216
Pleasure 148; pure states of 149
Poetry 178, 206
Polarity 122
Poles 159, 231, 253; ego-poles 14, 17
Possibility 127
Psychic 90, 151
Pour—autrui 208
Pour—soi 62, 86, 114, 208
Pre-conscious 54, 251, 257
Pre-objective 113, 114
Pre-personal 143, 160, 220, 268; emphasis 269; level 268

Pre-reflexive 171, 226, 231, 256
Presence 94, 95, 123, 124, 132, 136, 157, 181, 248, 258; of others 203; to self 234, 249; and the subject 247, 248; in-the-world 255
Present 123, 139, 180, 234
Process 244
Profiles 101, 102, 110
Project 124, 250, 252
Psychoanalysis 147, 150
Psychology 74, 79, 89, 118, 129, 131, 134, 135, 172, 187; and conscious being 257; psychological hypocrisy 153; relations 201

Rationality 39, 43, 227
Real, the 25, 120, 121
Reality 54, 113; and perception 237; and the world 59, 72
Reason 40, 217; essential 16, 17
Reduction 6, 8, 26, 27, 28, 32, 35, 236; eidetic 31, 32, 34; phenomenological 33, 110
Reflection 73, 119, 168, 200, 236, 256; beyond phenomenology 264; level of 264, 231; phenomenological 218; philosophical 256, 263; secondary 255
Reflex behavior 82
Reflexes 79, 80, 94, 148, 149
Reflexive behavior 82
Relation 97, 99, 118, 125, 135, 141, 144, 166, 169, 174, 247; ambiguous 259; existential 251; "related" 259; and the world 268
Relativism 266
Relativization 95
Representation 177
Response 126
Revocable forms 82, 83

Seeing 242, 243; contingent 244
Self 111, 112, 241; doubling 245
Sensation 82, 95, 128, 132, 145, 226; double-sensation 133
Senses 155, 157
Sense-organs 140, 152, 155
Sensism 31
Sexed 143; being 143, 147
Sexual 149; expression 166; meaning 169; pleasure 161
Sexuality 146, 147, 148, 149, 150, 158, 161, 164; as ambiguous 162, 165; as atmosphere 162, 169; as content of experience 163, 165; as dialectical 161

Sign 176, 183; conventional 189, 191, 192; natural 189, 191, 192
Signification 85, 104, 106, 111, 115, 118, 140, 141, 151, 157, 163, 169, 264; and body 101, 138, 181; and soul 116; and consciousness 103, 105; conventional 191; and existential 150, 158, 159; and expression 183, 139, 208; and ideas 117; and language 198, 199; and perception 102; and profile 107; and relation 185; and sign 182, 183
Signified 141, 183
Silence 186
Situation 155, 232; being-in-155, 156, 157, 232, 241; lived 241; present 251
Sleep 154
Social, the 233; as solicitation 234; and transcendence 234
Solipsism 15, 230; pluralistic 230; truth of 231
Soul 92, 93, 96, 112, 259; and body 97
Space 119, 120, 208, 218
Spatiality 136, 137, 139, 140
Speech 151
Spirit 89, 91, 93, 95, 97, 107, 157, 166; and life 116, 177; and man 257; and matter 97, 271
Stimulus 81, 84
Stimulus-response 81, 89, 94
Structure 79, 80, 84, 91, 96, 108, 116, 117, 153, 154, 188; of existence 253; forms 88; of intersubjectivity 269; and ontology 269
Structuration 87, 89, 150, 193; and love 238
Subject 48, 49, 50, 77, 92, 153, 271; being of the soul 213; as conscious 213, 218; as empirical 77; as living 222; plurality of 221, 225, 231; and solipsism 215; as speaking 197; as temporal 123, 124; as universal 246; and the world 247
Subjective 124, 148, 248
Subjectivity 18, 123, 213, 284; and being 247; and consciousness 135; as existential 246; as inalienable 227; as radical 214; as transcendental 233
Superior behavior 82
Syncretic forms 82, 83
Symbol 82

Symbolic forms 82, 83, 84, 85; as behavior 145
Synthesis 210, 211; dialectical 266; final 268; philosophical 272

Temporality 123, 138
Thought 169, 223, 284; absolute 248; of all thought 194, 210; certitude of 244; as existential 182; as expression 195, 197; genuine 174; incarnation of 171, 174, 176, 177, 202; nature of 180, 226, 237; as style 182; and word 157, 174, 176, 181, 199
Time 123, 124, 180, 203, 248
Transcendence 19, 105, 124, 163, 220, 230; and consciousness 244; as existential 246; and immanence 261; and liberty 249
Transcendent 199, 233, 236; subject 77; world 245
Transcendental 192, 204, 233, 255; judgment 244; idealism 244; subjectivity 233
Truth 44, 52, 139 203, 207, 246, 248, 258; and Hegel 210, 211; integral 210; of the "real" 245; search for 267; universal 265
Thing 94, 121, 141, 168, 226, 237; and body 136; and the Cogito 242; and encounter 268; and knowledge 135; and perception 243; and space 120

Understanding 150, 175, 178, 187, 188; bodily 188; and human existence 262; phenomenon of 175
Universal 208, 214; life 208, 215

Will 153, 154, 155, 156, 208; consciousness of 237
Word 152, 177, 180, 183; as authentic 175, 176, 179; as being of reason 173; and the body 180, 186, 199; and concept 181; and contingency 210; as creative 176, 178, 179, 186, 205; as empirical 175, 176, 178; living 98, 193; as phenomenon 202; and philosophy 201; as silence 205; as social 174; and thought 157, 174, 176, 181, 199
World 27, 29, 40, 51, 59, 71, 157, 246, 248, 250, 264, 271; being-in 235; and body 119, 128, 130, 137, 140, 141, 153, 181, 199, 222; certitute of 246; commitment to 26, 124; as constituted 202, 236, 248; as cultural 227; of experience 25, 71, 123, 191, 199; and knowledge 59, 120, 143; and life 157; and language 185; and man 195, 214, 220, 254, 255; and man-in-the- 255; and other people 268; and perception 119, 138, 217, 220, 221; pre-objective 32, 36; qualifications of 31, 287; and rationality 40, 59; and subjectivity 247; as transcendent 245, 260